The Best Algebra 2/ Precalculus Book Ever

Written by Jonathan Cheng

Table of Contents

ISBN: 9798646911897
Imprint: Independently Published

Email author.jonathan.cheng@gmail.com for any questions or concerns.

Cover Designer: Roland Zhang
Contributors: Caton Zhu and Kenny Chen

Special Acknowledgement to those who ever taught us math, our parents and teachers, and to those who have ever supported us, our friends and family.

Chapter 1 Introduction

Prerequisites and tips

Before you begin this book, I'd like to tell you some things. While the book may have been outlined based on my own experiences, I've tried to group concepts in general categories instead of based on chapters in the textbook I used.

In addition, this book is not meant to replace learning in the classroom. It's meant to supplement what you learned in class by working out example problems that your teacher may not have explained too clearly and offering a bunch of practice tests to help you get the best grades. Therefore I won't be going over formulas, rules or equations since I expect you'll learn that in class.

Now half of Algebra 2 isn't defined very clearly since it depends on each textbook. For this book, I expect that you have already mastered Parent Functions, Transformations, Quadratic Equations, and Polynomials. These are prerequisite concepts that will pop up from time to time in these problems. Below is a "diagnostic" test that you should be able to complete before beginning this book.

Every chapter will be split into several key concepts or problem types. For each problem type, I will give around several example exercises that will be fully worked out. Note that I won't go over the formulas or rules. I expect that you can learn this from your textbook or teacher. Instead, I offer you problem solving strategies for each problem. After the exercises are the practice tests. Each chapter has a different amount of practice tests based on importance with some only having 2 while Conics has 7! At the end of the book are answer keys for all the practice tests. But don't look at the answer keys after you've attempted the problems in a timed sitting.

Most tests should be doable in a 50 minute sitting with exception to Matrices, which are tedious. Matrices should be completed in 90 minutes. You can use scientific calculators for tests to prevent computation errors, but they shouldn't be defeating the purpose of the problem. Most chapters won't require you to use a calculator. So sometimes, I'll put answers in exact form. The point value for each problem indicates the approximate difficulty and complexity of each problem.

While I do provide full answer explanations and solutions for the example exercises, the practice tests, on the most part, only have answers. Why? I hope that you'll be able to work out problems with your own methods instead of just relying on my method every time. However, for the hardest problems, I will give you hints that may give you some ideas as to how you could possibly approach the problem. Test problems with hints will have the hint number bolded and underlined.

The only way to be good at math is through doing problems and I hope that this book provides exactly that. I created these problems originally to help my classmates do better, but through this book I hope you will also gain an appreciation for math.

Diagnostic Test

#1: (4 points each) Factor completely.

a) $32x^5 - 256x^2$

b) $48x^2 + 77x - 5$

c) $x^6 - y^6$

d) $2x^3 + 9x^2 + 13x + 6$

#2: (10 points each) Solve each:

a) $2x - 5y + 3z = 11$
$x + 3y - z = 0$
$3x + 2y + z = 7$

b) $2x^4 - 7x^3 - 2x^2 + 13x + 6 = 0$

c) $\left|x^2 - 4\right| + 1 \le 2x$ $\underline{\mathbf{6}}$

#3: (12 points) Find the axis of symmetry, vertex, x/y intercepts, and two additional points of the parabola: $g(x) = x^2 + 12x + 3$. What are the transformations that transform $f(x) = x^2$ to $g(x)$?

#4: (12 points) Using the discriminant, find the value(s) of k if $x^2 + \sqrt{2}kx + 2k + 2 = 0$ has exactly one real root.

#5: (15 points) A toy store normally sells 980 toys a week at 13 dollars a toy. For every dollar they increase the price of a toy (one upcharge), they sell 20 less toys. Calculate how many upcharges the store should place on their toy prices so that they will be making a maximum amount of money each week? What is the maximum amount of money they can make each week? **27**

#6: (15 points) Let r_1, r_2, r_3 be the roots of $f(x) = x^3 - ax^2 - 4x - 12$. If $\frac{1}{1+r_1} + \frac{1}{1+r_2} + \frac{1}{1+r_3} = -\frac{7}{6}$, find a. **2**

Chapter 2 Radical Functions

Rational Exponents/Radicals

Ex: 1 Simplify $\sqrt{\frac{9^{10}+3^{12}}{9^8+3^8}}$

$\sqrt{\frac{3^{20}+3^{12}}{3^{16}+3^8}}$ Expressing terms in base 3

$\sqrt{\frac{3^{12}(3^8+1)}{3^8(3^8+1)}}$ Factoring out greatest power of 3

$\sqrt{\frac{3^{12}}{3^8}}$ Cancelling out common factor

$\sqrt{3^4}$ Dividing out using exponent rules

> 9 Simplifying

Ex: 2 Factor $\sqrt[3]{54x^7y^{10}} + \sqrt{8x^5y^7}$

$\sqrt[3]{3^3 \cdot (x^2)^3 \cdot (y^3)^3 \cdot 2xy} + \sqrt{2^2 \cdot (x^2)^2 \cdot (y^3)^2 \cdot 2xy}$

Expressing factors in powers of 3 and 2.

$3x^2y^3\sqrt[3]{2xy} + 2x^2y^3\sqrt{2xy}$ Simplifying the powers

Remember that taking the n th root is the same thing as raising a quantity to the $\frac{1}{n}$ power, so the exponent and root cancel out.

> $x^2y^3(3\sqrt[3]{2xy} + 2\sqrt{2xy})$ Factoring

Ex: 3 Rationalize $\frac{3}{\sqrt[3]{4}+3\sqrt[3]{2}+9}$

Note that $\sqrt[3]{4} + 3\sqrt[3]{2} + 9 = \sqrt[3]{2^2} + 3\sqrt[3]{2} + 3^2$

$\frac{3}{\sqrt[3]{4}+3\sqrt[3]{2}+9}\left(\frac{\sqrt[3]{2}-3}{\sqrt[3]{2}-3}\right)$

Multiply $(a-b)$ to fulfill difference of cubes

$\frac{3\sqrt[3]{2}-9}{(\sqrt[3]{2})^3-3^3}$ Multiply numerators and denominators

> $\frac{9-3\sqrt[3]{2}}{25}$ Simplify

Remember $a^3 - b^3 = (a-b)(a^2+ab+b^2)$. It's important to see where you can factor things.

Ex: 4 Simplify $\sqrt[3]{7+\sqrt{50}} + \sqrt[3]{7-\sqrt{50}}$

Let $x = \sqrt[3]{7+\sqrt{50}} + \sqrt[3]{7-\sqrt{50}}$

When we see something taken to the cube root, we should immediately think of the difference/sum of cubes or taking everything to the third power. This way we can get rid of the cube root. However, in this case, the sum of cubes won't help since we would have to multiply both sides by a whole bunch of other radicals, which we don't want.

$x^3 = (\sqrt[3]{7+\sqrt{50}} + \sqrt[3]{7-\sqrt{50}})^3$ Cubing both sides

Remember that $(a+b)^3 = 3a^2b + 3ab^2 + b^3$.

$x^3 = 14 + 3(\sqrt[3]{(7+\sqrt{50})^2(7-\sqrt{50})} + \sqrt[3]{(7-\sqrt{50})^2(7+\sqrt{50})})$

We could cancel out the $\sqrt{50}$ after cubing.

$x^3 = 14 + 3(\sqrt[3]{(49-50)(7-\sqrt{50})} + \sqrt[3]{(49-50)(7+\sqrt{50})})$

Multiplying out difference of squares

$x^3 = 14 + 3(-1 \cdot \sqrt[3]{7-\sqrt{50}} - \sqrt[3]{7+\sqrt{50}}$

Factoring out -1

$x^3 = 14 - 3x$ Identifying $\sqrt[3]{7+\sqrt{50}} + \sqrt[3]{7-\sqrt{50}} = x$

$x^3 + 3x - 14 = 0$ Rewriting the polynomial

$(x-2)(x^2+2x+7) = 0$ Factoring

Since x obviously is a real number, $x = 2$.

> 2

Ex: 5 Rationalize $\frac{\sqrt{2}}{\sqrt{2}+\sqrt{3}-\sqrt{5}}$

$\frac{\sqrt{2}}{\sqrt{2}+\sqrt{3}-\sqrt{5}} \cdot \frac{\sqrt{2}+\sqrt{3}+\sqrt{5}}{\sqrt{2}+\sqrt{3}+\sqrt{5}}$ Multiply the conjugate by grouping $\sqrt{2}+\sqrt{3}$ together

$\frac{\sqrt{2}(\sqrt{2}+\sqrt{3}+\sqrt{5})}{(\sqrt{2}+\sqrt{3})^2-5}$ Multiplying

$\frac{\sqrt{2}(\sqrt{2}+\sqrt{3}+\sqrt{5})}{2+2\sqrt{6}+3-5}$ Expanding $(\sqrt{2}+\sqrt{3})^2$

$\frac{(\sqrt{2}+\sqrt{3}+\sqrt{5})}{2\sqrt{3}} \cdot \frac{\sqrt{3}}{\sqrt{3}}$ Simplify and Rationalize

$\frac{\sqrt{6}+3+\sqrt{15}}{6}$ Multiply

> $\frac{\sqrt{6}+3+\sqrt{15}}{6}$ Multiply

Ex: 6 Find the value of $\sqrt{6+\sqrt{6+\sqrt{6+\ldots}}}$

Now let's set this infinite radical to equal x.

Each time we have another square root, let's call that a layer. Losing the outermost layer does not matter at infinity, so essentially we can force the value of the expression inside the expression itself.

$\sqrt{6+x} = x$ The part after the first 6 is also x.

$x^2 - x - 6 = 0$ Squaring both sides and simplifying

$(x-3)(x+2) = 0$ Factoring

$x = 3$ Must be positive

> $x = 3$

Domain and Range of Radical Functions

The basic guideline for domain is that the radicand must always be greater than or equal to 0 for even indexes. For the range, if the radicand has a maximum above 0, replace the radicand for 0 and simplify to get the minimum of the function. If the radicand's minimum is below 0, the maximum is when the radicand equals 0 and if the radicand's minimum is above 0, the function approaches positive infinity.

Ex 1: $f(x) = 2\sqrt{-x^2 + 2x + 4} - 3$

Domain: $-x^2 + 2x + 4 \geq 0$

Radicand must be greater than or equal to 0

Critical points: $x = 1 \pm \sqrt{5}$

Find critical points by solving $-x^2 + 2x + 4 = 0$.

$x = \frac{-2 \pm \sqrt{4 - 4(-1)(4)}}{-2} = \frac{-2 \pm 2\sqrt{5}}{-2}$

$x = 1 \pm \sqrt{5}$

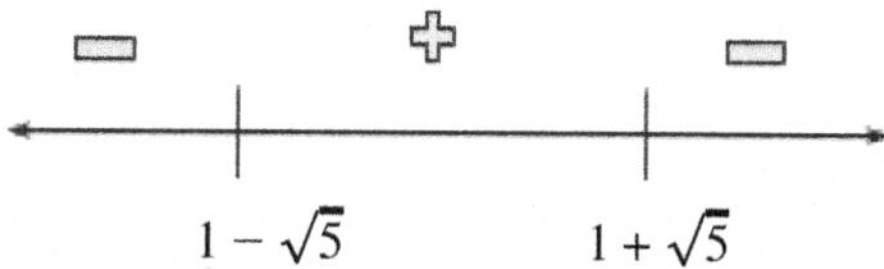

$1 - \sqrt{5}$ $\quad$ $1 + \sqrt{5}$

Create a number line and plot the critical values. Then test 0, a point between the two critical points. Find out that 0 meets the requirements. Therefore the domain is the interval between our two critical values.

Range: $f(x) = 2\sqrt{-(x^2 - 2x + 1) + 1 + 4} - 3$

Find the maximum of the radicand by expressing the radicand in vertex-form

$f(x) = 2\sqrt{-(x-1)^2 + 5} - 3$ Simplify

Since the maximum of the radicand is 5, the maximum of the function would be $2\sqrt{5} - 3$.

The lowest possible value of the function would occur when the radicand equals 0. Therefore the minimum of the function would be $2\sqrt{0} - 3 = -3$

> Domain: $1 - \sqrt{5} \leq x \leq 1 + \sqrt{5}$
> Range: $-3 \leq y \leq 2\sqrt{5} - 3$.

Ex: 2 $f(x) = \sqrt{-x^2 + 2x + \frac{7}{9}} - 1$

Domain: $-x^2 + 2x + \frac{7}{9} \geq 0$

Radicand must be greater than or equal to 0

Critical points: $x = -1/3, 7/3$

Find critical points by solving $-x^2 + 2x + \frac{7}{9} = 0$.

$(3x + 1)(3x - 7) = 0, x = -\frac{1}{3}, \frac{7}{3}$

Create a number line and plot the critical values. Then test 0, a point between the two critical points. Find out that 0 meets the inequality.

$-1/3$ $\quad$ $7/3$

Range: $f(x) = \sqrt{-(x^2 - 2x + 1) + 1 + \frac{7}{9}} - 1$

Find the maximum of the radicand by expressing the radicand in vertex-form

$f(x) = \sqrt{-(x-1)^2 + \frac{16}{9}} - 1$ Simplify

Since the maximum of the radicand is $\frac{16}{9}$, the maximum of the function is $\sqrt{\frac{16}{9}} - 1 = 1/3$ The lowest possible value of the function would occur when the radicand equals 0. Therefore the minimum of the function would be $\sqrt{0} - 1 = -1$.

> Domain: $-1/3 \leq x \leq 7/3$
> Range: $-1 \leq y \leq 1/3$

Ex: 3 $f(x) = \sqrt{|x^2 - 4| + |-2x + 10|}$

Foremost, the domain must be all real numbers because the absolute value ensures that whatever goes beneath the radicand is nonnegative.

In order to find range, we must first eliminate the absolute values and consider each interval for x.

If $x \leq -2, x \geq 2, x^2 - 4 \geq 0$; $|x^2 - 4| = x^2 - 4$.

If $-2 < x < 2, x^2 - 4 < 0$; $|x^2 - 4| = 4 - x^2$.

If $x \geq 5, -2x + 10 < 0; |-2x + 10| = 2x - 10$

If $x < 5, -2x + 10 > 0; |-2x + 10| = -2x + 10$

If $x \leq -2, 2 \leq x < 5, f(x) = \sqrt{x^2 - 4 - 2x + 10}$

$f(x) = \sqrt{x^2 - 2x + 1 + 5} = \sqrt{(x-1)^2 + 5}$

Minimum is achieved at $(1, \sqrt{5})$. However, 1 does not meet the x restriction of $x \leq -2, 2 \leq x < 5$. If we test out $-2, 2, 5$ (the "endpoints" of our interval), we see the minimum is at $(2, \sqrt{6})$. We test these numbers just like we would test the vertices in a system of inequalities. The maximum would obviously be at infinity, which is achievable since x includes negative infinity.

If $-2 < x < 2, f(x) = \sqrt{4 - x^2 - 2x + 10}$

$f(x) = \sqrt{-(x^2 + 2x + 1) + 15} = \sqrt{-(x+1)^2 + 15}$ so

the maximum is achieved at $(-1,\sqrt{15})$. The minimum would be when $-(x+1)^2+15=0$ If we solve we get $(x+1)^2=15, x=-1\pm\sqrt{15}$. Neither of which is included in the interval. The minimum would be achieved when $x=2$, which allows for the function to be $\sqrt{6}$ like before. For our last interval, we look at when $x\geq 5$.
If $x\geq 5, f(x)=\sqrt{x^2-4+2x-10}=\sqrt{x^2+2x-14}$.
In vertex form, $f(x)=\sqrt{(x+1)^2-15}$ so the minimum is at $f(x)=0$ which is achieved when $x=1\pm\sqrt{15}$, which is not in the interval. Plugging in $x=5$, we see the minimum is at $\sqrt{21}$. The maximum would be positive infinity since as x goes to positive infinity, $f(x)$ gets infinity large.

Domain: All Real Numbers
Range: $y\geq\sqrt{6}$

Radical Equations/Inequalities

General tips: Remember to isolate the radical before squaring and check for extraneous values. Make sure to see if terms can be cancelled anywhere. For inequalities, solve for critical values and remember to consider the domain of the radicand.

Ex: 1 $\sqrt{1+\sqrt{2+\sqrt{x}}}=2$

$1+\sqrt{2+\sqrt{x}}=4$ Square both sides

$\sqrt{2+\sqrt{x}}=3$ Subtract 1

$2+\sqrt{x}=9$ Square both sides

$\sqrt{x}=7$ Subtract 2

$x=49$ Square both sides

$x=49$

Ex: 2 Solve $\sqrt{x+7}=\sqrt{18-x}-1$

$x+7=(18-x)-2\sqrt{18-x}+1$

Square both sides to remove the radical

$-12+2x=-2\sqrt{18-x}$ Combine like terms

$x-6=\sqrt{18-x}$ Simplify/Divide by -2

$x^2-12x+36=18-x$ Square both sides

$x^2-11x+18=0$ Combine like terms

$(x-9)(x-2)=0$ Factor

$x=9,2$ Solve for x

$x=2$ Check for extraneous values

Ex: 3 Solve $4(x+1)^2-5(x+1)^{3/2}+(x+1)^{5/2}=0$

$(x+1)^{3/2}(4(x+1)^{1/2}-5+(x+1))=0$

Factor out greatest common factor $(x+1)^{3/2}$

$(x+1)^{3/2}(4\sqrt{x+1}-4+x)=0$ Distribute

$(x+1)^{3/2}=0, 4\sqrt{x+1}-4+x=0$ Factor Theorem

$4\sqrt{x+1}=-x+4$ Solving for x

$16x+16=x^2-8x+16$ Squaring

$0=x^2-24x$ Combining like terms

$0=x(x-24)$ Factoring

$x=-1,0$ Solve for x, 24 is extraneous

Ex: 4 Solve $\sqrt{x^2+9x+13}-\sqrt{x^2+9x}=1$

$\sqrt{x^2+9x+13}=1+\sqrt{x^2+9x}$ Isolate the radical

$x^2+9x+13=1+2\sqrt{x^2+9x}+x^2+9x$ Square

$6=\sqrt{x^2+9x}$ Combine like terms/Isolate radical

$x^2+9x-36=0$ Square/Standard quadratic form

$(x+12)(x-3)=0$ Factor

$x=-12,3$ Solve for x

Ex: 5 Solve $\sqrt{x^2+13x+30}=x+3+\sqrt{x+3}$

$x^2+13x+30=(x+3)^2+2(x+3)(\sqrt{x+3})+x+3$

Squaring both sides

$x^2+12x+27=x^2+6x+9+2(x+3)(\sqrt{x+3})$

Expanding/Combining like terms

$6x+18=2(x+3)(\sqrt{x+3})$ Combining like terms

$6(x+3)=2(x+3)(\sqrt{x+3})$ Factoring right side

$0=(x+3)(\sqrt{x+3}-3)$ Factoring out $x+3$

If $x+3=0, x=-3$ Factor Theorem

$\sqrt{x+3}-3=0$ Factor Theorem

$x+3=9$ Isolating radical and squaring both sides

$x=6$ Combining like terms

$x=-3,6$

Ex: 6 Solve $\sqrt{3x+2}=\sqrt{6x+5}-\sqrt{6x+3}$

If we let $3x+2=a$, we can express $6x+5$ as $2a-1$ and $6x+3$ as $2a+1$

$\sqrt{a} = \sqrt{2a+1} - \sqrt{2a-1}$ Rewriting equation
$a = 2a + 1 - 2\sqrt{(2a+1)(2a-1)} + 2a - 1$ Squaring
$2\sqrt{4a^2 - 1} = 3a$ Difference of Squares
$4(4a^2 - 1) = 9a^2$ Squaring both sides
$16a^2 - 4 = 9a^2$ Expanding
$a^2 = \frac{4}{7}$ Simplifying
$a = 0.755928$ Must be nonnegative
$3x + 2 = 0.755928$ Substituting for a
$x \approx -0.41469$

$x \approx -0.41469$

Remember to look for places where you can use substitution to greatly help.

Ex: 7 $\sqrt[3]{350 + 90\sqrt{x}} + \sqrt[3]{350 - 90\sqrt{x}} = 10$
Similar to Ex: 4 of the simplifying section, don't isolate the radical because cubing both sides allow us to cancel out the $90\sqrt{x}$.
$350 + 90\sqrt{x} + 3\sqrt[3]{(350 + 90\sqrt{x})^2(350 - 90\sqrt{x}}$
$+ 3\sqrt[3]{(350 - 90\sqrt{x})^2(350 + 90\sqrt{x}} + 350 - 90\sqrt{x} = 1000$
When we cube both sides, remember the coefficient of 3 for the middle terms.
$3(10)\sqrt[3]{(350^2) - (90\sqrt{x})^2} = 300$ Simplifying
What I did in this past step was use difference of squares to multiply $(350 + 90\sqrt{x})(350 - 90\sqrt{x})$ underneath both cube roots. When I factor out this common factor from both, I'm left with $\sqrt[3]{350 + 90\sqrt{x}} + \sqrt[3]{350 - 90\sqrt{x}}$ which we know equals 10.
$\sqrt[3]{122500 - 8100x} = 10$ Dividing by 30
$122500 - 8100x = 1000$ Cubing both sides
$x = 15$ Solving for x

$x = 15$

Ex: 8 Solve $\sqrt{10 - x^2} > x + 2$
$10 - x^2 > x^2 + 4x + 4$ Square both sides
$0 > x^2 + 2x - 3$ Combine like terms/Simplify
Critical Values: $x = 1$ Solve for x
Note that -3 is an extraneous solution.

Test 0. Since $\sqrt{10 - 0}$ is greater than $0 + 2$, the range of values is less that 1. However, you must also consider the domain of the radicand and make sure $10 - x^2 > 0$.

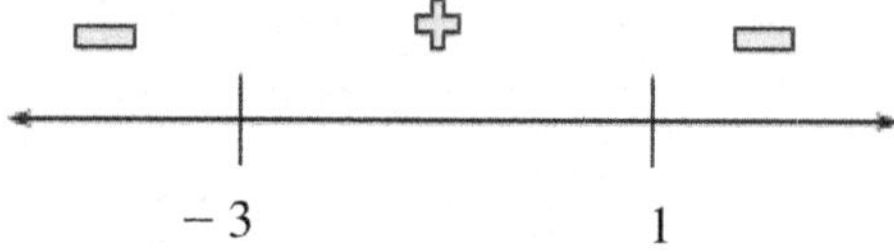

Find the critical values at $x = \pm\sqrt{10}$. Testing 0, you see that $-\sqrt{10} < x < \sqrt{10}$. Since $\sqrt{10} \approx 3.162$, it's less specific than 1. Therefore, it's redundant and we don't need to include it. However, the $-\sqrt{10}$ provides us with a new restriction. After looking at two sets of inequalities, we get:

$-\sqrt{10} < x < 1$

Ex: 9 Solve $\sqrt{3 - \sqrt{x+2}} > 1$
$3 - \sqrt{x+2} > 1$ Squaring both sides
$2 > \sqrt{x+2}$ Simplifying
$4 > x + 2$ Squaring both sides
$x < 2$ Simplifying
By domain restrictions, we have:
$x + 2 > 0$ so $x > -2$
$3 - \sqrt{x+2} > 0$ Beneath radicand must be greater than 0
$3 > \sqrt{x+2}$ Simplifying
$9 > x + 2$ Squaring both sides
$x < 7$ Simplifying
By looking at all the domain restrictions, we get: $-2 < x < 2$.

$-2 < x < 2$

Ex: 10 If a and b are the roots of $x^2 - 10x - 27$ find $\sqrt[3]{a} + \sqrt[3]{b}$.
We could try to find a and b but that's not fun. Instead, let's try to use Vieta's formulas and clever manipulation to find this value.
We know that the sum of the roots is equal to the negative of the coefficient of the x term. We know the product is equal to the constant term.
$a + b = 10, ab = -27$ Using Vieta's formulas
Like before, set $\sqrt[3]{a} + \sqrt[3]{b} = x$

$a+3(\sqrt[3]{a^2b}+\sqrt[3]{ab^2})+b=x^3$ Cubing both sides
$a+b+3\sqrt[3]{ab}(\sqrt[3]{a}+\sqrt[3]{b})=x^3$ Factoring
$10+3(-3)(x)=x^3$ Substituting in values
$x^3+9x-10=0$ Simplifying
$(x-1)(x^2+x+10)=0$ Factoring
$x=1$ Value must be real

1

Functions: Inverses and Operations

Remember that the inverse undoes a function. Therefore, the domain of the function equals the range of the inverse. The range of the function equals the domain of the inverse. If a function typically does not have an inverse function, the domain of the function must be restricted.

Ex: 1 Find the inverse of $f(x)=\sqrt{16-x^2}+2$ for $-4\leq x\leq 0$. What is the domain and range of the inverse?
$x=\sqrt{16-y^2}+2$ Swap the x and y
$x-2=\sqrt{16-y^2}$ Isolate the radical
$x^2-4x+4=16-y^2$ Square both sides
$y^2=-x^2+4x+12$ Combine like terms
$y=-\sqrt{-x^2+4x+12}$ Take the square root
We add the negative sign because the restricted domain shows that the range of the inverse must always be negative. When things are squared, negative signs can be "lost" so we add it back.

$f^{-1}(x)=-\sqrt{-x^2+4x+12}$

Domain: $-x^2+4x+12\geq 0$
Radicand must be greater than or equal to 0
Critical Values: $x=6,-2$. Testing 0, we see that $-0^2+4(0)+12$ is greater than 0. Therefore, the domain is between 6 and -2. The range of the inverse is just the domain of the function.

Domain: $-2\leq x\leq 6$ Range: $-4\leq y\leq 0$.

Ex 2: Let $b(x)=2x-3, o(x)=x+2, r(x)=\frac{x^2-3x+c+1}{2}$.
If $(b\circ r\circ o)(c)=-c$ and what is c

$b(r(o(c)))=b(r(c+2))$ Evaluating $o(c)$
$b(r(o(c)))=b(\frac{(c+2)^2-3(c+2)+c+1}{2})$ Evaluating $r(c+2)$
$b(r(o(c)))=b(\frac{c^2+4c+4-3c-6+c+1}{2})$ Expanding
$b(r(o(c)))=b(\frac{c^2+2c-1}{2})$ Simplifying
$b(r(o(c)))=c^2+2c-1-3$ Evaluating $b(\frac{c^2+2x-1}{2})$
$c^2+2c-4=-c$ Substituting $(b\circ r\circ o)(c)=-c$
$c^2+3c-4=0$ Combining like terms
$(c+4)(c-1)=0$ Simplifying
$c=-4,1$

$c=-4,1$

Ex: 3 Let $g(x)=\frac{3+g(x)}{2-x}$. If $g^{-1}(x)=3$, find x.
$g^{-1}(x)=3$ We want to isolate x to see what it is.
$g(g^{-1}(x))=g(3)$ Taking $g(x)$ on both sides
$x=g(3)$ So we want to find $g(3)$
$g(3)=\frac{3+g(3)}{2-3}$ Plugging in 3 to the function
$-g(3)=3+g(3)$ Simplifying
$g(3)=\frac{-3}{2}$

$x=-\frac{3}{2}$

Ex: 4 Let $f(x)=3g^{-1}(x)+2x-4$ where $g(x)$ is a linear function. If $f^{-1}(4)=2$ and $g^{-1}(3)=1$, find $f(g^{-1}(5))$.
$4=f(2), 3=g(1)$ Definition of Inverses
$f(2)=3g^{-1}(2)+2(2)-4$ Plugging $x=2$ into the equation that relates f with g
$4=3g^{-1}(2)$ Simplifying
$g^{-1}(2)=\frac{4}{3}$ Solving for $g^{-1}(2)$
$2=g(\frac{4}{3})$ Taking the function g on both sides
Because $g(x)$ is a linear function, we can use $g(\frac{4}{3})=2$ and $g(1)=3$ to find the function.
$m=\frac{2-3}{\frac{4}{3}-1}=-3$ Finding Slope
$g(x)-3=-3(x-1)$ Point slope form
$g(x)=-3x+6$ Simplifying
$g^{-1}(x)=\frac{6-x}{3}$ Finding the inverse
$f(x)=3(\frac{6-x}{3})+2x-4$ Plugging in $g^{-1}(x)$
$f(x)=6-x+2x-4$ Simplifying
$f(x)=x+2$ Simplifying
$f(g^{-1}(5))=f(\frac{6-5}{3})$ Evaluating $g^{-1}(5)$
$=f(\frac{1}{3})=\frac{1}{3}+2=\frac{7}{3}$

$\frac{7}{3}$

Ex: 5 Let $f(x) = x^2 + kx + 7$ and $g(x) = kx - 4$. If $(f \circ g^{-1})(5) + (f \circ g)(0) = 36$, find k.

$f(g^{-1}(5)) + f(-4) = 42$ Applying composition

Note that $g^{-1}(x) = \frac{x+4}{k}$ by simple inspection.

$f(\frac{9}{k}) + f(-4) = 42$ Simplifying

$\frac{81}{k^2} + 9 + 7 + 16 - 4k + 7 = 36$ Evaluating $f(x)$

$\frac{81}{k^2} - 4k + 3 = 0$ Combining like terms

$4k^3 - 3k^2 - 81 = 0$ Multiplying k^2

$(k-3)(4k^2 + 9k + 27) = 0$

$k = 3$

$k = 3$

Ex: 6 If $g(x) = ax + b$, find a and b such that $g(g(x)) = 9x + 32$.

$g(g(x)) = a(ax + b) + b$ Applying composition

$9x + 32 = a^2x + ab + b$ Simplifying

Now the x and constant terms must match up.

$9x = a^2x$ Matching up x term

$a = \pm 3$ Solving for a

$ab + b = 32$ Matching up constant terms

$3b + b = 32$ Plugging in $a = 3$

$b = 8$ Solving for b

$-3b + b = 32$ Plugging in $a = -3$

$b = -16$

$a = 3, b = 8$ and $a = -3, b = -16$

Ex: 7 If $f(x) = 4x - 7$ and $g(x) = 4\sqrt{x-3}$. Find c such that $f(g(c)) = 25$.

$4g(c) - 7 = 25$ Applying composition

$g(c) = \frac{32}{4}$ Isolating $g(c)$

$g(c) = 8 = 4\sqrt{c-3}$

$2 = \sqrt{c-3}$ Simplifying

$4 = c - 3$ Squaring both sides

$c = 7$ Solving for c

$c = 7$

Ex: 8 Let $f(x) = bx^2 + 5, g(x) = cx - 4$. If $f(g^{-1}(c)) = 32$ and $g^{-1}(f(3)) = 6b$, find c and b if c and b are both integers.

Let's first find the inverse of $g(x)$.

$g^{-1}(x) = \frac{x+4}{c}$ Definition of Inverse

$f(g^{-1}(c)) = f(\frac{c+4}{c})$ Evaluating $g^{-1}(c)$

$f(g^{-1}(c)) = b(\frac{c^2+8c+16}{c^2}) + 5$ Evaluating $f(\frac{c+4}{c})$

$b(\frac{c^2+8c+16}{c^2}) + 5 = 32$ Substituting $f(g^{-1}(c)) = 32$

$b(\frac{c^2+8c+16}{c^2}) = 27$ Simplifying

$g^{-1}(f(3)) = g^{-1}(9b + 5)$ Evaluating $f(3)$

$g^{-1}(f(3)) = \frac{9b+9}{c}$ Evaluating $g^{-1}(9b + 5)$

$\frac{9b+9}{c} = 6b$ Substituting $g^{-1}(f(b)) = 18$

$3 = 2bc - 3b$ Simplifying

$b = \frac{3}{2c-3}$ Simplifying

$(\frac{3}{2c-3})(\frac{c^2+8c+16}{c^2}) = 27$

$c^2 + 8c + 16 = 18c^3 - 27c^2$ Simplifying

$(c-2)(9c^2 + 4c + 4) = 0$ Factoring

$c = 2$ c is integer

$b = \frac{3}{4-3} = 3$

$c = 2, b = 3$

Ex: 9 Let $f(x) = 3x + 6$ and $g(f(x)) = 2x^2 + 3x - 2$. Find $g^{-1}(x)$ for $x \geq \frac{15}{4}$.

Remember that $f(x)$ and $f^{-1}(x)$ "cancel" out, so plugging in $x = f^{-1}(x)$ into $g(f(x))$ gets $g(x)$.

$f^{-1}(x) = \frac{x-6}{3}$ Solving for inverse

$g(x) = 2(\frac{x-6}{3})^2 + 3(\frac{x-6}{3}) - 2$ Substituting $f^{-1}(x)$

$g(x) = \frac{2x^2-24x+72}{9} + x - 6 - 2$ Expanding

$g(x) = \frac{2x^2-15x}{9}$ Simplifying

$x = \frac{2y^2-15y}{9}$ Swapping x and y

$9x = 2(y^2 - \frac{15}{2}y + \frac{225}{16} - \frac{225}{16})$ Completing the square

$9x + \frac{225}{8} = 2(y - \frac{15}{4})^2$ Simplifying

$\frac{72x+225}{16} = (y - \frac{15}{4})^2$ Simplifying

$\frac{3\sqrt{8x+25}}{4} = y - \frac{15}{4}$ Taking square root

Remember that because of our domain restriction of $x \geq \frac{15}{4}$ we use the positive square root.

$y = \frac{15+3\sqrt{8x+25}}{4}$ Isolating y

$f^{-1}(x) = \frac{15+3\sqrt{8x+25}}{4}$

Radical Functions Test 1

#1: (4 points each) Simplify.

a) $\frac{6}{3-\sqrt{7}}$

b) $\frac{2}{\sqrt[3]{9}+4\sqrt[3]{3}+16}$

c) $(32^{2/3} \cdot 2^{2/3})^{-2}$

d) $\frac{1}{3-\sqrt[4]{3}}$

#2: (16 points) Let $f(x) = 3x - 2$, $h^{-1}(x) = \frac{x-1}{2}$. If $(f^{-1} \circ g \circ h)(x) = \frac{12x^2+10x+1}{3}$, algebraically find and simplify $g^{-1}(x)$ if $g^{-1}(x)$ is always positive. **<u>34</u>**

#3: (12 points) Find the domain and range of $f(x) = \sqrt{|x^2 - 9| + 3x + 5} + 2$

#4: (16 points) Let $g(x) = b\sqrt{a + bx^2 - 2x}$. If it's domain is $-a \le x \le -b$ and range is $-2 \le y \le 0$, algebraically find a and b. **16**

#5: (10 points each) Algebraically solve each equation/inequality for x.

a) $3\sqrt{x+3} - 4 \le x$

b) $(x+1)^{1/2} + 3(x+1)^{-1/2} = 10(x+1)^{-3/2}$

c) $\sqrt{14 + x\sqrt{10}} - \sqrt{14 - x\sqrt{10}} = x$

d) $\sqrt[3]{4x-1} + \sqrt[3]{4-x} = \sqrt[3]{3x+3}$ **41**

Radical Functions Test 2

#1: (4 points each) Simplify.

a) $\frac{2}{3+\sqrt{7}}$

b) $\frac{4}{\sqrt[3]{9}+4\sqrt[3]{3}+16} - \frac{1}{\sqrt[3]{3}-4}$

c) $(8^{1/5} \cdot 4^{1/5})^{-2} \cdot \sqrt[3]{8(64)}$

#2: (12 points) Let $f(3x^2 + x) = 2x^3 + 3x^2 - 2x - 1$. Find $f(2)$ and $f^{-1}(2)$ for all real solutions. Note: This isn't really a function. **33**

#3: (14 points) Find $\sqrt{34 - 24\sqrt{2}} + \sqrt{43 - 30\sqrt{2}}$ **18**

#4: (14 points) If $\sqrt[3]{\frac{a}{b}} + \sqrt[3]{\frac{b}{a}} = \frac{5}{2}, a + b = 9$, find $|a - b|$. **20**

#5: (10 points each) Algebraically solve each equation/inequality for x.

a) $\sqrt{5-x^2}+1 \le x$

b) $\sqrt[3]{5+2\sqrt{x}}+\sqrt[3]{5-2\sqrt{x}}=1$

c) $x+1=\sqrt[4]{x^4+4x^3-x}$

d) $\sqrt{2x-\sqrt{x^2-15}}=3$

#6: (12 points) Let $f(x)=2x+1$, $g(f(x))=4x^2+2x-3$, and $h(x)=3x-b$. a) Find $g(x)$. b) If $f^{-1}(h^{-1}(g(-1)))=0$, what is b?

Radical Functions Test 3

#1: (3 points each) Simplify.

a) $\frac{3}{3+\sqrt{7}} - \frac{1}{3-\sqrt{7}}$

b) $\frac{2}{\sqrt[3]{9}+4\sqrt[3]{3}+16} + \frac{3}{\sqrt[3]{3}-4}$

c) $(16^{1/5} \cdot 8^{2/5})^{-\frac{1}{2}} \cdot \sqrt[3]{8(64)}$

#2: (3 points each) Find the following:

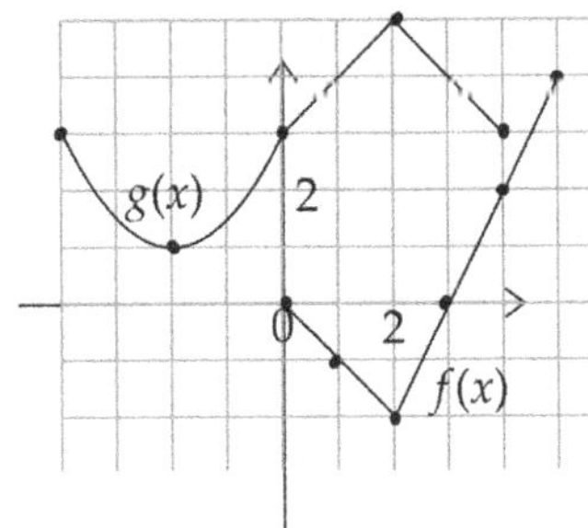

a) $f(2) + g(f(3))$

b) $g(f(5)) - f^{-1}(-2)$

c) $g(g(-2)) \cdot f(g(2))$

#3: (14 points) Write $f(x) = \sqrt{|x^2 - 4| + 3x}$ as a piecewise function.

#4: (14 points) If $f(x) = 3x + 6$ and $g(f(x) + g(x)) = 10x - 3$, find $g(x)$. **48**

#6: (10 points each) Algebraically solve each equation/inequality for x.

a) $3\sqrt{x-4}+\sqrt{x+4}=6$

b) $12(x-3)^{5/6}+4(x-3)^{1/2}-5(x-3)^{1/6}=0$

c) $x+2\geq 3\sqrt{x+3}$

#7: (12 points) If $\sqrt{x}-\sqrt{y}=\sqrt{2}, x^2+y^2=14,$ find and simplify $\sqrt[3]{(x+3)(y+3)+5}$.

#8: (12 points) What is the domain and range of $f(x)=4\sqrt{2x^2+x-6}+4$?

Chapter 3 Exponential/Logarithmic Functions

Exponential Growth and Decay

Ex 1: A teenager puts \$1000 of his allowance into a bank which compounds quarterly at an annual interest rate of 8%. How much money would he have in the account if he leaves the money in that account for 7 years?

The principal value is \$1000 and every quarter, it increases exponentially by $\frac{8}{4} = 2\%$ Therefore, the equation is $A = 1000(1.02)^{4t}$ where t is in years. Note that we have $4t$ because we are compounding interest 4 times in a year.

Plugging $t = 7$, we get:

$A = 1000(1.02)^{28} \approx \$1741.02$

Ex: 2 At the start of summer today, I have 320 grams of a radioactive element. During summer, it has a half life of 50 days. 90 days later, it's fall and the half life decreases to 20 days. How many days from today will the element reach 40 grams?

We can set up an exponential decay model for the element during its first 90 days (summer).

$s(t) = 320(\frac{1}{2})^{t/50}$ Definition of Half Life

$s(t) = 320(\frac{1}{2})^{9/5}$ Plugging in $t = 90$

$s(t) \approx 91.89586$ grams Evaluating the expression

Now we set up a decay model for fall.

$f(t) = 91.89586(\frac{1}{2})^{t/20}$ Definition of Half Life

$40 = 91.89586(\frac{1}{2})^{t/20}$ Setting $f(t) = 40$

$0.43528 = (\frac{1}{2})^{t/20}$ Simplifying

$\log_{1/2} 0.43528 = \frac{t}{20}$ Taking $\log_{1/2}$ on both sides

$t \approx 1.2 \cdot 20 = 24$ fall days

90 summer plus 24 fall days: 114 days

114 days

Ex: 3 A couple decides to put \$5000 into a savings account which compounds continuously at an annual interest rate of 4%. If the couple were to leave the money in the account, how much money would they have after 15 years?

Because this is a case of continuous interest, we use $A = Pe^{rt}$, where we use e, an irrational constant. Remember that r must be in decimal form. Therefore, the equation for this situation is $A = 5000e^{0.04t}$. Pluggin in $t = 15$:

$A = 5000e^{0.6} \approx \$9111.059$

Domain and Range of Logs/Exponents

Ex: 1 Algebraically find the domain and the range of $g(x) = 2^{\sqrt{-x^2-2x+5}} + 2$

Remember that whatever is beneath the radical must be nonnegative. Therefore, $-x^2 - 2x + 5 \geq 0$. Using the quadratic formula, $x = -1 \pm \sqrt{6}$ are the critical values. Testing $x = 0$, we can tell that the points in between $-1 \pm \sqrt{6}$ fulfill the inequality.

Domain: $-1 + \sqrt{6} \leq x \leq -1 - \sqrt{6}$

Now for the range. Let's find the maximum of the power of 2 by finding the maximum of the radical. Let's look at $\sqrt{-x^2 - 2x + 5}$.

If we complete the square, we get: $\sqrt{-(x^2 + 2x + 1) + 6}$. It is clear that the maximum power would thus be $\sqrt{6}$. So the maximum of the function would be $2^{\sqrt{6}} + 2$. Since the maximum of the radicand is 6, it's the clear the minimum is at 0. Plug in 0 for the radicand to get $2^0 + 2 = 3$.

Range: $3 \leq y \leq 2^{\sqrt{6}} + 2$

Ex: 2 Find the domain and range of $f(x) = 2^{\sqrt{-x^2-4x+8}} - 2$.

$-x^2 - 4x + 8 \geq 0$ because the value underneath a radical must be nonnegative. Let's find the critical points: $x = \frac{-4 \pm \sqrt{48}}{2}$. Simplifying, we get that the the critical points are at $-2 - 2\sqrt{3}$ and $-2 + 2\sqrt{3}$. Testing 0, we see that between these two critical points fulfills the inequality.

Domain: $-2 - 2\sqrt{3} \leq x \leq -2 + 2\sqrt{3}$

For the range, let's rewrite $-x^2 - 4x + 8$.
$-(x^2 + 4x + 4) + 8 + 4$
$-(x + 2)^2 + 12$
The maximum is 12. Therefore, the maximum of the function would be $2^{\sqrt{12}} - 2$. The minimum occurs when $-(x + 2)^2 + 12$ equals 0. The minimum would be at $2^0 - 2$.

$-1 \le y \le 2^{2\sqrt{3}} - 2$

Ex: 3 State the domain and range of $f(x) = \log_4(-x^2 + 4x)$.
You can only take the logarithm of a positive number. Therefore, $-x^2 + 4x > 0$. This can be factored into $-x(x - 4) > 0$ so the critical values are at $x = 0, 4$. Plotting these values on a number line and nothing that 1 works, the domain must be between 0 and 4. For the range, let's find the maximum of $-x^2 + 4x$.
$-(x^2 - 4x + 4) + 4$ Completing the square
$-(x - 2)^2 + 4$ Maximum is 4. Therefore, the maximum of this function is $\log_4 4 = 1$. The minimum would be negative infinity because as $-x^2 + 4x$ becomes a fraction and gets smaller and smaller and $\log_4(-x^2 + 4x)$ also gets smaller without bound.

Domain: $0 < x < 4$ Range: $y \le 1$

Ex: 4 Find the domain/range of $f(x) = \log_{x^2 - 4x + 8} 64$.
Remember that minimizing the base maximizes the function because you have to take the base to a greater number to get the 64. We can rewrite the base as $x^2 - 4x + 4 + 4$ and complete the square to get $(x - 2)^2 + 4$. Therefore, the minimum of the base is 4. $\log_4 64 = 3$ so the maximum of the function is 3. The base increases without bound, so the function does not have a minimum. For domain, the only restriction is that $x^2 - 4x + 8 > 0$ which is always achieved.

Domain: All Real Numbers, Range: $y \le 3$

Properties of Logarithms

Remember the logarithm rules are like the inverses of the exponent rules. Also, when in doubt, change the base!

Ex: 1 Simplify $e^{\ln 3.5} + 2\ln e^{1.5}$
Looking at the first expression, remember that e and ln cancel each other because $\ln x$ is $\log_e x$. So $e^{\ln 3.5} = 3.5$. For the second expression, remember that $\ln x$ is the inverse of e^x. When we take the natural log of something we're, trying to figure out what is the power of e. Therefore, $\ln e^{1.5} = 1.5$ Multiply that by 2 to get 3. Add it together to get 6.5.

6.5

Ex: 2 $\log_{27} 3^{2x} 9^{3-x} + \log_3 3^{x+1} 81^{2+3x}$
First, we can use product to sum to write this as:
$\log_{27} 3^{2x} + \log_{27} 9^{3-x} + \log_3 3^{x+1} + \log_3 81^{2+3x}$
Now we can use change of base to express everything in term of 3.
$\frac{\log_3 3^{2x}}{\log_3 27} + \frac{\log_3 9^{3-x}}{\log_3 27} + \log_3 3^{x+1} + \log_3 3^{4(2+3x)}$
Remember that $\log_3 x$ and 3^x are inverses and we can rewrite numbers in terms of base 3 by using exponent power rules.
$\frac{1}{3} \cdot 2x + \frac{1}{3}\log_3 3^{2(3-x)} + x + 1 + 8 + 12x$
$\frac{2x}{3} + \frac{6-2x}{3} + 13x + 9$

$13x + 11$

Ex: 3 Simplify $\log(32^{\log_2 10} \cdot 27^{\log_3 2} \cdot 343^{\log_{49} 25})$
$\log(2^{5\log_2 10} \cdot 3^{3\log_3 2} \cdot 7^{\frac{3\log_7 25}{\log_7 49}})$ Change of Base
Here we are also expressing 32, 27, 343 in terms of bases 2, 3, 5 to cancel out logarithms.
$\log(2^{\log_2 10^5} \cdot 3^{\log_3 2^3} \cdot 7^{\log_7 25^{3/2}})$ Simplifying
$\log(10^5 \cdot 2^3 \cdot 25^{3/2})$ Exponents/Logs Cancel Out
$\log(10^5 \cdot 2^3 \cdot 5^3)$ Simplifying
$\log(10^8)$ Multiplying exponents
8 Definition of Logarithm

8

Ex: 4 Simplify $5\ln 3e - \frac{3}{2}\ln\frac{1}{\sqrt{e}} + 2\ln 8$

Let's first rewrite some of these using product to sum. $5(\ln 3 + \ln e) - \frac{3}{2}\ln e^{-1/2} + 2\ln 8$

Now simplify the $\ln e$ terms.

$5\ln 3 + 5 - \frac{3}{2}(\frac{-1}{2}) + 2\ln 8.$

Use product to power on the first and last term.

$\ln 3^5 + \frac{23}{4} + \ln 8^2$

Now we can use sum to product to simplify.

$\ln 15552 + \frac{23}{4}$

Ex: 5 Let $\ln 8 = A$, $\ln 5 = B, \ln 6 = C$. Find $\ln 15$ in terms of A, B, and C.

Let's rewrite 15 in terms of $8, 5, 6$. Something to notice is that because $2^3 = 8$, it's fine if we find $\ln 15$ in terms of $\ln 2$ cause we can just use change of base to get to $\ln 8$.

It's easy to figure out that we can rewrite this as:

$\ln 15 = \ln(\frac{5 \cdot 6}{2})$.

$\ln 15 = \ln 5 + \ln 6 - \ln 2$ Using product to sum

$\ln 15 = B + C - \ln 8^{1/3}$

$\ln 15 = B + C - \frac{1}{3}\ln 8$ Using power to product

$\ln 15 = B + C - \frac{1}{3}A$

$\ln 15 = B + C - \frac{1}{3}A$

Ex: 6 If $\frac{\log_b a}{\log_c a} = \frac{15}{23}$ and $\frac{c^2}{b} = b^k$, what is k?

$\frac{\log_b a}{\frac{\log_b a}{\log_b c}} = \frac{15}{23}$ Using Change of Base on $\log_c a$

$\log_b c = \frac{15}{23}$ Dividing out $\log_b a$

$2\log_b c = \frac{30}{23}$ Multiplying by 2 for product to power

$\log_b c^2 - \log_b b = \frac{30}{23} - \log_b b$ Subtracting $\log_b b$

$\log_b(\frac{c^2}{b}) = \frac{7}{23}$ Difference to quotient, simplifying

$\frac{c^2}{b} = b^{7/23}$ Definition of logs

Therefore, $k = \frac{7}{23}$

$k = \frac{7}{23}$

Ex: 7 Find x and y if $\log_4 x + \log_{16} y^4 = 6$ and $\log_4 y^2 + \log_{16} x^4 = 9$.

Let's simplify our first equation.

$\log_4 x + 4\log_{16} y = 6$ Product to power

$\frac{\log_2 x}{\log_2 4} + \frac{4\log_2 y}{\log_2 16} = 6$ Change of Base

$\frac{1}{2}\log_2 x + \log_2 y = 6$ Simplifying

Now onto our second equation.

$2\log_4 y + 4\log_{16} x = 9$ Product to power

$\frac{2\log_2 y}{\log_2 4} + \frac{4\log_2 x}{\log_2 16} = 9$ Change of Base

$\log_2 y + \log_2 x = 9$ Simplifying

If we let, $a = \log_2 x$ and $b = \log_2 y$ we can set up a system of linear equations. Solving, we get $a = 6, b = 3$. Since $\log_2 x = 6, \log_2 y = 3$ we get that $x = 64, y = 8$ by the definition of logarithms.

$x = 64, y = 8$

Ex: 8 If $\frac{1}{\log_2 x} + \frac{1}{\log_3 x} + \frac{1}{\log_4 x} + \ldots + \frac{1}{\log_n x} = \log_x 5040$, find n.

Our goal is to express things in log base x.

$\frac{1}{\frac{\log_x x}{\log_x 2}} + \frac{1}{\frac{\log_x x}{\log_x 3}} + \frac{1}{\frac{\log_x x}{\log_x 3}} + \ldots + \frac{1}{\frac{\log_x x}{\log_x n}} = \log_x 5040$ COB

$\log_x 2 + \log_x 3 + \log_x 4 + \ldots \log_x n = \log_x 5040$ Simplify

$\log_x(2 \cdot 3 \cdot 4 \cdot \ldots \cdot n) = \log_x 5040$ Sum to Product

$2 \cdot 3 \cdot 4 \cdot \ldots \cdot n = 5040$ Taking x to the power of

The left side is n factorial and $7!$ is equal to 5040. Therefore $n = 7$.

$n = 7.$

The important concept here is that $\frac{1}{\log_a b} = \log_b a$.

Logarithmic and Exponential Equations/Inequalities

Ex: 1 Solve $(\frac{3}{x})^{-\log_3 x} = 27x$

$(\frac{x}{3})^{\log_3 x} = 27x$ Negative Exponent Rules

$\log_3(\frac{x}{3})^{\log_3 x} = \log_3(27x)$ Taking $\log_3$ on both sides

$\log_3 x \cdot (\log_3 x - \log_3 3) = \log_3 27 + \log_3 x$ Applying basic log properties

$\log_3 x \cdot (\log_3 x - 1) = 3 + \log_3 x$ Simplifying

Let $a = \log_3 x$ and substitute that in.

$a^2 - 2a - 3 = 0$ Combining like terms

$(a-3)(a+1) = 0$ Factoring

$a = 3, a = -1$ Solving for a

$\log_3 x = 3, \log_3 x = -1$ Substituting for a

$x = 27, x = \frac{1}{3}$

$x = 27, x = \frac{1}{3}$

Ex: 2 Solve $\log_{0.5}(x-1) > \log_{0.25}(x^2-3x+5)$

Use change of base to rewrite the left side.

$\log_{0.5}(x-1) > \frac{\log_{0.5}(x^2-3x+5)}{\log_{0.5}0.25}$

$\log_{0.5}(x-1) > \log_{0.5}\sqrt{x^2-3x+5}$

Now, we may think that $x-1 > \sqrt{x^2-3x+5}$

However, we must actually switch the sign. Why? Because the base is less than 1, taking the base of a really large number actually gets a really small negative number. Therefore, $x-1 < \sqrt{x^2-3x+5}$.

$x^2-2x+1 < x^2-3x+5$ Square both sides

$x < 4$ By combining like terms

However, now let's consider the domain. Based on the first logarithm, $x-1>0$ so $x>1$. For the second logarithm, $x^2-3x+5>0$. Finding the critical points, we get $x = \frac{3\pm\sqrt{9-20}}{2}$. Since there's no real solutions, it's never less than 0.

$1 < x < 4$

Ex: 3 Solve $\log_3(28-3^x) = 4^{\frac{1}{2}\log_2(3-x)}$

$\log_3(28-3^x) = (2^2)^{\frac{1}{2}\log_2(3-x)}$ Rewriting 4

$\log_3(28-3^x) = 2^{\log_2(3-x)}$ Exponent Properties

Remember again that exponents and logarithms cancel out, so we can simplify the right side.

$\log_3(28-3^x) = 3-x$

$28-3^x = 3^{3-x}$ Take 3 to the power of

$28(3^x) - 3^{2x} = 3^3$ Multiply 3^x

$3^{2x} - 28(3^x) + 27 = 0$. Rewriting the equation

$(3^x-27)(3^x-1) = 0$ Factoring the "quadratic"

$3^x = 27, x = 3$ Solving the first factor

$3^x = 1, x = 0$ Solving the second factor

Not that 3 is extraneous because it makes $\log_2(3-x)$ undefined

$x = 0$

Ex: 4 Solve $\log_2(\log_4(2^x+3)) < 2\log_4(x+1)$

$\log_2(\log_4(2^x+3)) < \frac{2\log_2(x+1)}{\log_2 4}$ Change of Base

$\log_2(\log_4(2^x+3)) < \log_2(x+1)$ Simplifying

$\log_4(2^x+3) < x+1$ Properties of Logs

$2^x+3 < 4^{x+1}$ Taking 4 to the power of

$4(2^x)^2 - 2^x - 3 > 0$ Using exponent rules

$(4(2^x)+3)(2^x-1) > 0$ Factoring

$2^x = -\frac{3}{4}, 2^x = 1$ Factor Theorem

Critical Value: $x = 0$

If we test $x = -1$, we see that $2^{-1}+3 > 4^0$ so all values $x<0$ meet this criteria. For considering domain, 2^x+3 must be positive, which is always true. $\log_4(2^x+3) > 0$ as well.

$2^x+3 > 1$ Taking 4 to the power of

$2^x > -2$ which is always true

$x+1 > 0$ Considering domain for $\log_4(x+1)$

$x > -1$ Subtracting 1 on both sides

$-1 < x < 0$

Ex: 5 Solve $\log_3 x + \log_x 9 = \frac{11}{3}$

$\log_3 x + \frac{\log_3 9}{\log_3 x} = \frac{11}{3}$ Change of Base

$\log_3 x + \frac{2}{\log_3 x} = \frac{11}{3}$ Simplifying

Let $\log_3 x = a$ and substitute in a.

$a^2 + 2 = \frac{11}{3}a$ Multiply by a on both sides

$3a^2 - 11a + 6 = 0$ Multiply by 3 on both sides

$(3a-2)(a-3) = 0$ Factoring

$a = \frac{2}{3}, 3$ Solving for a

$\log_3 x = \frac{2}{3}$ and $\log_3 x = 3$ Substituting for a

$x = 3^{2/3}, 27$ Solving for x

$x = 3^{2/3}, 27$

Ex: 6 Solve $\sqrt{\frac{\log_4\sqrt{a}}{\log_a 16}} + \sqrt{\frac{\log_a 16}{\log_4\sqrt{a}}} = \frac{13}{6}$.

$\frac{\log_4\sqrt{a}}{\log_a 16} + 2\sqrt{\left(\frac{\log_4\sqrt{a}}{\log_a 16}\right)\left(\frac{\log_a 16}{\log_4\sqrt{a}}\right)} + \frac{\log_a 16}{\log_4\sqrt{a}} = \frac{169}{36}$ Squaring

$\frac{\log_4\sqrt{a}}{\log_a 16} + \frac{\log_a 16}{\log_4\sqrt{a}} + 2 = \frac{169}{36}$ Simplifying

$\frac{\log_4\sqrt{a}}{\log_a 16} + \frac{\log_a 16}{\log_4\sqrt{a}} = \frac{97}{36}$ Subtracting 2 from both sides.

Using product to power, we can rewrite $\log_4\sqrt{a}$ as $\frac{1}{2}\log_4 a$. Using Change of Base, we can rewrite $\log_a 16$ as $\frac{\log_4 16}{\log_4 a}$ which simplifies to $\frac{2}{\log_4 a}$.

$\frac{\frac{1}{2}\log_4 a}{\frac{2}{\log_4 a}} + \frac{\frac{2}{\log_4 a}}{\frac{1}{2}\log_4 a} = \frac{97}{36}$ Rewriting the expression

Now, to make life easier let $x = \log_4 a$.

$\frac{1}{4}x^2 + \frac{4}{x^2} = \frac{97}{36}$ Making substitutions and simplifying

$9x^4 - 97x^2 + 144 = 0$ Multiplying by $36x^2$
$(x^2 - 9)(9x^2 - 16) = 0$ Factoring
$x = \pm 3, x = \pm \frac{4}{3}$ Solving for x
$\log_4 a = \pm 3, \log_4 a = \pm \frac{4}{3}$ Substituting for x
$a = 64, \frac{1}{64}, 4^{4/3}, 4^{-4/3}$

$$a = 64, \frac{1}{64}, 4^{4/3}, 4^{-4/3}$$

Ex: 7 Solve $\ln(x-4) + \log(x-4) = 2$
We have to use change of base to relate the base e and base 10.
$\frac{\log(x-4)}{\log e} + \log(x-4)$ Change of base
$\log(x-4)^{\frac{1}{\log e}} + \log(x-4) = 2$ Using product to power to move the $\log e$ as a power
$\log(x-4)^{1+\frac{1}{\log e}} = 2$ Using sum to product
$(x-4)^{1+\frac{1}{\log e}} = 100$ Taking 10 the power of
$(x-4)^{\frac{\log e+1}{\log e}} = 100$ Combining the fraction
$x - 4 = 100^{\frac{\log e}{1+\log e}}$ Isolating the $x-4$

$$x = 4 + 100^{\frac{\log e}{1+\log e}}$$

If you instead use COB to write things in terms of ln instead of the common logarithm, you would get a different answer that is equally valid.

Ex: 8 Solve $4\log_9\sqrt{x} - \log_3(x-2) = \log_{27}(\frac{32}{x})$ if x is an integer.
$2\log_9 x - \log_3(x-2) = \log_{27}(\frac{32}{x})$ Product to Power
$\frac{2\log_3 x}{\log_3 9} - \log_3(x-2) = \frac{\log_3(\frac{32}{x})}{\log_3 27}$ Change of Base
$\frac{2\log_3 x}{2} - \log_3(x-2) = \frac{\log_3(\frac{32}{x})}{3}$ Simplifying
$\log_3(\frac{x}{x-2}) = \frac{1}{3}\log_3(\frac{32}{x})$ Difference to Quotient
$\log_3(\frac{x}{x-2}) = \log_3(\sqrt[3]{\frac{32}{x}})$ Product to Power
$\frac{x}{x-2} = \sqrt[3]{\frac{32}{x}}$ Taking 3 to the power of
$\frac{x^3}{x^3-6x^2+12x-8} = \frac{32}{x}$ Cubing both sides
$x^4 - 32x^3 + 192x^2 - 384x + 256 = 0$ Simplifying
$(x-4)(x^3 - 28x^2 + 80x - 64) = 0$
$x = 4$ Solving for x, factor theorem to check that $x^3 - 28x^2 + 80x - 64$ does not have integer roots

$$x = 4$$

Ex: 9 Solve $x^{2\log_{x^2}(\log_x 4)} = 2$
$2\log_{x^2}(\log_x 4) = \log_x 2$ Taking $\log_x$ on both sides
$\frac{2\log_x(\log_x 4)}{\log_x x^2} = \log_x 2$ Change of base
$\frac{2\log_x(\log_x 4)}{2} = \log_x 2$ Simplifying
$\log_x(\log_x 4) = \log_x 2$ Simplifying
$\log_x 4 = 2$ Taking x to the power of
$x^2 = 4$ Definition of logarithm
$x = \pm 2$ Taking square root

$$x = 2, \text{Bases of Logarithm must be positive}$$

Ex: 10 Solve $2(9^{3x/2}) - 7(3^{2x}) + 6(3^{x-1}) + 3 = 0$.
$2(3^2)^{3x/2} - 7(3^x)^2 + 6(3^{-1})(3^x) + 3 = 0$ Exponent rules to rewrite things in terms of 3
$2(3^x)^3 - 7(3^x)^2 + 2(3^x) + 3 = 0$ Simplifying
We can see the structure of a polynomial. If we let $a = 3^x$, we get the cubic polynomial:
$2a^3 - 7a^2 + 2a + 3 = 0$
$(a-3)(2a+1)(a-1) = 0$ Factoring
$a = 3, a = -\frac{1}{2}, a = 1$ Solving for a
$3 = 3^x, -\frac{1}{2} = 3^x, 1 = 3^x$ Substituting $a = 3^x$
$x = 1, 0$ Taking log base 3 on both sides

$$x = 1, 0$$

Ex: 11 If $\log_9 x = \log_{15} y = \log_{25}(\frac{3x-5y}{2}) = a$, find $(\frac{9}{25})^a$.
$x = 9^a, y = 15^a, \frac{3x-5y}{2} = 25^a$ Definition of logarithm
$3(9^a) - 5(15^a) = 2(25^a)$ Substituting in for x and y
$3(\frac{3}{5})^a - 5 = 2(\frac{5}{3})^a$ Dividing by 15^a on both sides
$3x - 5 = \frac{2}{x}$ Substituting $(\frac{3}{5})^a = x$
$3x^2 - 5x - 2 = 0$ Multiplying by x on both sides
$(3x+1)(x-2) = 0$ Factoring
$x = -\frac{1}{3}, 2$ Solving for x
$a = \log_{3/5} 2$ Log isn't defined for negative numbers
$(\frac{9}{25})^{\log_{3/5} 2} = (\frac{3}{5})^{2\log_{3/5} 2}$ Rewriting $\frac{9}{25}$
$(\frac{9}{25})^{\log_{3/5} 2} = 2^2 = 4$ Properties of logs

$$4$$

Exponential/Logarithms Test 1

#1: (3 points each) Simplify.

a) $\log_{64}\frac{1}{32}$

b) $e^{-2\ln(3-2x)}$

c) $3\log a - 2\log b^3 + \log c - \frac{5}{2}\log 3$

d) $\log_{125}(5^{2x-1}25^{5x+1}) =$

#2: (10 points) Algebraically find the domain and the range of $g(x) = 4^{\sqrt{-4x^2+3x+7}} + 3$

#3: (10 points) If $a \cdot \log_{440}2 + b \cdot \log_{440}5 + c \cdot \log_{440}11 = n$ and $a + b + c = 15$, find $\log_n a^{bc}$.

#4: (10 points) If $f(x) = 3^x$ and $g(x) = \log_{\sqrt{3}}(\sqrt{2x+1}) + \frac{1}{\log_{x-1}3}$, rewrite $g(x)$ in terms of f. Then find the domain of $g(x)$.

#5: (10 points each) Solve each for x:

a) $5^{\log_x 25} = 625x^2$

b) $64^x = 16^{\frac{1}{4}+x} + 4^x - 2$

c) $8\log_9 x + 6\log_x 3 = 11$

d) $\log_{1.4}(x+5) > \log_{1.96}(x^2 + 3x - 1)$

#6: (10 points) If $128^{2y} \cdot 8^{-3x} = 64$, $81^{0.5x} \cdot 27^{-\frac{1}{9}y} = 2187$, find $\log_x(8y + 2x)$.

#7: (8 points) A man places $1200 into a savings account that has an annual interest rate of 4%. In exact form, how many <u>years</u> will it take for the man's savings to reach $1500 if interest is compounded every 3 months?

Exponents/Logarithms Test 2

#1: (4 points each) Simplify/Condense

a) $3(\ln x - 3\ln(x^2 - 2)) + 7\ln 2$

b) $(e^{-3\ln(1+6x)^{\sqrt{5}}})^2$

c) $3\log(\frac{a+3b}{2}) - 2\log 9 + \frac{3}{4}\log 16 + 4\log\frac{-3}{2a+6b}$

d) $\log_{64}(2^{2x-1}4^{\frac{3}{2}x+7}8^{3x}32^{\frac{2}{5}x+2})$

#2: (10 points) Algebraically find the domain and the range of $f(x) = \sqrt{\log_2(2-x) + \log_{\sqrt{2}}\sqrt{x+6}}$.

#3: (14 points) If $\log_a b + \log_b a = \frac{25}{12}$, $4^{\frac{a}{b}+\frac{b}{a}} = 32$, find all possible pairs of a and b. **40**

#4: (10 points each) Solve each for x:

a) $4^x + 6^x = 9^x$ **11**

b) $2^{3x+1} - 6(4^{x-0.5}) - 44(2^{x-2}) + 6 = 0$

c) $\sqrt{2x - \log_3(3^x - 18)} = 2$

d) $\sqrt{3}\log 10x = \sqrt{\log x^6 + 12}$

#5: (8 points) A certain chemical substance will decay by 17% every 3 days. a) In exact form, after how many days will there only be 20% of the substance left? b) How much of the chemical would be left after 5 days?

#6: (12 points) If you graphed $\log_b(1 + x^2 + y^2) \leq 1 + \log_b(x + y)$, the area of the resulting circle is 17π. What is b? **25**

Exponents/Logarithms Test 3

#1: (4 points each) Simplify/Condense

a) $5^{\log 2} \cdot 2^{\log 3} \cdot 5^{\log 12} \cdot 2^{\log 8}$

b) $(\log_2 5)(\log_5 14) + (\log_2 9)(\log_9 \frac{32}{7})$

c) $64^{[\log_2 x + 2\log_4 (x+1)]}$

d) $\log_3(3^{x-1} 9^{2x+1} 27^x)$

#2: (8 points) A sample of chemical decayed to 82% of its original amount after a year. What is the half life of the chemical in exact form?

#3: (12 points) Let the domain of $f(x) = a^{\sqrt{-x^2+ax+b}}$ be $-1 \leq x \leq 2a - 1$. What is the range of $f(x)$? **15**

#4: (10 points) Solve each for x.

a) $-\log_{25}(11x + 4) + \log_{\sqrt{5}}(16 - x) = \log_5 \sqrt{2x - 17}$

b) $16^x - 3(8^{x+1/3}) + 7(4^x) + 6(2^x) - 8 = 0$

c) $\log_3\sqrt{x-1} > \log_9(2x-3)$

d) $\log_2\sqrt{x} = \sqrt[3]{2\log_2 x}$

#5: (12 points) An equilateral triangle has side length $\log_2(4x^2) + \log_8 x$ units. Its area is $\frac{100\sqrt{3}}{9}$ units squared. If the radius of the triangle's inscribed circle is $\frac{5\sqrt{3}}{3}\log_{16} a$, what is $\log_x a$? **39**

#6: (12 points) If $\log_b 4 = A, \log_b 10 = B, \log_b 15 = C$ Find $\log_{b^2}(72b)$ in terms of A, B, C.

Chapter 4 Rational Functions

Rational functions are functions that represent a ratio of two polynomials. It is important to know how to condense rational functions as well as break them apart via partial fraction decomposition. Also make sure, you're familiar with the type of asymptotes and other features before you start. With this chapter, factoring skills will be used a lot! So make sure you're super good at factoring and expanding. There's a lot of work required and if you're not good at it, you'll run out of time.

Operations with Rational Expressions

Ex: 1 Simplify $\frac{3x+2}{x-1} + \frac{x-4}{x^2-1}$

$\frac{3x+2}{x-1} + \frac{x-4}{(x+1)(x-1)}$ Factor $x^2 - 1$

$\frac{(3x+2)(x+1)+(x-4)}{(x-1)(x+1)}$ Least common denominator

$\frac{3x^2+3x+2x+2+x-4}{(x+1)(x-1)}$ Expand

$\frac{3x^2+6x-2}{(x+1)(x-1)}$ Combine like terms

Ex: 2 Simplify $\frac{3x+5}{x-1} + \frac{x-4}{x+3} - \frac{x-1}{x^2+2x-3}$

$\frac{3x+5}{x-1} + \frac{x-4}{x+3} - \frac{x-1}{(x-1)(x+3)}$ Factor $x^2 + 2x - 3$

$\frac{(3x+5)(x+3)+(x-4)(x-1)-(x-1)}{(x-1)(x+3)}$ LCD

$\frac{3x^2+9x+5x+15+x^2-5x+4-x+1}{(x-1)(x+3)}$ Expand

$\frac{4x^2+8x+20}{(x-1)(x+3)}$ Combine like terms

Ex: 3 Simplify $\frac{2x^4+7x^3-16x^2-57x-36}{x^3-3x^2-x+3} \cdot \frac{x^3-1}{4x+6}$

$\frac{(x-3)(2x+3)(x+4)(x+1)}{(x-3)(x-1)(x+1)} \cdot \frac{x^3-1}{4x+6}$

Factor using synthetic division. You can also factor by grouping for the denominator.

$\frac{(x-3)(2x+3)(x+4)(x+1)}{(x-3)(x-1)(x+1)} \cdot \frac{(x-1)(x^2+x+1)}{2(2x+3)}$

Factor the difference of squares and the 2 out of $4x + 6$.

$\frac{(x+4)(x^2+x+1)}{2}$ Cancel out like terms

Ex: 4 Simplify $(\frac{1}{x-2} + \frac{1}{x+2})^{-1} \cdot \frac{8x^3(y^2-9)}{xy+3x+2y+6}$

$(\frac{x+2+x-2}{x^2-4})^{-1} \cdot \frac{8x^3(y^2-9)}{xy+3x+2y+6}$ Combining fractions

$\frac{(x+2)(x-2)}{2x} \cdot \frac{8x^3(y+3)(y-3)}{xy+3x+2y+6}$ Difference of Squares

$\frac{4x^2(x+2)(x-2)(y+3)(y-3)}{(x+2)(y+3)}$ Factoring the bottom

$4x^2(x-2)(y-3)$ Cancelling out factors

$4x^2(x-2)(y-3)$

You may encounter domain and range problems for rational functions. Remember that the denominator may never be 0 and solve rational inequalities when the rational function is underneath a square root.

Solving Rational Equations/Inequalities

Remember that any number that makes the denominator of a fraction equal 0 is an extraneous solution. Also remember that for word problems work equals rate multiplied by time.

Ex: 1 Solve $\frac{2x^2-3x+1}{x^2-x-6} = \frac{x}{x+2} + \frac{2}{x-3}$

$\frac{2x^2-3x+1}{(x+2)(x-3)} = \frac{x}{x+2} + \frac{2}{x-3}$ Factor the denominator

$2x^2 - 3x + 1 = x(x-3) + 2(x+2)$

Multiply $(x+2)(x-3)$ on both sides. You don't have to worry about losing solutions here because $-2, 3$ would not be valid solutions.

$x^2 - 2x - 3 = 0$ Distributing and simplifying

$(x-3)(x+1) = 0$

$x = -1$ because 3 is extraneous

Ex: 2 Solve $(\frac{1}{x+1} + \frac{1}{x-1})^2 = \frac{64}{225}$

$(\frac{x+1+x-1}{x^2-1})^2 = \frac{64}{225}$ Common denominator

$\frac{2x}{x^2-1} = \pm\frac{8}{15}$ Taking the square root

$30x = 8x^2 - 8$ Cross Multiplying (Positive)

$0 = 2(x-4)(4x+1)$ Factoring

$x = 4, -\frac{1}{4}$ Solving for x

$-30x = 8x^2 - 8$ Cross Multiplying (Negative)

$0 = 2(4x-1)(x+4)$ Factoring

$x = \frac{1}{4}, -4$

$x = \pm 4, \pm\frac{1}{4}$

Ex: 3 Simplify $\dfrac{2}{1+\frac{2}{1+\frac{2}{\dots}}}$.

This is an infinite repeating fraction. The key to solving these fractions is to try to set a part of the fraction equal to itself. What does that mean? Let this fraction's value equal x. If you look think about it, we can actually rewrite the fraction as $\frac{2}{1+x}$ by replacing the fraction with numerator 2 from the denominator. We can do this because adding one extra "layer" does not matter when there is an infinite amount of layers.

$\frac{2}{1+x} = x$ Equating the fraction to itself

$2 = x^2 + x$ Cross Multiplying

$0 = (x-1)(x+2)$ Factoring

$x = 1$ The fraction's value must be positive.

1

Ex: 4 During the triathlon, Aryan first ran 16 miles. Then, he swam 2 miles at a rate of 7 miles per hour slower than his running rate. Then, he biked 48 miles at a rate triple the running rate. The total time of the triathlon was 6 hours. What is Aryan's running speed in miles per hour?

Let x be Aryan's running speed. Therefore, his swimming speed would be $x-7$ and his biking speed would be $3x$. Using these variables, set up a rational equation. Remember distance equals rate times speed

$\frac{16}{x} + \frac{2}{x-7} + \frac{48}{3x} = 6$

$\frac{32}{x} + \frac{2}{x-7} = 6$ Simplification

$32(x-7) + 2(x) = 6(x)(x-7)$ Multiply the LCD

$0 = 3x^2 - 38x + 112$ Combining like terms

$0 = (3x-14)(x-8)$ Factoring

$x = \frac{14}{3}, 8$ Solve for x.

$\frac{14}{3}$ would make the swimming speed negative so it does not make sense in this situation.

Running Speed: 8 miles per hour

Ex: 5 Cedar Point is 240 miles away from Kings Island. Two cars leave Kings Island at the same time, heading for Cedar Point, but one averages 8 mph faster than the other. If the faster car reaches Cedar Point one hour earlier than the slower car, what is the average speed of the faster car?

Let the average speed of the faster car be x. The time it takes to get to Cedar Point would be $\frac{240}{x}$. The slower car has average speed $x-8$. The time it takes would be $\frac{240}{x-8}$. We can set up the equation:

$\frac{240}{x-8} - \frac{240}{x} = 1$ Difference in time is 1

$\frac{240x-240(x-8)}{x(x-8)} = 1$ Combining denominators

$\frac{240x-240x+1920}{x^2-8x} = 1$ Expanding

$1920 = x^2 - 8x$ Cross multiplying

$0 = (x-48)(x+40)$ Factoring

$x = 48, -40$ Solving

48 mph (must be positive)

Ex: 6 Colin takes one hour shorter than Kenny to create a code. Jonathan, who sucks at coding, takes 2 hours to destroy a code. If it takes 12 hours to complete the code when all three people are "coding", how long does it take for Colin to finish the code by himself?

Let Colin take x hours to finish the code and Kenny $x+1$ hours. Therefore, Colin completes $\frac{1}{x}$ of the code per hour. Kenny would complete $\frac{1}{x+1}$ of the code per hour. Jonathan would destroy $\frac{1}{2}$ of the code per hour. Therefore, we set up the equation: $12(\frac{1}{x} + \frac{1}{x+1} - \frac{1}{2}) = 1$ since it takes 12 hours to complete one code.

$\frac{1}{x} + \frac{1}{x+1} - \frac{1}{2} = \frac{1}{12}$ Dividing 12

$\frac{x+1+x}{x(x+1)} = \frac{7}{12}$ Simplifying

$24x + 12 = 7x^2 + 7x$ Cross multiplying

$0 = 7x^2 - 17x - 12$ Simplifying

$0 = (7x+4)(x-3)$ Factoring

$x = \frac{-4}{7}, 3$ Solving

3 hours

Ex: 7 I can normally walk to school in 24 minutes so I will be exactly on time. One day, after I had walked 540 meters, I suddenly got a stomach ache. Because of that, my walking speed decreased by 18 meters a minute and I got to school 8 minutes late. How far is my school in meters?

Let d be how far my school is and r be my normal walking speed in meters/minute.

$d = 24r$ Definition of distance

Now let's use the situation to set up an equation.

$\frac{540}{r} + \frac{d-540}{r-18} = 32$ Setting up equation for time

$\frac{540}{r} + \frac{24r-540}{r-18} = 32$ Substituting in $d = 24r$

$540(r-18) + r(24r-540) = 32r(r-18)$

Multiplying least common denominator

$540r - 9720 + 24r^2 - 540r = 32r^2 - 576r$ Simplify

$0 = 8r^2 - 576r + 9720$ Combining like terms

$0 = r^2 - 72r + 1215$ Dividing by 8

$0 = (r-45)(r-27)$ Factoring

$r = 45, 27$ Solving for r

$d = 24(45) = 1080, d = 24(27) = 648$

1080 or 648 meters

Ex: 9 Jolie goes on a roadtrip to a national park. On the way there, she averages 12 miles per hour faster than on the way back. If the total average speed for her trip (to and from), is $\frac{160}{3}$ miles per hour, what was average speed on the way there?

Let the distance to the park be d. The total distance Jolie has traveled to and from the park is $2d$. Let x be the average speed on the way there. $\frac{d}{x}$ would be the time it takes to drive to the park while $\frac{d}{x-12}$ will be the time it takes to drive back.

$\frac{2d}{\frac{d}{x}+\frac{d}{x-12}} = \frac{160}{3}$ Setting up our equation for average speed (Total distance over total time)

$\frac{1}{\frac{1}{x}+\frac{1}{x-12}} = \frac{80}{3}$ Dividing out common factors $(d, 2)$

$3 = \frac{80}{x} + \frac{80}{x-12}$ Cross Multiplying

$3x(x-12) = 80(x-12) + 80x$ Multiplying $x(x-12)$

$3x^2 - 196x + 960 = 0$ Combining like terms

$(x-60)(3x-16) = 0$

$x = 60$ Can't be $\frac{16}{3}$ since $x - 12$ would be negative

60 miles per hours

Ex: 10 Solve $\frac{2x+1}{x-2} + 2 > 0$

$\frac{2x+1}{x-2} + \frac{2(x-2)}{x-2} > 0$ Create common denominator

$\frac{4x-3}{x-2} > 0$ Combine terms into one fraction

Critical values: $\frac{3}{4}$, 2

Find critical values by finding what makes the denominator and numerator equal to 0.

Test 0: $\frac{4(0)-3}{0-2}$ is indeed greater than 0.

$x < \frac{3}{4}, x > 2$

Ex: 11 Find the domain and range of $f(x) = \sqrt{\frac{2-x-x^2}{(x+1)^2}} - 2$. As we dealt with in chapter 2, the value under the radicand must be positive. $\frac{2-x-x^2}{(x+1)^2} \geq 0$. We know that $(x+1)^2$ will always be positive since we're squaring so we can simplify the inequality to get $2 - x - x^2 \geq 0$ Solve for critical points $x = 1, -2$. We can plot these values on a number line and test 0. Since $2 \geq 0$, we know the range from -2 to 1 fulfills the value. However, remember that -1 does not work because it makes the denominator of the fraction equal to 0.

Domain: $-2 \leq x < -1$ and $-1 < x \leq 1$

Now to find the range. We know that the rational expression beneath the radical can equal 0 so the minimum is -2. Now, the maximum is actually infinity. The reason why we know this because $f(x)$ has a asymptote at $x = -1$ where the denominator equals 0 and $f(x)$ is thus undefined. As $f(x)$ approaches closer and closer to -1, the graph gets infinitely big.

Range: $y \geq -2$

Graphing Rational Functions

Ex: 1 Graph $y = \frac{x^2+x-2}{x^3+3x^2-4x-12}$.

$y = \frac{(x+2)(x-1)}{(x+2)(x+3)(x-2)}$ Factor the top and bottom

Hole: Because the $x+2$ term cancels out, there's a hole at $x = -2$. Plug -2 in $y = \frac{x-1}{(x+3)(x-2)}$ to get the hole to be $(-2, \frac{3}{4})$.

Vertical Asymptote: There is a vertical asymptote where the denominator is 0.

$x = -3, x = 2$

Horizontal Asymptote: The horizontal asymptote is $y = 0$ because the degree of the numerator is less than the degree of the denominator.

Slant Asymptote: None

x − intercept: $(1, 0)$

y − intercept: $\frac{0-1}{3(-2)} = \frac{1}{6}$. $(0, \frac{1}{6})$

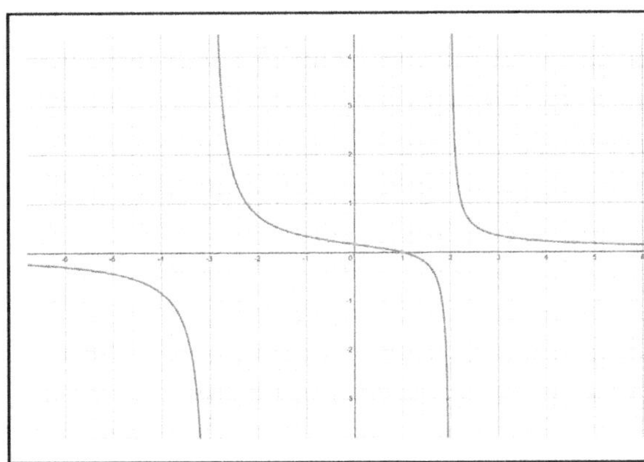

Ex: 2 Graph $y = \frac{x^4+2x^3+3x^2-2x-4}{x^3+3x^2-4}$.

$y = \frac{(x+1)(x-1)(x^2+2x+4)}{(x+2)(x+2)(x-1)}$ Factor the top and bottom.

Hole: Because the $x-1$ term cancels out, there's a hole at $x = 1$ Plug 1 in $y = \frac{(x+1)(x^2+2x+4)}{(x+2)(x+2)}$ to get the hole to be $(1, 14/9)$.

Vertical Asymptote: $x = -2$ which makes the denominator equal 0.

Horizontal Asymptote: None

Slant Asymptote: Divide the two polynomials and find that the quotient is $x-1$. So the slant asymptote is $y = x - 1$.

Intersection: Because of the slant asymptote, the graph intersects the asymptote at $(-\frac{4}{3}, \frac{-7}{3})$. You can find this by solving $x - 1 = \frac{(x+1)(x^2+2x+4)}{(x+2)(x+2)}$

$(x-1)(x^2+4x+4) = (x+1)(x^2+2x+4)$

$x^3+3x^2-4 = x^3+3x^2+6x+4$ Expanding

$-8 = 6x$ Cancelling out like terms

$x = \frac{-4}{3}, y = \frac{-4}{3} - 1 = \frac{-7}{3}$

x − intercept: $(-1, 0)$ since x^2+2x+4 only has complex roots.

y − intercept: $(0, 1)$

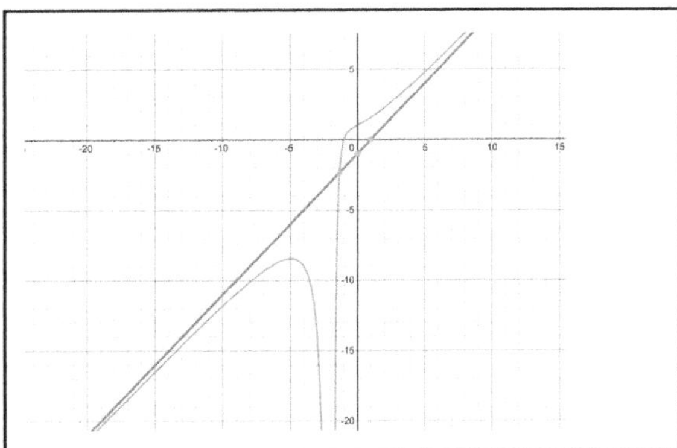

Note: The line is the slant asymptote.

Ex: 3 Write the equation of the rational function $f(x)$ such that the following conditions are met.

- Horizontal Asymptote: $y = -2$
- Vertical Asymptote: $x = 2$
- Hole at $(1, -3)$

Because the horizontal asymptote is $y = -2$, the degree of the top and bottom must be the same. In fact, the leading coefficient divided by the leading coefficient of the bottom must be -2. Because of the vertical asymptote at $x = 2$, $(x-2)$ must be a factoron the denominator. Because of the hole, $(x-1)$ must be a factor in both the numerator and denominator that gets cancelled out. After we cancel out this common factor and plug in $x = 1$, we must get -3.

$f(x) = \frac{(-2x+a)(x-1)}{(x-2)(x-1)}$ Putting the information together

$f(x) = \frac{-2x+a}{x-2}$ Cancelling out common factor

$f(1) = -3 = \frac{-2+a}{1-2}$ Definition of a hole

$3 = -2 + a$ Simplifying

$a = 5$ Solving for a

Therefore, $f(x) = \frac{(-2x+5)(x-1)}{(x-2)(x-1)}$

$f(x) = \frac{-2x^2+7x-5}{x^2-3x+2}$ Expanding

Partial Fraction Decomposition

Ex: 1 Find the partial fraction decomposition of $\frac{x-1}{x^2-7x+10}$.

$\frac{x-1}{(x-5)(x-2)}$ Factor the denominator

$\frac{x-1}{(x-5)(x-2)} = \frac{A}{x-5} + \frac{B}{x-2}$

Write out the fractions for each linear factor.

$x - 1 = A(x-2) + B(x-5)$

Multiply both sides by $(x-5)(x-2)$.

$x - 1 = (A+B)x - 2A - 5B$ Simplify

$1 = A + B, -1 = -2A - 5B$

Set up a system of equations by matching up coefficients.

Solve to get $A = 4/3, B = -1/3$

$\frac{x-1}{x^2-7x+10} = \frac{4/3}{x-5} - \frac{1/3}{x-2}$ Write out answer

Ex: 2 Find the partial fraction decomposition of $\frac{x+2}{x^3-8}$.

$\frac{x+2}{(x-2)(x^2+2x+4)}$ Factor the denominator

$\frac{x+2}{(x-2)(x^2+2x+4)} = \frac{A}{x-2} + \frac{Bx+C}{x^2+2x+4}$

Write out fractions for each factor. For the quadratic factor, you need two variables instead of one.

$x + 2 = A(x^2 + 2x + 4) + (x - 2)(Bx + C)$

Multiply both sides by $(x - 2)(x^2 + 2x + 4)$

$x + 2 = (A + B)x^2 + (2A - 2B + C)x + 4A - 2C$

$0 = A + B, 1 = 2A - 2B + C, 2 = 4A - 2C$

Set up a system of equations by matching coefficients.

Solve to get $A = 1/3, B = -1/3, C = -1/3$

$\frac{x+2}{x^3-8} = \frac{1/3}{x-2} - \frac{\frac{1}{3}x+\frac{1}{3}}{x^2+2x+4}$

Ex: 3 Find the partial fraction decomposition of $\frac{5x^2+20x+6}{x^2+2x+1}$.

First notice that this is not a proper fraction because the degree of the numerator is greater than the degree of the denominator. Use long division to get a proper fraction.

$\frac{5x^2+20x+6}{x^2+2x+1} = 5 + \frac{10x+1}{x^2+2x+1}$

Now we can proceed with the standard process:

$\frac{10x+1}{(x+1)^2} = \frac{A}{x+1} + \frac{B}{(x+1)^2}$

Because the $(x + 1)$ factor has a multiplicity of 2, it occupies a partial fraction for each factor.

$10x + 1 = A(x + 1) + B$

$10x + 1 = Ax + A + B$

Matching up like terms, we see that

$10 = A, 1 = A + B$

Therefore, $A = 10, B = -9$

$5 + \frac{10}{x+1} - \frac{9}{(x+1)^2}$

Direct and Inverse Variation

With these problems, just carefully define your variables and keep track of your changes. Most teachers won't allow you to directly plug in numbers but you can use that to check your work.

Ex: 1 The luminosity I of a light varies inversely as the square of the distance d from the light. If a certain lamp has intensity of 800 candelas at a distance of 20 meters, what is the intensity of this lamp at a distance of 8 meters?

$I \cdot d^2 = k$ where k is the constant

Plug in 800 for I and 20 for d to get:

$k = 800 \cdot 20^2 = 320{,}000$

$320{,}000 = I \cdot 8^2$ Plug in variables

5000 candelas Solve for I

Ex: 2 Let a be directly proportional to b, b directly proportional to the square of c, and c inversely proportional to the cube of d. If d is doubled and c and b are kept constant, how will a be changed?

$a = b \cdot k_1$, $b = c^2 \cdot k_2$, $c = \frac{k_3}{d^3}$ Set up an equation of proportionality for each.

$b = \frac{(k_3)^2 \cdot k_2}{d^6}$ Substitute c for the second equation

$a = \frac{(k_3)^2 \cdot k_2 \cdot k_1}{d^6}$ Substitute b for the first equation.

k_1, k_2, k_3 are all constants so they can be grouped together into one constant of proportionality. Now we can see the relationship between a and d. a is inversely proportional to the sixth power of d.

Therefore, if d is doubled, a must be divided by 64

Ex: 3 If a varies directly as the square of b and inversely as the cube of c, how is the value of a changed when the values of b and c are halved?

$a = \frac{kb^2}{c^3}$ Statement of proportionality

Now let's add the changes.

$\frac{k(\frac{1}{2}b)^2}{(\frac{1}{2}c)^3} = \frac{k(\frac{1}{4})b^2}{\frac{1}{8}c^3} = \frac{2kb^2}{c^3}$

After simplifying with our changes , we see that the our new expression is double a so a must be doubled.

a is doubled

Rational Functions Test 1

#1: (10 points each) Simplify.

a) $\frac{2x^3+9x^2+x-12}{x^4-x^2} \cdot \frac{2x^2-3x}{x^2+x-12} \div \frac{4x^2-9}{x^2-2x-3}$

b) $2x + 3 + \frac{3x+2}{x-1} + \frac{2x^2-1}{x+1}$

c) $2b(\frac{1}{a} + \frac{1}{b})^{-1}(1 - \frac{a^2-3b^2}{2a^2-ab-3b^2})^{-1}$

#2: (16 points) Find all asymptotes, holes, x and y intercepts, and intersections of $f(x) = \frac{x^3+x^2-36x-36}{x^3+8x^2+9x-18}$ Then graph.

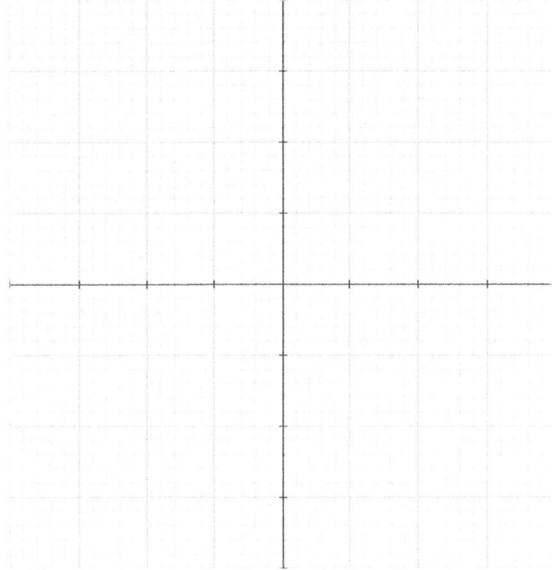

#3: (10 points each) Find the partial fraction decomposition for each.

a) $\frac{x^3+2x+6}{x^2-5x-6}$

b) $\frac{x^2-3x+5}{x(x+1)^2}$

#4: (12 points) Set up a system of rational equations and solve. Matthew's hose takes 20% less time to fill up the neighborhood pool compared to Ryan's hose. Together they can fill up the pool in 4 hours. a) How long does it take for Matthew and Ryan to each fill up the pool? b) Both hoses run for 108 minutes before Matthew takes his hose away. How many more hours would it take for Ryan to fill up his pool alone?

#5: (10 points) The force applied on a car rounding a corner to keep it from skidding is jointly proportional to the car's weight and velocity and inversely proportional to the square of the radius of the curve. a) Define variables and set up an equation of proportionality. If the force required to keep a 1500 lb car traveling at 30 mph from swerving around the curve of radius 15 meters is 4500 newtons, b) what is the constant of proportion? c) What would be the force required to keep a 1200 lb car from skidding around a 20 meter curve at 40 miles per hour?

#6: (12 points) Solve the rational inequality and express your answer in interval notation. $\frac{x+3}{x-2} \leq 2$

Rational Function Test 2

#1: (10 points each) Simplify.

a) $\frac{m^2-2m-8}{m^2-5m+6} \div \frac{m^2-3m-4}{m^2-9}$

b) $\dfrac{\frac{1}{y}-\frac{y-2}{y^2+y-2}}{\frac{1}{y^2-4}+\frac{1}{y^2+2y}}$

c) $\frac{1}{x+1} + \frac{3x}{6x^2+11x-7} - \frac{2x+1}{2x^2+x-1}$

#2: (16 points) Find all asymptotes, holes, x and y intercepts, and intersections of $f(x) = \frac{2x^2+x-6}{x^3+2x^2-x-2}$. Then graph.

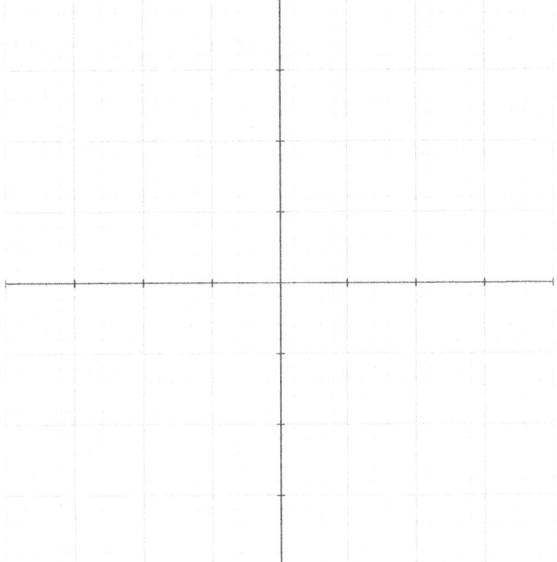

#3: (10 points each) Find the partial fraction decomposition for each.

a) $\frac{4x-3}{x^3-5x^2-6x}$

b) $\frac{-4x^4-26x^2-2x^3-8x-44}{(x+1)(x^2+3)^2}$

#4: (12 points) Set up a system of rational equations and solve. A tank can be filled by Pipe A in 8 hours and by Pipe B in 12 hours. It can be drained, from full, by Pipe C in 20 hours. a) How long would it take to fill the tank from empty with all three pipes open? b) Suppose Pipe A and C are opened to fill the tank from empty for 4 hours. Then Pipe B is added to speed up the process. How much longer will all 3 pipes need to be running for the tank to be filled?

#5: (10 points) The selection index of a student applying to MIT is jointly proportional to the SAT score, cube of the GPA, the square of the extra curricular rating, and inversely proportional to the total number of students applying from the school. a) Define variables and set up an equation to represent this variation. b) If the selection index of a student with a 4.0 GPA, 1500 SAT, 2 extra curricular rating, and total of 4 students applying from the same school is 3200. What is the constant of proportionality? c) If a student has a 3.0 GPA, 1600 SAT, extracurricular rating of 4 and 2 students applying from the same school, what is the selection index?

#6: (12 points) Solve the rational inequality and express your answer in interval notation. $\frac{1-x}{2x+3} \leq 3$

Rational Function Test 3

#1: (10 points each) Simplify.

a) $\frac{m^3-2m^2-5m+6}{m^2-1} \div \frac{m^2+7m+10}{m^2+m-20}$

b) $\frac{\left(\frac{1}{a}-\frac{1}{b}\right)^{-1}}{a-b} \cdot \frac{a+b}{ab} \cdot (a^2-b^2)$

c) $\frac{3x-1}{3x^2+2x-5} + \frac{x+2}{x^2-1} + \frac{x}{3x^2+8x+5}$

#2: (16 points) Find all asymptotes, holes, x and y intercepts, and intersections of $f(x) = \frac{2x^3-5x^2-4x+3}{x^2+4x+3}$. Then graph.

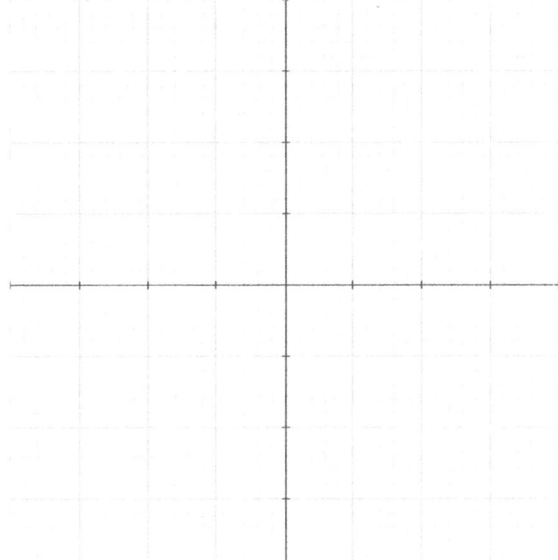

#3: (10 points each) Find the partial fraction decomposition for each.

a) $\frac{2x-1}{x^3-x^2+2x-2}$

b) $\frac{2x^4+3x^3-8x^2-9x-10}{x(x^2+1)(x^2-5)}$

#4: (12 points) Set up a system of rational equations and solve. If Aaron drives at an average of x miles per hour, he will be late by 3 minutes to work. If he drives at an average of $(x+20)$ miles per hour, he will be early by 3 minutes. a) If his company is 12 miles away, what is x? b) How many miles per hour does Aaron need to drive to get to work exactly on time?

#5: (10 points) The grade of an English paper is jointly proportional to the style rating, the square of the evidence rating, the cube of the analysis rating, and inversely proportional to error rating and the square of the redundancy rating. a) Define variables and set up an equation of proportionality. b) If an essay with style rating 6, evidence rating 6, analysis rating 4, error rating 8, and redundancy rating 4 receives a grade of 72, what is the constant of proportionality? c) What grade does an essay with style rating 8, evidence rating 3, analysis rating 5, error rating 5, and redundancy rating 4 receive?

#6: (12 points) Solve the rational inequality and express your answer in interval notation.

$\sqrt{\frac{2x+4}{x-1}} \geq x-2$

Rational Function Test 4

#1: (10 points each) Simplify:

a) $3+\frac{6}{1+\frac{6}{1+\frac{6}{\cdots}}}$

b) $\frac{2m^3+5m^2-14m-8}{mn+5m-2n-10}\cdot\left(\frac{1}{n+5}+\frac{1}{n-5}\right)^{-1}$

c) $\left(2+\frac{1}{2+\frac{1}{x}}\right)^{-1}\cdot\frac{25x^2-4}{8x^3+1}$

#2: (16 points) Find all asymptotes, holes, x and y intercepts, and intersections of $f(x)=\frac{3x^3+x^2-12x-4}{2x^3-3x^2-3x+2}$. Then graph.

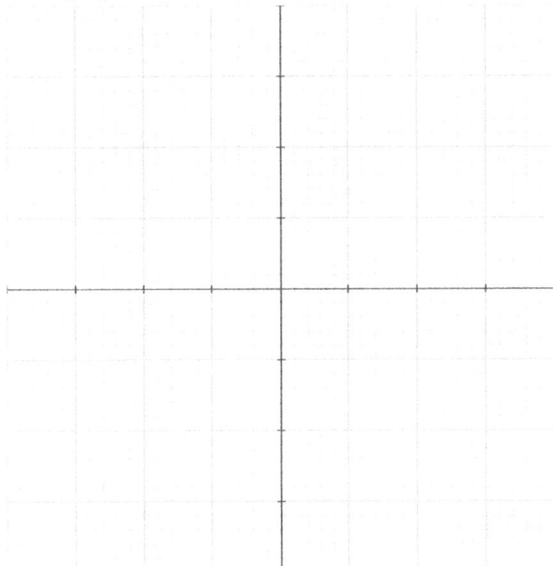

#3: (10 points each) Find the partial fraction decomposition of each.

a) $\frac{6x^2+9x-9}{4x^2+2x-2}$

b) $\frac{x^3-5x^2+11x+10}{x^4-3x^2-4}$

#4: (12 points) Dorcas and Justice have two types of walking speeds: one for when they are normal and one for when they are tired. On the way to the park, Dorcas first walks normally for the first 640 meters. Then she gets tired, decreasing her speed by 6 meters per second, and walks the last 360 meters at the tired speed. Justice's normal speed is 30 meters per minute faster than Dorcas's but his tired speed is 12 meters per minute slower. On the way to the movie theater, Justice first walks 720 meters normally but then walks the last 400 meters at a tired speed. If Dorcas's trip takes 1040 seconds, how much time does Justice's trip take?

#5: (10 points) Suppose that a group of coders all work at the same constant speed. a) Write an equation that represents the amount of workers required in terms of the number of hours working, the number of codes written, and the individual rate of a worker (constant of proportionality). b) If 25 coders can write 24 codes in 8 hours, how many coders would it take to write 96 codes in 20 hours?

#6: (12 points): Solve the rational inequality and express your answer in interval notation:

$\sqrt{\frac{3x+9}{x+2}} \geq x+1$

Chapter 5 Sequences and Series

Explicit Formulas

Ex: 1 Find an explicit formula for $\frac{1}{-2}, \frac{1+5}{4}, \frac{1+5+9}{-12}, \frac{1+5+9+13}{48}$... starting with n=1.
Look at the numerator. It's easy to see that the second differences are constant so it can be modelled by a quadratic. Let $a_n = xn^2 + yn + z$
Plugging in x for 1,2,3, gets the equations: $1 = x + y + z,\ 6 = 4x + 2y + z,\ 15 = 9x + 3y + z$.
Solving for coefficients, you get $x = 2, y =- 1, z = 0$ so $a_n = 2n^2 - n$. For the denominator, you see the alternating negative signs, starting with negative, which implies $(-1)^n$. Then you see that the numbers are being multiplied by 2, then 3, then 4. This implies a factorial. Since it starts at 2, it's $2!$.

$a_n = \frac{2n^2-n}{(-1)^n \cdot 2n!}$ Putting it all together

Ex: 2 Find an explicit formula for $\frac{2}{3}, \frac{2+5}{6}, \frac{2+5+8}{18}, \frac{2+5+8+11}{72}$... starting with $n = 1$.
The numerator shows constant second differences, meaning it's a quadratic. Similar to example 1, we set up a system of equations: $x + y + z = 2, 4a + 2b + z = 7, 9a + 3b + z = 15$.
Solving, we get that the numerator can be modelled by $\frac{3}{2}n^2 + \frac{1}{2}n$. For the denominator, we can see that it starts with 3 and it doubles, triples, etc. This is $3!$. When the number is being multiplied by $n, n+1, n+2$..., that's a factorial.

$a_n = \frac{\frac{3}{2}n^2+\frac{1}{2}n}{3n!}$ Putting it all together

Ex: 3 Find an explicit formula for $\frac{1+3}{4}, \frac{9}{2+7}, \frac{6+3}{16}, \frac{25}{24+7}, \frac{120+3}{36}$, ... starting with n=1.
The style of the fraction seems to alternate with the summation going top, bottom, top, bottom, etc. That means we're going to have to take thing to the power of $(-1)^n$ to get the reciprocals. If you look at the solo number, it's clear that it's $(n+1)^2$ since it starts with $2^2, 3^2, 4^2$... For the first part of the sum, the numbers are $1, 2, 6, 24, 120$... This clearly is $n!$ since we're multiplying 2, then 3, then 4... Now for the second part of the sum, we seem to alternate between 3 and 7. The alternating suggests that we must have $(-1)^n$ since that allows for alternation (between -1 and 1). If we think about it, the midpoint between 3 and 7 is 5, so it's like we're starting at 5 but we alternate between subtracting and adding 2. This can be represented by $5 + 2(-1)^n$ since we start off with adding $5 - 2 = 3$. Putting these all together:

$a_n = \left(\frac{(n+1)^2}{n!+5+2(-1)^n}\right)^{(-1)^n}$

Arithmetic and Geometric Sequences

Ex 1: The following is an arithmetic progression: $a, 6, a + 2d$. The following is a geometric progression: $a + 1, 6, a + 2 + 2d$ Find a and d.
Since the mean of the first and last term must equal the middle term for an arithmetic sequence, we get $12 = 2a + 2d$ or $6 = a + d$. Since the geometric mean of the first and last term must equal the middle term for a geometric sequence, we get $36 = (a+1)(a+2+2d)$. Expanding and simplifying, we get, $36 = a^2 + 3a + 2ad + 2d + 2$.
Square the $6 = a + d$ to get $36 = a^2 + 2ad + d^2$.
Subtract this new equation from the other to get $0 = 3a + 2d + 2 - d^2$.
$0 = 3(6-d) + 2d + 2 - d^2$ Substituting $a = 6 - d$,
$d =- 5, 4$ Solving after factoring
Therefore, $a = 6 - (-5)$ or $a = 6 - 4$.

$d = 4,\ a = 2$ or $d =- 5, a = 11$

Ex: 2 Let a_n be an arithmetic sequence such that $a_4 + a_7 + a_{10} = 17$ and $a_4 + a_5 + a_6 + ... + a_{14} = 77$. If $S_k = 175$, what is k?
Rewrite each term of the two equations in terms of the first term and the common difference to get $a_1 + 3d + a_1 + 6d + a_1 + 9d = 17$. Simplifying we get, $3a_1 + 18d = 17$. For the other, we get $11a_1 + (3 + 4 + 5 + ... + 13)d = 77$. By using the sum formula we get, $11a_1 + \frac{16(11)}{2}d = 77$. This simplifies to $11a_1 + 88d = 77$. With these two system of equations, we get $a_1 = \frac{5}{3}$ and $d = \frac{2}{3}$.
$S_k = \frac{(\frac{5}{3}+a_k)k}{2}$ Definition of the sum
$a_k = \frac{5}{3} + \frac{2}{3}(k-1) = \frac{2}{3}k + 1$ Solving for a_k

$S_k = \frac{(\frac{5}{3}+\frac{2}{3}k+1)k}{2} = 175$ Substituting a_k

$350 = \frac{8}{3}k + \frac{2}{3}k^2$ Simplifying

$2k^2 + 8k - 1050 = 0$ Simplifying

$2(k-21)(k+25) = 0$ Factoring

$k = 21$ Term number must be positive

Ex: 3 Find integer k such that when it is subtracted from each of the numbers $203, 291,$ and 411, you'll obtain the squares of three consecutive terms of an arithmetic sequence.

So the three terms of the arithmetic sequence in terms of k is: $\sqrt{203-k}, \sqrt{291-k}, \sqrt{411-k}$. Therefore, $\sqrt{203-k} + \sqrt{411-k} = 2\sqrt{291-k}$ because the middle number of an arithmetic sequence is the average of the numbers directly before and after it. Square both sides to get:

$614 - 2k + 2\sqrt{(203-k)(411-k)} = 4(291-k)$

$\sqrt{(203-k)(411-k)} = 275 - k$ Simplifying

$(203-k)(411-k) = 75625 - 550k + k^2$ Squaring both sides again

$83433 - 614k + k^2 = 75625 - 550k + k^2$ Expanding

$7808 = 64k$ Combining like terms

$k = 122$

$k = 122$

Ex: 4 If $9, a, b, ab$ is an arithmetic progression, what are a and b?

First, let's look at the first 3 terms. Because $a - 9 = b - a$, we get that $a = \frac{1}{2}(b+9)$. Similarly using the next three terms, we see that $ab - b = b - a$. Simplifying, we get $a(b+1) = 2b$. Substituting in $a = \frac{1}{2}(b+9)$, we get the quadratic: $(b+9)(b+1) = 4b$. After expanding and combining like terms, we get $b^2 + 6b + 9 = 0$. This shows that $b =- 3$. Substituting $b =- 3$, we get $a = 3$:

$a = 3, b =- 3$

Ex: 5 If the sum of the first n terms in an arithmetic sequence is represented by $4n^2 + 5n$, find the formula for the nth term.

For the sum of an arithmetic sequence, we need take the average of the first and last term and multiply that by n or the number of terms. The first term is a_1 and the last term is $a_1 + d(n-1)$. Therefore, the sum is $\frac{n(2a_1+nd-d)}{2}$.

$\frac{n(2a_1+nd-d)}{2} = 4n^2 + 5n$

$2a_1 + nd - d = 8n + 10$

Similar to what we did for partial fraction decomposition, we must match up like terms.

$nd = 8n$ so $d = 8$ by matching up n term.

$2a_1 - 8 = 10$ Matching up constants

$a_1 = 9$ by solving the equation

Since $a_n = a_1 + (n-1)d$, $a_n = 8n + 1$

$a_n = 8n + 1$

Ex: 6 An infinite geometric series has sum 72. If the first term was increased by 3 and the ratio decreased by $\frac{1}{12}$, the sum would be 60. What is the first term and ratio of the geometric series.

$\frac{a_1}{1-r} = 72$ Sum of infinite geometric series

$a_1 = 72 - 72r$ Solving for a_1

$\frac{a_1-3}{1-(r-\frac{1}{12})} = 60$ Sum after new conditions

$\frac{72-72r-3}{\frac{13}{12}-r} = 60$ Substituting in for a_1

$69 - 72r = 65 - 60r$ Simplifying

$r = \frac{1}{3}$ Solving for r

$a_1 = 72 - 72(\frac{1}{3})$ Solving for a_1

$a_1 = 48$ Simplifying

$a_1 = 45, r = \frac{1}{3}$

Ex: 7 If $\frac{96}{5}, x, y$ is a geometric sequence while $x, y, 36$ is an arithmetic sequence, what is x and y?

In a geometric sequence, the geometric mean of two terms is the equal to the number exactly in between. Therefore, $x^2 = \frac{96}{5}y$. For an arithmetic sequence, the arithmetic mean of two terms is equal to the number exactly in between the terms. Therefore, $2y = x + 36$. We can rewrite this to $x = 2y - 36$.

$(2y-36)^2 = \frac{96}{5}y$ Substituting x

$4y^2 - 144y + 1296 = \frac{96}{5}y$ Expanding

$5y^2 - 204y + 1620 = 0$ Simplifying

$(y-30)(5y+54)=0$
$y=30$ Solving for $y, y=-\frac{54}{5}$ is extraneous
$x=24$ Plugging in y into $x^2=\frac{96}{5}y$

$x=24$ ($x=-24$ is extraneous)

Ex: 8 A finite decreasing geometric sequence has 6 terms and sum 189. If the number of terms was infinite, the sum of the geometric sequence would be 192. What is the first term?
Using the two types of geometric series formulas, we can set up two equations.
$S_6=189=\frac{a(r^6-1)}{r-1}$ First 6 terms
$S=\frac{a}{1-r}=192$ Infinite series
We can substitute $\frac{a}{1-r}=192$ into the finite sequence equation.
$S_6=189=-\frac{a}{1-r}\cdot(r^6-1)$
$189=-192(r^6-1)$ Substituting
$1-\frac{189}{192}=r^6$ Isolating r^6
$\frac{1}{64}=r^6$ Simplifying
$r=\frac{1}{2}$ Must be positive ratio in order to be always decreasing
$192=\frac{a}{1-\frac{1}{2}}$ Substituting into equation
$a=96$ Solving for a

$a=96$

Summations

Ex: 1 Write the series using summation notation and then find the sum:
$3(8)^3+3(9)^3+3(10)^3+\ldots+3(29)^3$
Since every term is being multiplied by 3, you can take out this common factor from the summation. We see that summation starts from cubing 8 and all the way to cubing 29. In order to find this summation that begins with 8, we can rewrite the summation as:
$3\sum_{n=1}^{29}n^3-3\sum_{n=1}^{7}n^3$. By using the sum of the first n cubes formula, we get: $\frac{3\cdot29^2\cdot30^2}{4}-\frac{3\cdot7^2\cdot8^2}{4}$.

$3\sum_{n=8}^{29}n^3=565323$ Simplifying

Ex: 2 Find the sum of $\sum_{n=5}^{21}(3n^3-n^2+2n+1)$.
Since the summation begins at 5 instead of 1, we can rewrite this summation as
$\sum_{n=1}^{21}(3n^3-n^2+2n+1)-\sum_{n=1}^{4}(3n^3-n^2+2n+1)$.
By using the common sum formulas, the first summation can be written as
$\frac{3(21^2)(22^2)}{4}-\frac{21(22)(43)}{6}+\frac{2(21)(22)}{2}+21$. This simplifies to 157255. Similarly, the second summation be written as $\frac{3(4^2)(5^2)}{4}-\frac{4(5)(9)}{6}+\frac{2(4)(5)}{2}+4=294$.

156961 By subtracting the two

Ex: 3 Evaluate the infinite sum: $\sum_{n=1}^{\infty}\frac{2n+3}{5^n}$.
Let's first split the infinite sum into two parts ($\sum_{n=1}^{\infty}\frac{2n}{5^n}$ and $\sum_{n=1}^{\infty}\frac{3}{5^n}$) and evaluate each part separately. At first glance, the first summation seems tricky. Let's let the first sum be A. If we write out the first few terms, we can see:
$A=\frac{2}{5}+\frac{4}{25}+\frac{6}{125},\ldots$ If only the numerators were 2 throughout. Now what if all the numerators were 2: $\frac{2}{5}+\frac{2}{25}+\frac{2}{125},\ldots$ That can be summed up by the infinite geometric sequence to be $\frac{2}{1-\frac{1}{5}}=\frac{5}{2}$.
$A=\frac{2}{5}+\frac{4}{25}+\frac{6}{125},\ldots$
$\frac{5}{2}=\frac{2}{5}+\frac{2}{25}+\frac{2}{125},\ldots$
Now if we subtracted the second equation from the first we would get $A-\frac{5}{2}=\frac{2}{25}+\frac{4}{125}+\frac{6}{625}\ldots$ The right side looks familiar. It's exactly $\frac{1}{5}$ of the original summation. So now we have $A-\frac{5}{2}=\frac{1}{5}A$. Solve to get $A=\frac{25}{8}$. Now the second part of the summation is easy. It's just an infinite geometric series starting from $\frac{3}{5}$ with a common ratio $\frac{1}{5}$. The sum therefore is $\frac{3/5}{1-1/5}=\frac{3}{4}$.

$\frac{31}{8}$ Adding the summations together

Ex: 4 Evaluate the sum $\sum_{n=2}^{24}\frac{x^3+6x^2+11x+7}{x^2+5x+6}$.
When we see a rational expression, we should think to use partial fraction decomposition.
$x+1+\frac{1}{x^2+5x+6}$ Using polynomial long division
$\frac{1}{x^2+5x+6}=\frac{A}{x+2}+\frac{B}{x+3}$ Setting up partial fractions

$1 = A(x+3) + B(x+2)$ Multiplying $x^2 + 5x + 6$
$1 = AX + 3A + BX + 2B$ Expanding
$A + B = 0, 3A + 2B = 1$ Matching like terms
$A = 1, B =- 1$ Solving for A and B
$\sum_{n=2}^{24} x + 1 + \frac{1}{x+2} - \frac{1}{x+3}$ Rewriting summation
$\sum_{n=2}^{24} x + 1 + \sum_{n=2}^{24} \frac{1}{x+2} - \frac{1}{x+3}$ Splitting summation
$\frac{23(2+24)}{2} + 1(23) + \sum_{n=2}^{24} \frac{1}{x+2} - \frac{1}{x+3}$ Simplifying
$322 + \frac{1}{4} - \frac{1}{5} + \frac{1}{5} + \ldots + \frac{1}{26} - \frac{1}{27}$ Writing out terms
By writing out the first few terms, a pattern quickly emerges. Consecutive terms cancel out because of our partial fractions that alternate in signs. This is known as telescoping.
$322 + \frac{1}{4} - \frac{1}{27}$ Simplifying
$322\frac{23}{108}$ Simplifying

$\frac{34799}{108}$

Induction

The key with induction is that you must be able manipulate your assumption. For equality, just add the $k+1$ "part" on both sides and start from the assumption. For divisibility, it's usually easier to start from what it means for $k+1$ to be true and proving it. For inequality, it will depend. Inequality induction will require a lot of intuition and logic in order to make the right manipulations.

Ex: 1 Prove by induction:
$1(1+4) + 2(2+4) + \ldots + n(n+4) = \frac{n(n+1)(2n+13)}{6}$
$n = 1 : 1(1+4) = 5, \frac{1(2)(15)}{6} = 5$ True for $n = 1$
$n = k :$ Assume that
$1(1+4) + 2(2+4) \ldots + k(k+4) = \frac{k(k+1)(2k+13)}{6}$
Now we want to prove it works for $n = k+1$.
$1(1+4) + 2(2+4) \ldots + k(k+4) + (k+1)(k+5) =$
$\frac{n(n+1)(2n+13)}{6} + (k+1)(k+5)$ since we add $(k+1)(k+5)$ to both sides of our assumption.
Working on the right side, we get:
$\frac{2k^3+2k^2+13k^2+13k}{6} + k^2 + 6k + 5$ Expanding
$\frac{2k^3+21k^2+49k+30}{6}$ Combining into one fraction
$\frac{(k+1)(k+2)(2k+15)}{6}$ Factoring
$\frac{(k+1)((k+1)+1)(2(k+1)+13)}{2}$ Rewriting the equation
Now it is clear that indeed the equation holds true for $n = k+1$.

Ex: 2 Prove by induction:
$5^{2n+1} + 2^{2n+1}$ is divisible by 7 for all $n \geq 0$
$n = 1 : 5^3 + 2^3 = 19(7)$ True for $n = 1$
$n = k :$ Assume that $5^{2k+1} + 2^{2k+1} = 7a$ for some integer a.
Now we want to prove it works for $n = k+1$.
$5^{2(k+1)+1} + 2^{2(k+1)+1}$ Plugging in $k+1$
$5^{2k+3} + 2^{2k+3}$ Simplifying
$5^2(5^{2k+1}) + 2^2(2^{2k+1})$ Using exponent rules
$25(5^{2k+1}) + 25(2^{2k+1}) - 21(2^{2k+1})$
Rewriting the $4(2^{2k+1})$ to factor out the 25
$25(5^{2k+1} + 2^{2k+1}) - 7(3)(2^{2k+1})$ Factoring
$25(7a) - 7(3 \cdot 2^{2k+1})$ From assumption
$7(25a - 3(2^{2k+1}))$ Since k and a are both integers, $25a - 3(2^{2k+1})$ is an integer as well. So we have proved that $5^{2(k+1)+1} + 2^{2(k+1)+1}$ is divisible by 7 so we're done with our proof.

Ex: 3 Prove by induction:
$9^n \geq 6n$ for $n \geq 1$
$n = 1 : 9^1 \geq 6(1)$ So it's true for $n = 1$.
$n = k :$ Assume $9^k \geq 6k$ is true for $k \geq 1$
Now we want to prove it's true for $n = k+1$:
$9^k \geq 6k$ From assumption
$9 \cdot 9^k \geq 54k$ Multiply 9 on both sides
$9^{k+1} \geq 6k + 48k$ Rewriting both sides
Since $k \geq 1$, $48k$ is greater than 6.
$9^{k+1} \geq 6k + 48k \geq 6k + 6$
$9^{k+1} \geq 6(k+1)$ This way we proved that the inequality holds for $k+1$.

Ex: 4 Prove by induction:
$2^n < n!$ for $n \geq 4$
$n = 1 : 2^4 < 4!$ It's true since $16 < 24$
$n = k :$ Assume $2^k < k!$ for $k \geq 4$
Now we want to prove it's true for $n = k+1$:
$2^k < k!$ From assumption
$2(2^k) < 2(k!)$ Multiply 2 on both sides
Since we know $k \geq 4$, 2 must be less than $k+1$
$2^{k+1} < 2(k!) < (k+1)(k!)$
Therefore, we get: $2^{k+1} < (k+1)!$
This proves that our inequality holds for $n = k+1$.

Sequences and Series Test 1

#1: (4 points each) Find an explicit formula for each sequence starting with $n = 1$:

a) $\frac{-2}{1 \cdot 1}, \frac{3}{2 \cdot 2}, \frac{-5}{3 \cdot 6}, \frac{8}{4 \cdot 24}, \ldots$

b) $1(3-2), 8(5+4), 27(8-12), 64(12+48), \ldots$

c) $1(3), -\sqrt{4(6)}, \sqrt[3]{9(18)}, -\sqrt[4]{16(72)}, \ldots$

#2: (12 points) Calculate $\sum_{n=1}^{\infty}(\frac{n^2+n+2}{3^n})$ **23**

#3: (12 points) a_n and b_n are two arithmetic sequences. Let the sum of any two corresponding terms (same n) in the sequences be $c_n = 5n + 4$. If $a_3 + b_4 + a_5 + b_6 + \ldots + a_{17} + b_{18} = 456$ and $a_{26} = 57$ find the explicit formulas for a_n and b_n. **46**

#4: (12 points) Let a_n be an infinite geometric series with first term 56 and sum S_a. Let b_n be an infinite geometric series with second term 32 and sum S_b. The common ratio of both can be expressed as $\frac{1}{x}$ where x is an integer. Let $S_a + S_b = \frac{496}{3}$. If every term in a_n was halved, while every term in b_n was squared, the sum of the two series becomes 5480. What is $S_b - 3S_a$? **14**

#5: (15 points each) Prove two of the following by induction:

a) $5^n + 9 < 6^n$ for all positive integers $n \geq 2$

b) $17n^3 + 103n$ is divisible by 6 for all integers n.

c) $1^2 + 3^2 + 5^2 + ... + (2n - 1)^2 = \frac{4n^3 - n}{3}$

#6: (12 points) Let a, b, c be a geometric progression. If we increase the first and second term by 1, it becomes an arithmetic progression. Let $a + b + c = 19$. Find all possible $a, b,$ and c.

#7: (5 points each) Simplify each:

a) $1 + 2 + 3 - 4 + 5 + 6 + 7 - 8 + ... + 97 + 98 + 99 - 100$

b) $12 + 8 - 6 - 6 + 3 + \frac{9}{2} - \frac{3}{2} - \frac{27}{8} + ...$

Sequences and Series Test 2

1: (4 points each) Find an explicit formula for each sequence:

a) $7\sqrt{2}, 8\sqrt[3]{4}, 11\sqrt[4]{12}, 16\sqrt[5]{48}, 23\sqrt[6]{240}, \ldots$

b) $\frac{2}{3}, \frac{1}{4}, \frac{0}{6}, \frac{1}{9}, \frac{2}{13}, \frac{3}{18}, \frac{4}{24}$

c) $\frac{-1}{1}, \frac{8}{1}, \frac{-27}{2}, \frac{64}{6}, \frac{-125}{24} \ldots$

#2: (12 points) Suppose there is an arithmetic sequence where $a_4 + a_7 + a_{10} = 18$. Let S_n represent the sum of the first n terms. If $S_x = 55$ and $x \cdot (a_1 + a_{x+1}) = 121$ find x.

#3: (12 points) A ball is dropped from a height of $\frac{x}{4}$ feet and rebounds x% of the distance fallen each time it hits the ground. Algebraically find x if the the total distance (up and down) the ball travels before coming to a rest is 60 feet.

#4: (10 points) If $\sum_{x=1}^{n} \frac{1}{x^2+9x+20} = \frac{8}{45}$, find $\sum_{x=1}^{n} x$.

#5: (15 points each) Prove two of the following with induction:

a) $9+13+17+\ldots+(4n+5)=n(2n+7)$

b) 5^n-3^n is divisible by 2

c) $8^n \geq 4n$ for $n \geq 1$

#6: (12 points) If $\sqrt[3]{3\sqrt[3]{9\sqrt[3]{27\sqrt[3]{81\ldots}}}}=3^x$, find x. **7**

#7: (12 points) The following is an arithmetic progression: $\frac{a}{b}$, ab, $a-b$, $a+b$. Find the next term. **10**

Chapter 6 Counting and Probability

Basic Counting

For most basic counting problems, you can just multiply the number of choices for each "option". However, sometimes you may need to do casework if there are restrictions.

Ex: 1 A diner offers three appetizers, four entrees, and two deserts. How many diner orders are there possible?

Simply multiply the number of cases for each option $3 \cdot 4 \cdot 2$.

24 orders possible

Ex: 2 How many four digit numbers are there that begin or end with an even digit?

For numbers that begin with an even digit, there will be 4 choices for the first number (2,4,6,8) and 10 choices for the other three numbers. That's $4 \cdot 10^3 = 4000$ numbers. For numbers that end with an even digit, there are 9 choices for the first digit (1-9), 10 choices for the next two digits, and then 5 choices for the last digit. That's a total of $9 \cdot 10^2 \cdot 5 = 4500$ numbers. However, you must subtract out the overlap since that those are double counted. Four digit numbers that both begin and end with even numbers would have 4 choices for the first number, 10 choices each for the next two, and 5 choices for the last number. That's of 2000 numbers. In total, there would be $4000 + 4500 - 2000$ numbers:

6500 numbers

Ex: 3 A state's license plates have three letters in a row and then 2 numbers. The numbers must be even and the letters cannot contain vowels. How many possible license plates are there?

For the letters, there are $26 - 5 = 21$ choices each. While for the numbers, there 5 choices each. Therefore, the number of license plates:

$21^3 \cdot 5^2 = 231525$ License Plates

Ex: 4 How many 5 digit odd palindromes exist? Remember that a palindrome is a number that is the same when read forwards and backwards. In the case of a 5 digit palindrome, the first digit would be the same as the last digit. Then the second digit would be the same as the fourth digit, so we are really only choosing 3 digits total. For the first digit, we can have 5 choices (1,3,5,7,9). Remember that because the last digit must be odd, the first digit must be odd as well. For the second/fourth digit, we have 10 choices. For the third digit, we also have 10 choices.

$5 \cdot 10 \cdot 10 = 500$ palindromes

Ex: 5 You draw 3 marbles out of a bag without replacement. The bag consists of 6 unique marbles. How many ways can you draw out the marbles?

For the first marble, you have 6 choices to choose from. However, with the second marble, you only have 5 choices left since you are not replacing the marbles. For the third marble, you are only left with 4 choices.

$6 \cdot 5 \cdot 4 = 120$

Ex: 6 After a call, the 8 members are placed into 3 breakout rooms such that each breakout room has at least 1 person. How many ways can the people be sorted into the unique breakout rooms?

Each member has three options into which breakout room they will get placed into.

That represents $3^8 = 6561$ choices. However, this may allow for some breakout rooms to have nobody. If everybody goes to one breakout room, that represents 3 cases. If everybody goes to 2 breakout rooms and leaves the last breakout empty, they will have $2^8 = 256$ ways to distribute themselves. However, there are 3 choices as to which breakout room will be empty. So the number of cases where one room is empty is $3 \cdot 256 = 768$.

$6561 - 3 - 768 = 5790$ cases

Permutations and Combinations

The basic of permutations is that you are finding the number of ways to order n distinct objects in certain number ways. If there are indistinct (identical) objects in the mix, you must divide the number of permutations formed by just those indistinct objects.

Ex: 1 Find the number of ways to arrange 5 dimes and 2 nickels in a line.
If all the coins were different from each other, you would have 7 choices for the first coin, 6 choices for the second coin and so on which equals $7!$. However, because the 2 nickels are considered identical and the 5 dimes are identical, you must divide out the permutations of those.
$\frac{7!}{2!5!} = 21$

21 Ways

Ex: 2 How many ways can Alicia, Bhavesh, Cindy, Diane, and Esther sit at the movie theaters if Diane must sit next to Cindy?
Since Diane and Cindy must sit next to each other, first consider them as one "person". Now the number of permutations for the 4 "people" would be $4! = 24$. However, because Diane and Cindy can still switch spots, so you would double that. Therefore the number of ways is:

$4! \cdot 2 = 48$ ways

Combinations involve choosing a subgroup out of a set of objects where the order in which you choose the group does not matter. Remember that $nCk = nC(n-k)$.

Ex: 3 Out of the five juniors, two will be selected to be co-presidents. For the rest of 15 members in the club, one will be vice president, one will be secretary, and one will be treasurer. How many ways are there to choose officers for the club?
First for the five juniors, you would need to choose two of them for the co-president positions. That can be calculated by $\frac{5!}{2!3!}$ which equals 10 ways. For the other three positions, there's 15 possibilities for the VP, 14 for the secretary, and 13 for the treasurer. Multiply all the possible ways together to get:

$10 \cdot 15 \cdot 14 \cdot 13 = 27300$ ways

Ex: 4 On a salad bar, you can choose 0 to 8 toppings to place on your salad. You must choose exactly 2 out of the 6 protein options. Then you must choose one salad dressing out of the 7 options. How many salads can you make?
For toppings, it's a bit tricky since you can choose any number of toppings to put on your salad. However, for each topping you can think of it having two options: being on your salad or off. So therefore if you multiply the options for each topping, there's $2^8 = 256$ ways to put on toppings. For the protein options, you must choose 2 out of the 6 proteins. That would be 6 choose 2 or 15. For salad dressings, you have 7 choices. In total, the number of salads you can make:

$256 \cdot 15 \cdot 7 = 268800$ salads

Ex: 5 For the play, there are 6 female characters and 6 male characters. There are 14 females and 10 males auditioning. How many ways are there to create a cast?
The number of ways to choose the female characters is $\frac{14!}{6!8!} = 3003$ ways. The number of ways to choose the male characters is $\frac{10!}{4!6!} = 210$ ways. In total you would multiply the two possibilities to get:

$3003 \cdot 210 = 630630$ ways to create a cast

Remember to always consider when the objects are considered distinct and when they are considered indistinct.

Ex: 6 How many ways can you distribute 14 identical pencils to 3 people if each must get at least 2 pencils?
Now let's assume each person starts off with two pencils (the restriction states that each person

must get at least two). So we are now distributing 8 pencils without restriction. Suppose we let each pencil be a circle and let a bar represent the distribution of pencils for each person.

All the circles left of the first bar go to the first person, between the bars goes to the second person, etc. The number of ways to distribute the pencils would just be the number of ways we rearrange these circles and bars in a row. If the bars were to go on the very side, that's okay because we are already ensured that everybody has at least 2.
The number of ways would be $\frac{10!}{2!8!}$.

$\frac{10!}{2!8!} = 45$ ways

Ex: 7 There are 18 teams in league A who all play each other once throughout the season. There are 14 teams in league B who all play each other once as well. The top 3 teams of each league go to the championships, where they will all play each other again twice. How many games are played in total?
For league A, because each team plays each other once, the number of games within league A is 18 choose 2 or $\frac{18!}{2!16!} = 153$ since we want to count the number of ways to choose pairs of teams. For league B that would be $\frac{14!}{2!12!} = 91$. During championships, we now have 6 teams who will play each other twice. The number of ways to choose pairs of 2 teams to play against each other would be 6 choose 2 or $\frac{6!}{2!4!} = 15$. They play each other twice so we multiply by 2 to get 30.

$153 + 91 + 30 = 274$ games

Probability

Remember that probabilities that are linked together should be multiplied. Two probabilities that are not linked together but instead represent two parts of the fulfilling cases should be added.

Ex: 1 If you roll two dice, what is the probability that the numbers on top sum up to 8?
For the sample space, there are a total of 36 possibilities because there are 6 options for each die. Then listing out the ways the dice can add up to 8, $(6,2)(5,3)(4,4)(3,5)(2,6)$, you can see how there's 5 ways to get a sum of 8.
Therefore the probability is:

$\frac{5}{36}$

Ex: 2 If you draw 3 random cards from a standard deck of 52 cards, what is the probability that they are all the same suit?
First find the total sample size. The total number of 3 card sets possible is $\frac{52!}{49!3!}$. Now we must choose the suit that the cards are. Since there's 4 total suits, that represents 4 choices. For each suit, there's 13 cards. Therefore, we must choose 3 cards out of those 13. Therefore the total number of cases is $4 \cdot \frac{13!}{3!10!}$. Dividing the number of cases by the total sample size:

$\frac{1144}{22100} \approx 0.051764$

Ex: 3 The probability that I will reply to someone's text is 80% if I'm in a good mood. If I'm in a bad mood, the probability is 30%. If on any given day, there's a 60% probability I'm in a good mood, what's the probability that I'll respond to someone's message today?
Split it into cases. Given that I'm in a good mood today (60%), the probability that I'll respond to someone's text will be (80%). So the probability that both will happen is $60\% \cdot 80\% = 48\%$. If I'm not in a good mood (40%), the probability I'll respond drops to 30%. So multiply to get that both will happen with a 12% chance.

60% by adding up the probabilities

Ex: 4 The Zhangs own 14 movies. If Frederick and Roland each choose 5 movies to watch during quarantine, what is the probability that they watch exactly 2 of the same movies?

Now for these types of problems, we can assume that one person can choose whatever set of 5 movies. As long as the second person fulfills the requirements, it doesn't matter what the first person chose. So suppose Frederick chooses 5 movies. Out of those 5, Roland must choose 2 of them as well. That's $\frac{5!}{2!3!} = 10$ ways.
Not out of the 9 movies Frederick did not choose, Roland must then choose 3 movies from there. That's $\frac{9!}{3!6!} = 84$ ways. Multiplying the two cases leads to 840 ways to choose the books so that they watch exactly two of the same movies. The total number of ways Roland can choose movies is 14 choose 5 or $\frac{14!}{9!5!}$.

$\frac{840}{2002} \approx 0.4196$

Ex: 5 The probability that a teenager is afraid of spiders is 32%. If you interview 6 students, what is the probability that exactly 2 of them are afraid of spiders?
Notice that these types of probability problems are called binomial probabilities. There's a formula but you should understand why it works. For the 2 that are afraid and the 4 that aren't afraid, you must figure out how many ways you can arrange them. The number of ways you can arrange them is $\frac{6!}{2!4!}$. The probability that the two are afraid is $(0.32)^2$ and the probability that the other four are not afraid is $(0.68)^4$. Then multiply them together.

$15 \cdot (0.32)^2 \cdot (0.68)^4 \approx 0.3284$

Ex: 6 A square with side length 2 is placed within a circle of radius 3. If you choose a random point in the circle, what is the probability that it is within the square?
The area of the square is $2^2 = 4$. The area of the circle is $3^2\pi = 9\pi$. So the geometric probability is:

$\frac{4}{9\pi} \approx 0.1415$

Ex: 9 Jerry randomly chooses an integer from 1-9. Barry randomly chooses an integer from 1-6. Barry wins if his number is within 2 of Jerry's number. What is the probability Jerry wins?
Jerry has 9 choices and Barry has 6 choices so in total there are 54 ways for the numbers to be chosen. If Jerry chooses a 9, there's no way Barry wins. If he chooses a 8, Barry must get a 6 (1 choice). If Jerry chooses a 7, Barry must get a 5 or 6 (2 choices). If Jerry gets a 6, Barry has 3 choices. If Jerry gets a 5, Barry has 4 choices. If Jerry gets a 4 or 3, Barry has 5 choices (two above, two below, the number itself). If Jerry gets a 2, Barry has 4 choices and Jerry get a 1, Barry has 3 choices.

$\frac{1+2+3+4+2(5)+4+3}{54} = \frac{1}{2}$

Ex: 10 Hasan and Marie randomly choose an integer from 1-9. Hasan wins if his number is greater than Marie's or he chooses a prime number. What is the probability Hasan wins?
From 1-9, there are 4 prime numbers. So if Hasan chooses one of them, he automatically wins. That's a $\frac{4}{9}$ probability. There are the other 5 non prime numbers, combined with the 9 choices that Marie has, that forms 45 ways for them to choose their numbers. Now let's do some casework. If Hasan gets a 1, there's zero cases from him to win. If he gets a 4, Marie has 3 choices. If Hasan gets a 6, Marie can pick a 1-5. If Hasan gets a 8, Marie can pick 1-7. If Hasan gets a 9, Marie can pick 1-8. That's a total of 23 cases.

$\frac{5}{9} \cdot \frac{23}{45} + \frac{4}{9} = \frac{59}{81}$

Ex: 11 I choose two numbers from 0 to 3. What is the probability that their sum is less than 2?
Because the numbers are not specified to be integers, we have to use geometric probability to represent this. Let the first number be x and the second number be y. We can draw a square on the coordinate grid that is 3 by 3 to represent the "area" for choosing our numbers. We want $x + y < 2$ so we can graph this line.

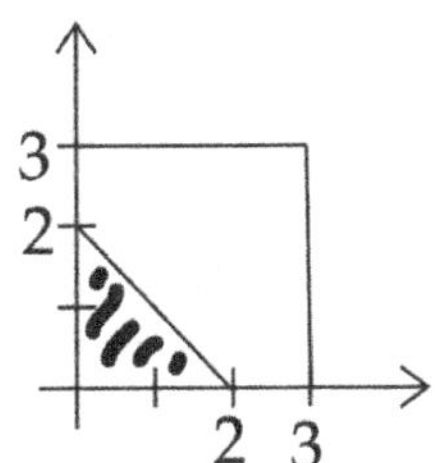

The area of the triangle that represents our valid choosings is $\frac{1}{2}(2)(2) = 2$. The total area that we can choose from is $3(3) = 9$.

$\frac{2}{9}$

Ex: 12 Anne, Barry, Cindy, Dennis, and Esther randomly sit in a row of 5 chairs. What is the probability Anne will not sit with Cindy?
In this case, let's use complementary counting. Suppose Anne is guaranteed to sit with Cindy. We can group them together as one item we are permuting around. Therefore, we are really just permuting around 4 items with Anne and Cindy together counting as one. That's $4! = 24$ ways. However, we can also switch Anne and Cindy's spot for any of the cases so we get $24 \cdot 2 = 48$. There is $5! = 120$ total ways for the 5 people to sit. If we subtract out all the cases with Anne and Cindy together, we get 72 cases left.

$\frac{72}{120} = \frac{3}{5}$

Binomial Expansion

Remember that when expanding $(A + B)^n$ the $(r + 1)st$ term is defined by $nCrA^{n-r}B^r$ since we start with $r = 0$ for the first term.

Ex: 1 Find the 4th term of $(2x - \frac{1}{x})^7$
$r = 3$ since we're looking at the 4th term
$\frac{7!}{3!4!}(2x)^4(-\frac{1}{x})^3$ Using the formula
$35 \cdot 16x^4 \cdot (-\frac{1}{x^3})$ Simplifying

4th Term: $-560x$

Ex: 2 Find the 3rd term of $(4x^2 - \frac{3}{x})^9$.
$r = 2$ since we're looking at the 3rd term.
$\frac{9!}{2!7!}(4x^2)^7(-\frac{3}{x})^2$ Using formula
$36 \cdot 16384x^{14} \cdot \frac{9}{x^2}$ Simplifying

3rd term: $5308416x^{12}$

Ex: 3 Find the coefficient of x^3 in $(2x - \frac{1}{x})^7$
First we need to find what term this is. Let the term with x^3 be represented as $a(2x)^b(-\frac{1}{x})^c$. Because the powers of the $2x$ and $-\frac{1}{x}$ cancel out the $x's$, we must have $b - c = 3$. Since we know $b + c = 7$, solving this system gets $c = 2$ and $b = 5$. Therefore, our term is $\frac{7!}{2!5!}(2x)^5\ (-\frac{1}{x})^2$. Simplifying, we get $21 \cdot 32x^5 \cdot \frac{1}{x^2}$. Therefore:

Coefficient of x^3 term is $21 \cdot 32 = 672$

Ex: 4 Find the constant term in $(3x^2 + \frac{2}{x})^9$
The constant term has x^0 so the term can be expressed as $n(3x^2)^a(\frac{2}{x})^b$. Because each $3x^2$ contributes $2a$ for the power of x and each $\frac{2}{x}$ contributes $-b$ power of x, $2a - b = 0$. As always, $a + b = 9$. Solving this, we get $a = 3$, $b = 6$. Therefore the constant term is $\frac{9!}{6!3!}(3x^2)^3(\frac{2}{x})^6$. Simplifying we get, $84 \cdot 27x^6 \cdot \frac{64}{x^6}$

Constant term: 145152

Do you see how this is related to binomial probabilities? The choose function in the beginning refers to the number of ways to arrange the two "choices" and the powers represent the probabilities of each. The number of objects that are involved represents the "degree" of the binomial. Looking at example 5 in probabilities, that is an example of a binomial probability because there are two options.

Counting and Probability Test 1

#1: (10 points) Find the coefficient of the x^4 term in the expansion of $(2x - \frac{3}{x})^{12}$.

#2: (5 points) There are twelve roller coasters to ride at the amusement park. Roland and Jongwon each chose to ride 7 of them. What is the probability that they ride exactly 4 of the same coasters?

#3: (5 points) Nicholas, Colin, Colin, and Ryan are to sit in a coaster car that consists of 3 rows with 2 seats in a row. If the Colin's are to sit next to each other, how many ways can the 4 guys occupy the 6 seats?

#4: (5 points) Nicholas stays at Six Flags from 10:30 am to 9 pm. He spends 45 minutes waiting in line for El Toro, 72 minutes waiting for Kingda Ka, and 24 minutes on average waiting in line for each of the other 8 coasters. At a random time, what is the probability that he's waiting in line for a coaster?

#5: (5 points) The probability that Jonathan will be too scared to ride El Toro is 15%. The probability that Colin will be too scared to ride El Toro is 45%. However, if Jonathan is brave enough to ride El Toro, there's a 75% chance Colin will ride El Toro. What is the probability that exactly one of these guys is brave enough to ride El Toro?

#6: (5 points) In Kenny's 6 day vacation in New York/New Jersey, Kenny randomly chooses one day for Great Adventure and one day for touring Columbia and NYU. What is the probability that he tours the colleges and goes to Great Adventure on two consecutive days?

#7: (5 points) Bhavesh must deal with the fact that Six Flags does not allow you to choose your seats on a ride since he only wants to ride back or front row. Suppose the ride attendant randomly chooses one of the 12 rows on Full Throttle for Bhavesh to ride. What is the probability that after 5 rides on Full Throttle, he gets a row he likes exactly twice?

#8: (5 points) There's a 80% chance Top Thrill Dragster will break down today, 40% chance for Steel Vengeance, 20% chance for Millenium Force. What is the probability that exactly one of these coasters will break down today?

#9: (5 points) Ryan's plan for his Six Flags trip: Ride 8 roller coasters, 2 water rides, use the bathroom 2 times, eat 2 meals. Assume that Ryan won't use the bathroom twice in a row. How many ways can he arrange his schedule?

#10: (5 points): A group of 8 friends have decided to board different trains in order to duel on Twisted Colossus. How many ways are there for the group to split into 2 groups (green and blue train) of 4 if Roland must be with Bhavesh and Colin must not be with Frederick?

#11: (5 points) In how many ways can 6 girls and 4 boys walk through a doorway single file if the girls must all walk through before the boys?

#12: (5 points) 40% of a sample has their favorite coaster as Steel Vengeance, 40% has El Toro as, and 20% has Railblazer . If you randomly choose 4 people, what is the probability that two of them have Railblazer as their favorite, one person has SV, and the last has ET?

#13: (5 points) The probability that a student at Irvington is taking at least one AP Class is 70%. If you interview 7 students, what is the probability that exactly 5 students are taking at least one AP Class?

#14: (5 points) 15 male and 10 female actors audition for a show. If the cast consists of 4 males and 5 females, how many ways can the cast be made?

#15: (5 points) A bag contains 2 red marbles, 6 green marbles, and 3 yellow marbles. Max draws three marbles one by one without replacement. What is the probability he draws exactly 2 green marbles?

#16: (5 points) At a park, there are 3 wooden coasters, 8 steel coasters, and 4 flat rides. If Jonathan chooses to ride exactly 10 rides (assume he doesn't ride anything more than once), what is the probability that he rides 6 steel coasters, 2 wooden coasters, and 2 flat rides?

#17: (5 points) How many ways can you arrange 8 marbles in a row if 2 are black, 4 are yellow, 1 is white, and 1 is purple?

#18: (5 points) If you chose a 4 digit number whose sum of digits is 34, what is the probability the number is divisible by 7?

#19: (5 points) Two six-sided dice are rolled. What is the probability that the sum of the numbers on top is prime?

Counting and Probability Test 2

#1: (10 points) Find the coefficient of the x^6 term in the expansion of $(3x^2 - \frac{2}{x})^{15}$.

#2: (5 points) Kailen rolls a 9-sided dice with numbers 1-9. Kenny rolls a 11-sided dice with numbers 1-11. Kailen wins if he rolls a number greater or equal to Kenny's number. What is the probability Kailen wins?

#3: (5 points) Colin randomly chooses an integer from 1-200. What is the probability he chooses a perfect square or a perfect cube?

#4: (5 points) Caton has 5 strings, with lengths $1, 2, 3, 4, 5$ centimeters. If he takes three random strings, what is the probability it can form a triangle?

#5: (6 points) Jessie chooses a random digit from 1-8 to be the 10s digit of her new number. Then she chooses a random digit from 0-7 to be the unit's digit of her new number. What is the probability that her new number is divisible by 7?

#6: (5 points) There are 2 available sauces and 10 toppings at a pizza place. If at least one topping and one sauce is required, how many combinations are there for pizzas?

#7: (5 points) On the first day, Colin decides to eat carrot fries. From then on, he does the same thing as the previous day (eat carrot fries or not) with probability ⅔. What is the probability he eats carrot fries on day 3?

#8: (5 points) Bhavesh has 10 marbles: 2 red, 4 blue, 3 green, and 1 yellow with same colored marbles considered indistinguishable. If he chooses 4 marbles at random, what is the probability that the gumballs he chooses consist of at least 2 colors and at most 3 colors?

#9: (6 points) A package of 15 calculators contains 4 defective units. The math department has ordered 5 calculators to be randomly selected from the package. What is the probability that exactly three units are good?

#10: (5 points) A point is randomly chosen within the square with vertices $(0,0)(0,1)(1,0)(1,1)$ The probability that the point lies within d units of a vertex is 0.6. What is d?

#11: (5 points) 7 men occupy a row of 7 seats at a movie theater. If Colin A. must sit next to Colin B. and Bhavesh must not sit next to Frederick, how many ways can the 7 men sit?

#12: (5 points) A standard dice is rolled two times. What is the probability that either the sum of the two numbers or the product of the two numbers on top is a perfect square?

#13: (5 points) If $8 \cdot {}_nP_2 = {}_{n+1}P_3$, what is $n! + (n-2)!$?

#14: (5 points): Ryan chooses two distinct integers from 1 to 6. Roland chooses one integer from 1 to 12. What is the probability that Roland's number is greater than the sum of Ryan's two numbers?

#15: (5 points) Roland, Kenny, Colin, and Jonathan each choose a number from 1 to 24. What is the probability that Roland's number is greater than Colin's but less than Jonathan's?

#16: (5 points) A class is given 24 study problems from which 20 will be chosen as part of an upcoming exam. Nicholas knows how to solve 18 of those 24 problems. What is the probability that Nicholas will be able to get an B (greater than or equal to 80%) on the test?

#17: (5 points) Five cards are chosen from a standard deck of 52 cards. How many five-card combinations contain two royal cards and three aces?

#18: (5 points) From a pool of 15 members, two members will be selected to be co-presidents and for VP, secretary and treasurer one member will be selected. How many ways can an officer team be chosen?

#19: (5 points) Mrs. Mohandas takes the 19 problems in a practice test. If she selects 4 of them to make a warm up, 6 of them to make a quiz, and 9 of them to make a review, how many ways can she create a warm up, quiz, and review?

Counting and Probability Test 3

#1: (10 points) Find the 3rd term in the expansion of $(2x - \frac{3}{x})^{11}$.

#2: (5 points) A weighted coin is three times as likely to show up as heads as supposed to tails. Mary drops 6 coins. What is the probability that exactly 4 are heads?

#3: (5 points) Colin draws three cards from a standard deck. What is the probability that they are all the same suit or the same number?

#4: (5 points) Two real numbers between 0 and 2 are chosen. What is the probability that their sum is greater than 3?

#5: (5 points) How many 3 digit odd palindromes are there less than 700?

#6: (5 points) If Roland is productive, there's a 60% chance he will study. If he is not productive there's a 10% chance he will study. If Bhavesh is active on Messenger, there's a 20% chance he will be productive. If he isn't active, there's a 70% chance Roland will be productive. If the probability that Bhavesh is active is 45%, what is the probability that Roland will not study?

#7: (5 points) A box of 24 textbooks contains 10 used ones. Ms. Tav randomly draws 18 textbooks. What is the probability that at least 8 are in new condition?

#8: (5 points) Samuel has 5 pairs of socks, 10 shirts, and 8 pants. How many sock-shirt-pants combinations can he make?

#9: (5 points) In how many ways can 3 pennies, 4 nickels, 2 dimes and 3 quarters be arranged in a row if the dimes must be together?

#10: (5 points) A box contains 10 red marbles numbered 1-10 and 8 blue marbles numbered 1-8. What is the probability of drawing a blue marble or prime-numbered marble?

#11: (5 points) What is the probability that if you draw 5 cards from a deck of cards, they will all be the same suit?

#12: (5 points) The probability of Jonathan getting into Harvard, Stanford, and Princeton is 10%. The probability of getting into MIT and CalTech is 12%. What is the probability he gets into at least one of these colleges?

#13: (5 points) How many ways can 5 men and 5 women sit in a row if they are to be seated alternately by gender?

#14: (5 points) There are 4 nonfiction and 6 nonfiction books on a shelf. What is the probability he chooses to read 2 nonfiction and 2 fiction if he chooses to read 4 books this month?

#15: (5 points) How many ways can 6 people sit around a circular table if rotations are considered the same

#16: (5 points) A class is given 23 study problems from which 16 will be chosen as part of an upcoming exam. Nicholas knows how to solve 18 of those 23 problems. What is the probability that Nicholas will be able to get at least a 90% on the test?

#17: (5 points) Frederick randomly chooses a number (A) from 1 to 7. Then he randomly chooses an operation (multiplication, division, subtraction, division). Finally, he randomly chooses as number (B) from 0-3. After clicking on the equal button, what is the probability he gets a prime number?

#18 (5 points) There are currently 24 blue marbles and 16 yellow marbles in an urn. At least, how many yellow marbles should be added so that the probability of getting a yellow marble is doubled?

#19: (5 points) A license plate consists of 4 letters and 3 numbers. How many license plates can be formed?

Chapter 7 Trigonometric Functions

Right Triangle Trigonometry

Ex: 1 Find $\csc 150^\circ$.

First, we know that csc is just the reciprocal of sin so we need to find $\sin 150^\circ$ first. Plotting 150° on the unit circle, we can see that it forms a 30° with the negative x axis. Since sin measures the "y" value and 150° is above the x axis, we know that $\sin 150^\circ = \sin 30^\circ = \frac{1}{2}$.

> $\csc 150^\circ = 2$ by taking the reciprocal

Ex: 2 Find $\cot \frac{5\pi}{2}$.

Remember that the unit circle repeats itself ever 2π so this equals $\cot \frac{\pi}{2}$. cot is defined as adjacent over hypotenuse or $\frac{x}{y}$ in unit circle terms. Graphing it out, it's easy to see:

> $\cot \frac{5\pi}{2} = \cot \frac{\pi}{2} = 0$

Ex: 3 During quarantine, a bored person standing at a window in Building A, stares at Building B, located directly across the street. She observes the top of Building B at an angle of elevation of 74° and observes the base of the building at an angle of depression of 52°. If the height of building B is 238 feet, how wide is the street?

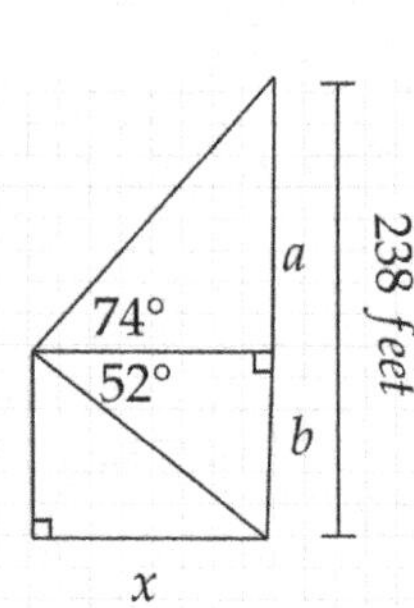

Using the information, we create this diagram where we want to find x. We know that $a + b = 238$ since that's the total height of the building. Using trigonometric ratios, $\tan 74^\circ = \frac{a}{x}$ and $\tan 52^\circ = \frac{b}{x}$. This leads to $a = x \cdot \tan 74^\circ$ and $b = x \cdot \tan 52^\circ$. Plugging these values into the original equation, we get $x(\tan 74^\circ + \tan 52^\circ) = 238$.

> $x = \frac{238}{\tan 74^\circ + \tan 52^\circ} \approx 49.9228$ feet

Ex: 4 Two boats leave a port at the same time. One travels with a bearing of $N40^\circ E$ and the other with a bearing of $N50^\circ E$. If they travel at the same speed, how far apart will they be when they are both 20 miles away from the port?

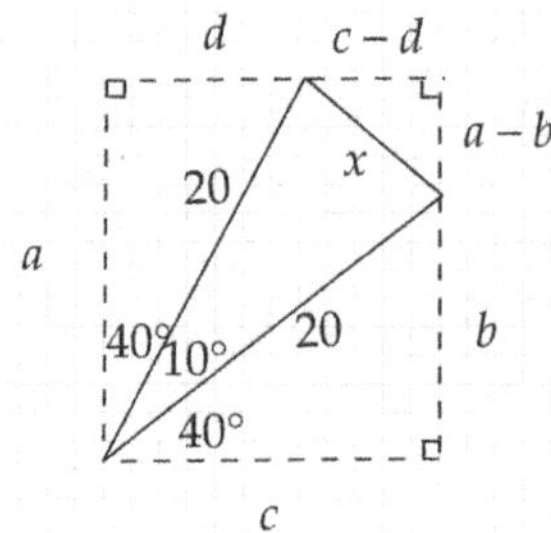

Using the information, we create this diagram. Our goal is to try to find $c - d$ and $a - b$ and then use the pythagorean theorem to find x. Using basic right angle trig, we know $\sin 50^\circ = \frac{a}{20}$ so $a = 20 \sin 50^\circ$. Repeating this process, we get $d = 20 \sin 40^\circ$, $b = 20 \sin 40^\circ$, and $c = 20 \sin 50^\circ$. Therefore $c - d = a - b = 20 \sin 50^\circ - 20 \sin 40^\circ$. Because this is an isosceles right triangle the hypotenuse is $\sqrt{2}$ times the legs.

> $\sqrt{2}(20 \sin 50^\circ - 20 \sin 40^\circ) \approx 3.4862$ miles

Using Law of Cosines would be way easier, but the point is that you understand how to use basic right triangle trigonometry.

Arc Length/Sector Area

Ex: 1 The rear windshield wiper of a car rotates 120 degrees. Find the area cleared by the wiper.

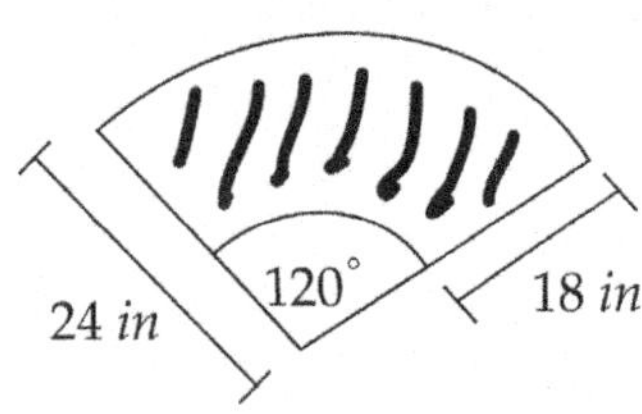

We need to find the area of the larger sectors and subtract it from the area of the smaller sector. The larger sector has radius 24 so the area is $\frac{120}{360} \cdot 24^2 \cdot \pi = 192\pi$. The smaller sector has radius $24 - 18 = 6$. Therefore, the area of the smaller sector is $\frac{120}{360} \cdot 6^2 \cdot \pi = 12\pi$.

180π Subtracting

Ex: 2 If you increase the radius of a circular sector by 1, the perimeter and area of the sector increase by the same numerical amount. If the perimeter of a sector with a radius one less than double the original is 8, find the original radius and θ.
Normally, the perimeter of the circular sector is $2r + r\theta$ (radii plus arc length). If radius increases by 1, the perimeter becomes $2(r+1) + (r+1)\theta$ or $2r + 2 + r\theta + \theta$. Subtracting from our normal perimeter, the perimeter has increased by $2 + \theta$. Normally the area of the sector is $\frac{1}{2}r^2\theta$. With the radius increasing by 1, the area is $\frac{1}{2}(r+1)^2\theta$ which simplifies to $\theta \cdot \frac{r^2+2r+1}{2}$. Subtracting from the original area, the area has increased by $r\theta + \frac{\theta}{2}$.
$2 + \theta = r\theta + \frac{\theta}{2}$ Setting up an equation
$4 = 2r\theta - \theta$ Combining like terms
$\theta = \frac{4}{2r-1}$ Simplifying
If the radius is changed to $2r - 1$, the perimeter would be $2(2r-1) + \frac{4(2r-1)}{2r-1} = 4r + 2$
$4r + 2 = 8$ Perimeter of sector is 8
$r = \frac{3}{2}$ Solving
$\theta = 2$ Plugging in r value into $\theta = \frac{4}{2r-1}$

$r = \frac{3}{2}, \theta = 2$

Ex: 3 A circular sector with radius r cm has a central angle of θ radians. If the perimeter of the sector is 16 cm. For which value of r is the area of the sector a maximum? What is the maximum area?
Let's first find the equation that represents the area of the sector in terms of r. Using the formula of arc length in terms of radians, the perimeter of the sector is $r + r + r\theta$.
$2r + r\theta = 16$ Perimeter equals 16
$r\theta = 16 - 2r$ Manipulation
$\theta = \frac{16-2r}{r}$ Solving for θ in terms of r
Because the area of a sector is $\frac{1}{2}r^2\theta$, plug in θ in terms of r to get: $\frac{1}{2}r^2(\frac{16-2r}{r})$
Simplify to get $A = r(8-r)$. Remember that the vertex of a function is exactly in between the two zeroes. In this case, the zeroes of the function for area are 0 and 8. Therefore, the maximum area occurs at $r = \frac{8+0}{2} = 4$. Plugging in $r = 4$, we get the area to be 16.

$r = 4, A = 16$

Ex: 4 Equilateral triangle ORS has side lengths of 2 cm. If PQ is the arc of a circle that has center O and PQ divides the triangle into two regions of equal area, find the length of OP and PQ.

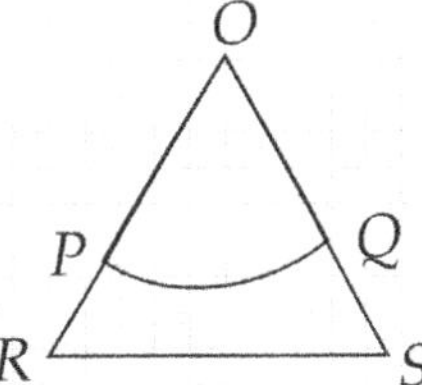

Since the equilateral triangle has side length 2, the area is $\frac{\sqrt{3}}{4} \cdot 2^2 = \sqrt{3}$. Therefore, the area of each region is $\frac{\sqrt{3}}{2}$. Since angle O is $\frac{\pi}{3}$ radians, we can set up this equation with $OP = x$.
$\frac{\sqrt{3}}{2} = \frac{1}{2}x^2 \cdot \frac{\pi}{3}$
$x^2 = \frac{3\sqrt{3}}{\pi}$ Simplifying
Therefore, $OP = \sqrt{\frac{3\sqrt{3}}{\pi}}$. Now that we know the radius, the arc length can be found by $s = r\theta$.
$PQ = \sqrt{\frac{3\sqrt{3}}{\pi}} \cdot \frac{\pi}{3}$
Simplify to get $PQ = \frac{\sqrt{3\pi\sqrt{3}}}{3}$.

$OP = \sqrt{\frac{3\sqrt{3}}{\pi}}$ $PQ = \frac{\sqrt{3\pi\sqrt{3}}}{3}$

Ex: 5 If $\theta = \frac{2\pi}{3}$ and sector ABO has a perimeter 4 units more than ABO, what is the length of AO?

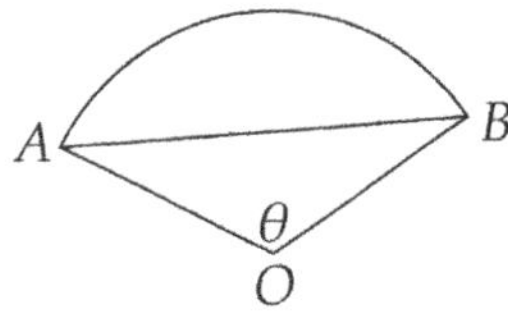

Let the radius (AO, BO) of the circle be x. The perimeter of the sector would be $2x + \frac{2\pi x}{3}$. If you draw down the altitude from O to AB, you get two $30-60-90$ triangles. Therefore, if $AO = x$, which represents the hypotenuse, $AB = 2 \cdot \frac{x\sqrt{3}}{2} = x\sqrt{3}$. The perimeter of the triangle would be $2x + x\sqrt{3}$.

$2x + \frac{2\pi x}{3} = 4 + 2x + x\sqrt{3}$ Relating perimeters

$x(\frac{2\pi}{3} - \sqrt{3}) = 4$ Combining like terms

$x = \frac{4}{\frac{2\pi}{3} - \sqrt{3}}$ Isolating x

$x = \frac{12}{2\pi - 3\sqrt{3}} \approx 11.039$

$\frac{12}{2\pi - 3\sqrt{3}} \approx 11.039$

Angular and Linear Speed

Ex: 1 A train is traveling at the rate of 12 miles per hour on a curve of radius 4000 feet. There are 5280 feet in a mile. a) Find the linear speed of the train in feet/minute. b) Find the angular speed of the train in radians/minute. c) Through what angle, in degrees, will the train turn in 20 minutes?

For a), use dimensional analysis with the speed.

$\frac{12mi}{hr} \cdot \frac{5280ft}{1mi} \cdot \frac{1hr}{60min} =$

$1056\frac{ft}{min}$

For b) remember than 2π radians $= 1$ revolution $=$ circumference $= 8000\pi$.

$\frac{1056ft}{min} \cdot \frac{2\pi\ radians}{8000\pi\ ft} =$

$0.264\frac{rad}{min}$

For c) remember than $180^\circ = \pi\ radians$.

$0.264\frac{rad}{min} \cdot \frac{180^\circ}{\pi\ rad} \cdot 20min =$

$\frac{950.4^\circ}{\pi}$

Ex: 2 A pulley is wrapped around two wheels. If the smaller wheel has angular speed of 10 revolutions per minute, find:

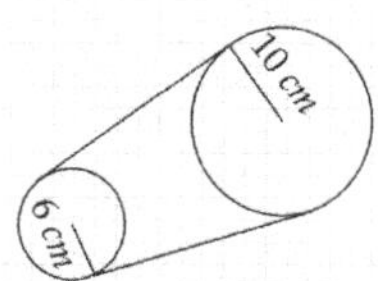

a) the angular speed, in radians/minute of the smaller wheel

$\frac{10\ rev}{min} \cdot \frac{2\pi\ rad}{1\ rev} =$

$\frac{20\pi\ radians}{minute}$

b) the linear speed, in cm/min, of a point on the smaller wheel

Remember that the linear speed equals the angular speed times the radius. Therefore:

Linear Speed= $\frac{20\pi\ radians}{minute} \cdot 6cm = \frac{120\pi cm}{minute}$

c) the angular speed, in radians/minute, of the larger wheel

Because the pulley goes around both wheels, they must have the same linear speed. Therefore, we can set up the equation:

$\frac{120\pi cm}{minute} = 10cm \cdot x$ because the angular speed times the radius $(10cm)$ equals linear speed.

$x = \frac{12\pi\ rad}{minute}$ Solving the equation

Modeling with Trigonometric Functions

Ex: 1 Joyce's circular bike tire has a piece of gum stuck on it. At $t = 0$, the gum is halfway between the ground and its maximum height. The gum reaches its maximum height of 72 cm from the ground $\frac{\pi}{18}$ seconds later before reaching the ground $\frac{\pi}{9}$ seconds after that. Find the sine and cosine function for the distance between the gum and the sidewalk after t seconds.

Because the minimum and maximum are 72 apart, the amplitude is 36. Since it takes $\frac{\pi}{18}$ seconds to go from the midpoint to the maximum, the period would be $4 \cdot \frac{\pi}{18} = \frac{2\pi}{9}$. Therefore, the "$b$" value equals 9. The "d" value is 36 because that's the midline of the function. Putting this information together:

$d(t) = 36\sin(9t) + 36$. In order to get the cosine version, replace t with $t - \frac{\pi}{18}$ since at $\frac{\pi}{8}$ the graph is at a maximum. Normally, cos curves begin at the maximum point so this is the transformation.

$d(t) = 36\sin(9t) + 36, d(t) = 36\cos(9t - \frac{\pi}{2}) + 36$

Ex: 2 A Ferris wheel has a radius of 10 meters and the bottom of the wheel passes 3 meters above the ground. It turns clockwise and makes one complete revolution every 40 seconds. Let $t = 0$ be when the person is at the "3 o'clock" position 13 meters high where the passengers load/unload. Find the sine and cosine equation that gives the height in meters above the ground as a function of time in seconds.

Because the radius is 10 meters, the amplitude is 10. Since it takes 40 seconds to go through one revolution, the period would be found by solving $\frac{2\pi}{b} = 40$. Therefore, the "b" value equals $\frac{\pi}{20}$. The "d" value is 13 because that's the midline of the function where the riders board. Since the Ferris wheel turns clockwise, the rider goes down then up. Therefore we must negate: $d(t) =- 10\sin(\frac{\pi}{20}t) + 13$. In order to get the cosine version, replace t with $t - 10$ since that's the transformation required to move the cos curve.

$$d(t) =- 10\sin(\tfrac{\pi}{20}t) + 13 =- 10\cos(\tfrac{\pi}{20}t - \tfrac{\pi}{2}) + 13$$

If you're struggling to find this "transformation" from sine to cosine, sketch a rough graph, label the key points, and see how much you need to shift the sine curve to get a cosine curve or vice versa.

Graphing Trigonometric Functions

Ex: 1 Find all relevant characteristics and graph:
$y =- 3\cot(3x - \frac{\pi}{4}) + 2$

The amplitude is clearly 3 while the midline is at 2. A normal period of $\cot$ is usually between 0 and π. Solving $3x - \frac{\pi}{4}$ for 0 and π gets that the left and right endpoints of a period will be at $\frac{\pi}{12}$ and $\frac{5\pi}{12}$. $\frac{\pi}{12}$ also represents the phase shift since that is the horizontal translation that transforms $y = \cot x$ to this graph. These are also where the asymptotes of the graph will be at. The period is $\frac{\pi}{3}$.

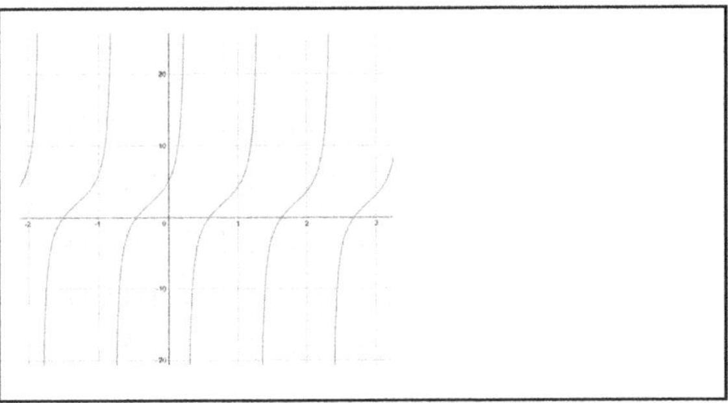

Ex: 2 Find all relevant characteristics and graph:
$y = 2\sin(\frac{\pi x}{2} + \frac{\pi}{3}) - 1$

The amplitude is 2, while midline is at -1. A period of $\sin$ has right and left endpoints at 0 and 2π. Solving $\frac{\pi x}{2} + \frac{\pi}{3}$ for 0 and 2π gets that the left and right endpoints of a period will be at $x = \frac{-2}{3}$ (also the phase shift) and $x = \frac{10}{3}$. The period is $\frac{2\pi}{\pi/2} = 4$.

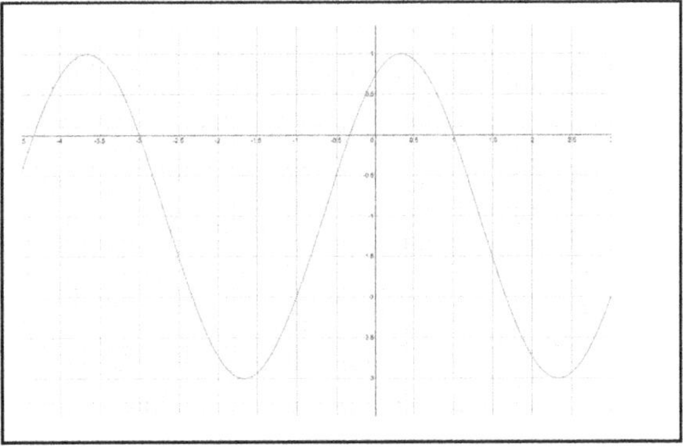

Ex: 3 Find all relevant characteristics and graph:
$y = 2\sec(\frac{\pi}{2}x - \frac{\pi}{3}) + 1$

For graphing this function, we need to first graph the helper function: $y = 2\cos(\frac{\pi}{2}x - \frac{\pi}{3}) + 1$. The zeroes of this helper function are where the asymptotes of our graph will lie. Look at this helper function, the amplitude is 2 and the midline is 1. The normal period goes from 0 to 2π so solving $\frac{\pi}{2}x - \frac{\pi}{3} = 0, 2\pi$ gives us the start and ending points. Solving, you get $x = \frac{2}{3}, \frac{14}{3}$. This is also where the graph will be tangent to the helper function. $\frac{2}{3}$ is also the phase shift. The period is $\frac{2\pi}{\pi/2} = 4$. Now after we graph in the helper function, we can draw out asymptotes and draw in the curve of the $\sec$.

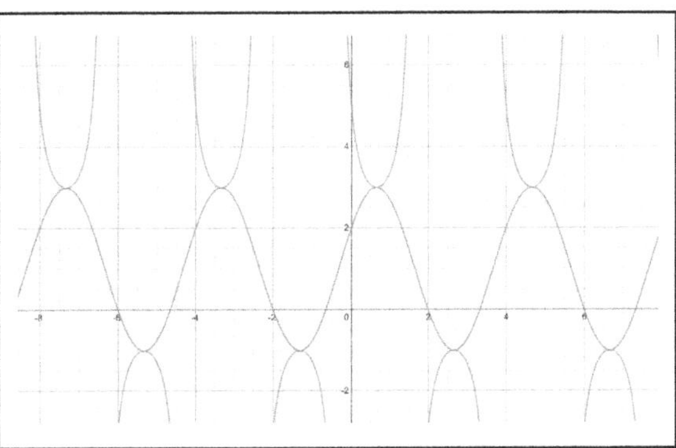

Trigonometric Functions Test 1

#1: (2 points each) Simplify.

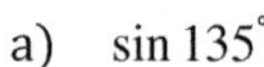

a) $\sin 135^\circ$

b) $\sec 210^\circ$

c) $\cot 135^\circ$

d) $\cos 510^\circ$

e) $\csc - 5\pi/4$

f) $\tan - 2\pi/3$

g) $\sin 5\pi/6$

h) $\sec 7\pi/3$

i) $\tan 5\pi/2$

#2: (12 points) Find the period, phase shift, midline, and asymptotes, of $y = \cot(\pi x + \frac{\pi}{2}) + 1$ Then graph 2 periods.

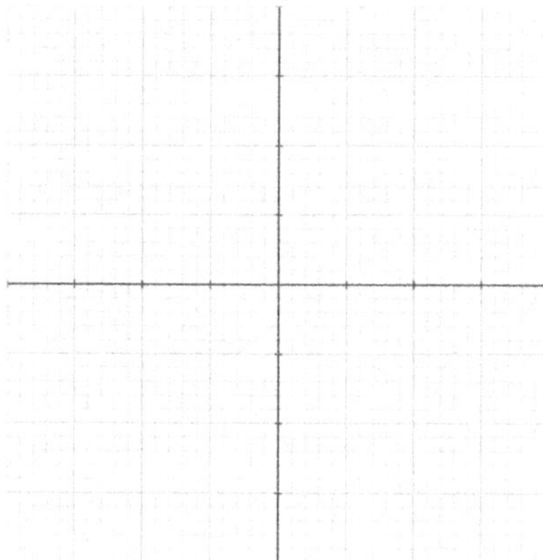

#3: (18 points) The wheels of a truck with diameter 2 feet spin at a rate of 200 revolutions a minute. a) Find the angular speed of the wheels in radians per minute b) Find the linear speed of the wheels in yards per second c) Suppose at $t = 0$, a pebble, which is caught in the tire, is at the tire's minimum point (0 feet above the ground) Express the pebble's height from the ground in feet as the tire spins with both a cos and sin function where t is in seconds.

#4: (10 points) From the top of the Eiffel tower, the angle of depression to the top of Twisted Timbers is 45 degrees. From the bottom of the Eiffel tower, the angle of elevation to the top of Twisted Timbers is 60 degrees. a) If Twisted Timbers is $60\sqrt{3}$ feet tall, how far is the Eiffel tower from Twisted Timbers? b) How tall is the Eiffel tower? c) How many feet down from the top of the Eiffel tower must you descend so that your angle of depression to the top of Twisted Timbers is 30 degrees?

#5: (14 points) A slice of cake is in a shape of a 3D circular sector with radius 2 cm, central angle of θ radians, and height h cm. The surface area of the slice of cake (including bottom) is 16 cm squared. If the height was decreased by 1 cm and θ increased by 1 radian, the surface area stays the same. What is θ and h? **47**

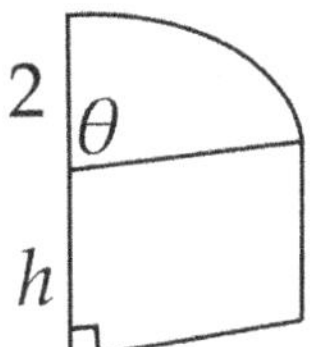

#6: (18 points) The bicycle wheel of radius of 12 inches has a linear speed of 48 inches per second a) Find the angular speed in radians per second. b) Find the angular speed in revolutions per second. c) If a piece of gum gets stuck at the bottom of the wheel at $t = 0$ seconds, express the height above the ground as the wheel spins clockwise with both a cos and sin function.

#7: (10 points) The bearing of a lighthouse (Point X) from a ship (Point Y) 8 km away is $N30^{\circ}E$. a) How far must the ship sail, due North to Point Z, for the bearing of the lighthouse to be $N135^{\circ}E$? b) What is the area formed by the triangle XYZ?

Trigonometric Functions Test 2

#1: (2 points each) Simplify.

a) 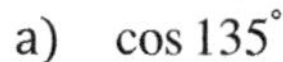 $\cos 135^\circ$

b) $\csc 210^\circ$

c) $\tan 135^\circ$

d) $\sin 510^\circ$

e) $\sec -5\pi/4$

f) $\cot -2\pi/3$

g) $\cot \pi$

h) $\csc 17\pi/6$

i) $\sin 35\pi$

#2: (12 points) Find the period, amplitude, phase shift, midline, and asymptotes, of $y = \csc(2\pi x + \frac{\pi}{2}) - 1$ Then graph 2 periods.

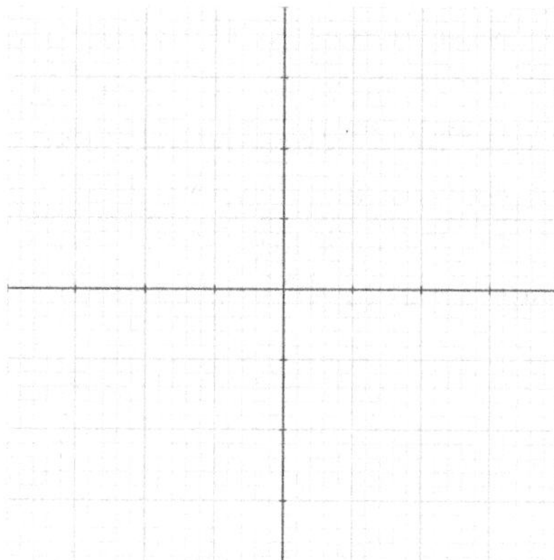

#3: (10 points) From the top of Kingda Ka, the angle of depression to the top of El Toro is 60°. From the bottom of Kingda, the angle of elevation to the top of El Toro is 45°. If the distance from the top of Kingda Ka to the bottom of El Toro is $100\sqrt{15 + 6\sqrt{3}}$ feet. Find the height of both El Toro and Kingda Ka.

#4: (10 points) A spiral staircase has 15 steps. Each step is a sector with a radius of 42 inches and a central angle of $\pi/8$. a) What is the length of the arc formed by the outer edge of a step? b) Through what angle would you rotate by climbing the stairs? c) How many square inches of carpeting would you need to cover the 15 steps?

#5: (18 points) The wheels of a truck with diameter 4 feet spin at a rate of 180 revolutions a minute. a) Find the angular speed of the wheels in radians per minute b) Find the linear speed of the wheels in yards per second c) Suppose at $t = 0$, a pebble, which is caught in the tire, is at the tire's minimum point (0 feet above the ground) Express the pebble's height from the ground as the tire spins with both a cos and sin function where t is in seconds.

#6: (18 points) The bicycle wheel of radius of 11 inches has a linear speed of 33 inches per second a) Find the angular speed in <u>radians</u> per second. b) Find the angular speed in <u>revolutions</u> per second. c) If a piece of gum gets stuck at the bottom of the wheel at $t = 0$ seconds, express the height above the ground as the wheel spins clockwise with both a cos and sin function.

#7: (14 points) AO_1B, CO_1D are circular sectors with angle $\frac{\pi}{3}$. AO_2B is a circular sector with angle $\frac{\pi}{6}$. If the perimeter of the entire figure is $\frac{5\pi}{3} + 16$ units and the area is $\frac{17\pi}{3}$, find the length of AO_1 and AC. **<u>17</u>**

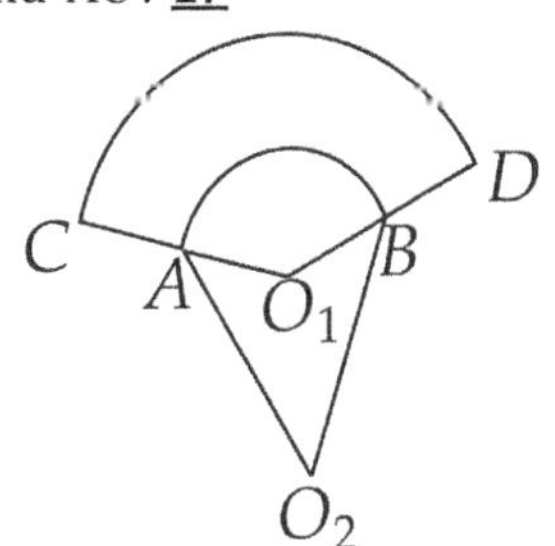

Trigonometric Functions Test 3

#1: (2 points each) Simplify.

a) 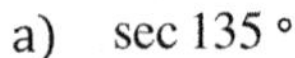 sec 135 °

b) sin 210 °

c) cot 225 °

d) sec 510 °

e) sin− 5π/4

f) tan− 4π/3

g) tan π

h) cos 17π/6

i) csc 35π

#2: (12 points) Find the period, phase shift, midline, amplitude, and asymptotes, of $y = 2\sec(\frac{\pi}{2}x - \frac{3\pi}{2}) + 1$ Then graph 2 periods.

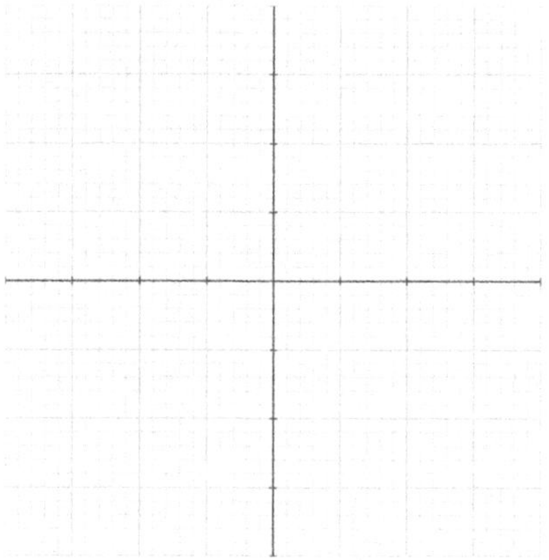

#3: (10 points) A roller coaster travels around a circular helix of radius 280 feet at a rate of 54 miles per hour. a) What is the linear speed of the coaster in yards/minute? b) What is the angular speed in radians/minute. c) What angle, in degrees, will the train turn in 25 minutes? d) How long in seconds will it take for the coaster to go through the entire helix?

#4: (12 points) AO_1B, CO_1D are circular sectors with angle $\frac{\pi}{3}$. AO_2B is a circular sector with angle $\frac{\pi}{6}$. A and B are the midpoints of CO_1 and DO_1 respectively. If the perimeter of the entire figure is 4π, what is the length of AO_1?

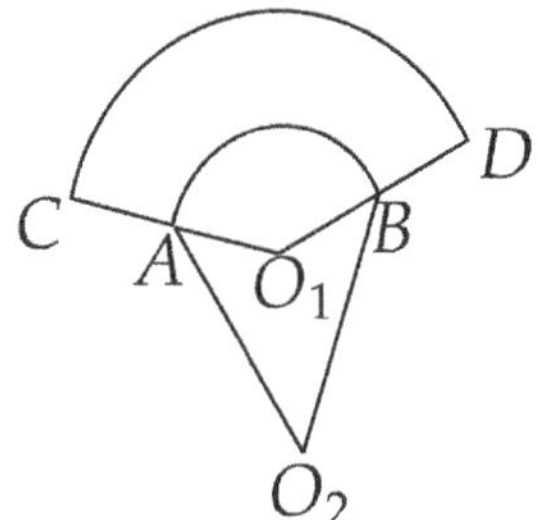

#5: (18 points) A clock with a 14 inch diameter has a minute hand that is 6 inches long and an hour hand that is 4 inches long. The bottom of the clock is hung 100 inches above the ground. a) What is the angular speed of the hour hand in radians/minute? b) What is the linear speed of the minute hand in feet/hour? c) Find a sine and cosine function that models the elevation h (in inches) of the minute hand as a function of time (minutes past the hour).

#6: (18 points) A ferris wheel has a radius of 70 feet. You board a car at the bottom of the ferris wheel, which is 10 feet above the ground. a) From your current spot $(t = 0)$, the ride moves at an angular speed of 12 radians per minute. In seconds, model the height of the car above the ground in minutes with a sine and cosine function. b) Suppose the ride rotates 240° counterclockwise before the ride temporarily stops. How high above the ground are you when the ride stops?

#7: (12 points) A pilot, who was supposed to fly 120 miles at a bearing of $N20^\circ W$ mistakenly flies 80 miles at a bearing of $N40^\circ E$, before realizing her mistake. a) In exact form, how far is she from her original destination? b) At what bearing should she fly to head directly to her original destination?

Chapter 8 Trig Identities/Equations

Before you begin, know the trig identities. You won't have to memorize all of them, but being familiar with them will greatly help. Oftentimes, people will struggle to determine which identity to use to solve a problem.
Below is a reference for the trig identities:

Pythagorean Identities
$\sin^2 u + \cos^2 u = 1$
$\tan^2 u + 1 = \sec^2 u$
$1 + \cot^2 u = \csc^2 u$

Sum and Difference
$\sin(u+v) = \sin u \cdot \cos v + \cos v \cdot \sin u$
$\sin(u-v) = \sin u \cdot \cos v - \cos u \cdot \sin v$
$\cos(u+v) = \cos u \cdot \cos v - \sin v \cdot \sin v$
$\cos(u-v) = \cos u \cdot \cos v + \sin u \cdot \sin v$
$\tan(u+v) = \frac{\tan u + \tan v}{1 - \tan u \cdot \tan v}$
$\tan(u-v) = \frac{\tan u - \tan v}{1 + \tan u \cdot \tan v}$

Double-Angle
$\sin(2u) = 2\sin u \cdot \cos u$
$\cos(2u) = \cos^2 u - \sin^2 u = 2\cos^2 u - 1 = 1 - 2\sin^2 u$
$\tan(2u) = \frac{2\tan u}{1 - \tan^2 u}$

Power-Reducing Formulas
$\sin^2 u = \frac{1-\cos(2u)}{2}$ $\cos^2 u = \frac{1+\cos(2u)}{2}$ $\tan^2 u = \frac{1-\cos(2u)}{1+\cos(2u)}$

Half-Angle Formulas
$\sin(\frac{u}{2}) = \pm\sqrt{\frac{1-\cos u}{2}}$ $\cos(\frac{u}{2}) = \pm\sqrt{\frac{1+\cos u}{2}}$
$\tan(\frac{u}{2}) = \frac{1-\cos u}{\sin u} = \frac{\sin u}{1+\cos u}$

Product-to-Sum Formulas
$\sin u \sin v = \frac{1}{2}[\cos(u-v) - \cos(u+v)]$
$\cos u \cos v = \frac{1}{2}[\cos(u-v) + \cos(u+v)]$
$\sin u \cos v = \frac{1}{2}[\sin(u+v) + \sin(u-v)]$
$\cos u \sin v = \frac{1}{2}[\sin(u+v) - \sin(u-v)]$

Sum-to-Product Formulas
$\sin x + \sin y = 2\sin(\frac{x+y}{2})\cos(\frac{x-y}{2})$
$\sin x - \sin y = 2\cos(\frac{x+y}{2})\sin(\frac{x-y}{2})$
$\cos x + \cos y = 2\cos(\frac{x+y}{2})\cos(\frac{x-y}{2})$
$\cos x - \cos y = -2\sin(\frac{x+y}{2})\sin(\frac{x-y}{2})$

Inverse Trig

Ex: 1 Simplify $\csc(\arccos(x+3))$
By the definition of inverse cosine, you know the cosine of some angle θ equals to $x+3$. Therefore, you can construct this right triangle.

$x+3$ θ 1
$\sqrt{1-(x+3)^2}$

Using the pythagorean theorem, you find out that the other side length is $\sqrt{1-(x+3)^2} = \sqrt{-8-x^2-6x}$. Therefore, the $\csc\theta$ equals:

$\frac{1}{\sqrt{-8-x^2-6x}}$ by dividing opposite by hypotenuse

Ex: 2 $\tan(\arcsin(x+1))$
Similarly, construct a right triangle, knowing that the sin of angle θ equals $x+1$.

$x+1$ 1 θ
$\sqrt{1-(x+1)^2}$

Using the pythagorean theorem, you find out that the other side length is $\sqrt{1-(x+1)^2} = \sqrt{-x^2-2x}$. Therefore, $\tan\theta$ equals:

$\frac{x+1}{\sqrt{-x^2-2x}}$ by dividing opposite over adjacent

Ex: 3 Solve for x : $\cos^{-1}x = \sin^{-1}(2x)$
Take the sin of both sides to get:
$\sin(\cos^{-1}x) = 2x$. Similar to above, construct a right triangle with adjacent x and hypotenuse 1 to find out that $\sin(\cos^{-1}x) = \sqrt{1-x^2}$
After solving $\sqrt{1-x^2} = 2x$, we get:

$x = \frac{\sqrt{5}}{5}$

Basic Identities

Ex: 1 Verify

$(\sin x - \tan x)(\cos x - \cot x) = (\sin x - 1)(\cos x - 1)$

Manipulating the right side only we get:

$(\sin x - \frac{\sin x}{\cos x})(\cos x - \frac{\cos x}{\sin x})$ Rewriting the $\tan x$

$\sin x \cos x - \cos x - \sin x + 1$ Expanding

$(\sin x - 1)(\cos x - 1)$ Factoring

This is equivalent to the right side so we have verified the identity.

Ex: 2 What is the maximum of

$f(x) =- 2\tan^2 x + 4\sec x + 1$

$f(x) =- 2(\sec^2 x - 1) + 4\sec x + 1$

Using pythagorean identity to rewrite $\tan^2 x$

$f(x) =- 2\sec^2 x + 4\sec x + 3$. Simplifying

$f(x) =- 2(\sec^2 x - 2\sec x + 1 - 1) + 3$

$f(x) =- 2(\sec x - 1)^2 + 5$ Completing the square

> The maximum is 5

Ex: 3 Verify $\frac{\sin^3 x - \cos^3 x}{\sin x + \cos x} = \frac{\csc^2 x - \cot x - 2\cos^2 x}{1 - \cot^2 x}$

Let's first rewrite the left side.

$\frac{(\sin x - \cos x)(\sin^2 x + \sin x \cos x + \cos^2 x)}{\sin x + \cos x}$ Factoring the top

$\frac{(\sin x - \cos x)(1 + \sin x \cos x)}{\sin x + \cos x}$ Applying Pythagorean Identity

Now moving on to the right side:

$\frac{\frac{1}{\sin^2 x} - \frac{\cos x}{\sin x} - 2\cos^2 x}{1 - \frac{\cos^2 x}{\sin^2 x}}$ Rewriting everything in $\sin$ and $\cos$

$\frac{1 - \sin x \cos x - 2\cos^2 x \sin^2 x}{\sin^2 x - \cos^2 x}$ Multiplying by $\frac{\sin^2 x}{\sin^2 x}$

$\frac{(1 + \sin x \cos x)(1 - 2\sin x \cos x)}{(\sin x + \cos x)(\sin x - \cos x)}$ Factoring top and bottom

$\frac{(1 + \sin x \cos x)(\sin^2 x + \cos^2 x - 2\sin x \cos x)}{(\sin x + \cos x)(\sin x - \cos x)}$ Rewriting 1

$\frac{(1 + \sin x \cos x)(\sin x - \cos x)^2}{(\sin x + \cos x)(\sin x - \cos x)}$ Factoring Again

$\frac{(1 + \sin x \cos x)(\sin x - \cos x)}{\sin x + \cos x}$ Cancelling out like terms

Ex: 4 Solve $\cot x + 2\cos x = 3\csc x \cdot \tan x$

$\frac{\cos x}{\sin x} + 2\cos x = \frac{3}{\sin x} \cdot \frac{\sin x}{\cos x}$ Expressing in $\sin$ and $\cos$

$\frac{\cos x + 2\sin x \cos x}{\sin x} = \frac{3}{\cos x}$ Simplifying

$\cos^2 x(1 + 2\sin x) = 3\sin x$ Cross Multiplying

$(1 - \sin^2 x)(1 + 2\sin x) = 3\sin x$ $\cos^2 x + \sin^2 x = 1$

$1 + 2\sin x - \sin^2 x - 2\sin^2 x = 3\sin x$ Expanding

$2\sin^3 x + \sin^2 x + \sin x - 1 = 0$ Combining like terms

$(2\sin x - 1)(\sin^2 + \sin x + 1) = 0$ Factoring

$\sin x = \frac{1}{2}, \sin^2 + \sin x + 1$ does not have real roots

$x = 30^\circ + 360^\circ k, 150^\circ + 360^\circ k$

$\sin^2 + \sin x + 1$ does not have real roots

> $x = 30^\circ + 360^\circ k, 150^\circ + 360^\circ k$

Ex: 5 Solve $\sin^3 x + \cos^3 x + \sin x \cos x = 1$.

$(\sin x + \cos x)(\sin^2 x - \sin x \cos x + \cos^2 x) + \sin x \cos x = 1$

Factoring sum of cubes

$(\sin x + \cos x)(1 - \sin x \cos x) - (1 - \sin x \cos x) = 0$

Using pythagorean identity and simplifying

$(\sin x + \cos x - 1)(1 - \sin x \cos x) = 0$ Factoring

$\sin x + \cos x = 1, \sin x \cos x = 1$ Factor theorem

$\sin x + \sqrt{1 - \sin^2 x} = 1$ Using pythagorean identity

$1 - \sin^2 x = 1 - 2\sin x + \sin^2 x$ Squaring both sides

$2\sin x(\sin x - 1) = 0$ Combining like terms

$\sin x = 0, \sin x = 1$ Factor theorem

$x = 180^\circ k, x = 90^\circ k$

$\sin x \cos x = 1$ does not have real solutions

> $x = 90^\circ k$

Sum/Difference/Double/Half Angle

Ex: 1 Simplify $\sin 52.5^\circ$

Express this as $\sin(22.5 + 30)^\circ$

$\sin 22.5^\circ \cos 30^\circ + \sin 30^\circ \cos 22.5^\circ$

Applying angle addition formula

Using the half angle formula we know

$\cos 22.5^\circ = \sqrt{\frac{1 + \cos 45^\circ}{2}} = \frac{\sqrt{2 + \sqrt{2}}}{2}$ and

$\sin 22.5^\circ = \sqrt{\frac{1 - \cos 45^\circ}{2}} = \frac{\sqrt{2 - \sqrt{2}}}{2}$. Plugging this back to the original expression we get:

$\sin 52.5^\circ = \frac{\sqrt{2 - \sqrt{2}}}{2} \cdot \frac{\sqrt{3}}{2} + \frac{1}{2} \cdot \frac{\sqrt{2 + \sqrt{2}}}{2}$

> $\frac{\sqrt{6 - 3\sqrt{2}} + \sqrt{2 + \sqrt{2}}}{4}$ Simplifying

Ex: 2 If $\sin x - \cos x = 1/3$, what is the value of $\sin(2x)$?

$(\sin x - \cos x)^2 = \frac{1}{9}$ Squaring both sides

$\sin^2 x + \cos^2 x - 2\sin x \cos x = \frac{1}{9}$ Expanding

$1 - \sin(2x) = \frac{1}{9}$ Applying pythagorean and double angle identities

> $\sin(2x) = \frac{8}{9}$ Solving the equation

Ex: 3 Solve $\cos(4x) + 4\sin x \cdot \cos x = 1$.
$1 - 2\sin^2(2x) + 2\sin(2x) = 1$ Double Angles
$-2\sin^2(2x) + 2\sin(2x) = 0$ Subtracting 1
$\sin(2x)[-2\sin(2x) + 1] = 0$ Factoring
$\sin(2x) = 0$ Setting the first factor to 0
$2x = \pi k$ so $x = \frac{\pi k}{2}$
$-2\sin(2x) + 1 = 0$ Setting the second factor to 0
$\sin(2x) = \frac{1}{2}$ Simplifying
$2x = \frac{\pi}{6} + 2\pi k, 2x = \frac{5\pi}{6} + 2\pi x$ so $x = \frac{\pi}{12} + \pi k, \frac{5\pi}{12} + \pi k$

$x = \frac{\pi}{12} + \pi k, \frac{5\pi}{12} + \pi k, \frac{\pi k}{2}$ where k is an integer

Ex: 4 Solve for $x: \cos^{-1}x = 2\sin^{-1}(1 - x)$
To isolate the x, take the cos of both sides to get:
$x = \cos(2\sin^{-1}(1 - x))$.
Now apply the double angle formula for cos to get:
$x = 1 - 2\sin(\sin^{-1}(1 - x))^2$
Simplifying, that leads to $x = 1 - 2(1 - x)^2$.
$x = 1 - 2x^2 + 4x - 2$ Expanding
$(2x - 1)(x - 1) = 0$ Factoring

$x = \frac{1}{2}, 1$ Solving for x

Ex: 5 Verify $\sin^4(\frac{x}{2}) = \frac{1}{8}(3 - 4\cos x + \cos(2x))$
Using the half angle identity we get that the left side equals: $(\sqrt{\frac{1-\cos x}{2}})^4$. Multiplying the power out we get, $\frac{(1-\cos x)^2}{4}$. Expanding we get $\frac{1-2\cos x+\cos^2 x}{4}$.
Applying the power identity, $\frac{1-2\cos x+\frac{1+\cos(2x)}{2}}{4}$.
Multiplying 2 on both sides and simplifying we get, $\frac{1}{8}(3 - 4\cos x + \cos(2x))$.

Ex: 6 Simplify $\cos(2\sin^{-1}(0.6) + \cos^{-1}(0.8))$
Using the angle sum identity for cos, we get
$\cos(2\sin^{-1}(0.6))\cos(\cos^{-1}(0.8)) -$
$\sin(2\sin^{-1}(0.6)\sin(\cos^{-1}(0.8)$
Applying double angle theorems, we get:
$(1 - 2\sin(\sin^{-1}(0.6))^2) \cdot 0.8 -$
$2\sin(\sin^{-1}(0.6))\cos(\sin^{-1}(0.6)) \cdot (\sin(\cos^{-1}(0.8))$
Simplifying the the $\sin(\sin^{-1})$ we get:
$(1 - 2(0.6)^2) \cdot 0.8 - 2(0.6)\cos(\sin^{-1}(0.6)) \cdot \sin(\cos^{-1}(0.8))$

Now construct a $3 - 4 - 5$ right triangle to see $\cos(\sin^{-1}(0.6)) = 0.8$ and $\sin(\cos^{-1}(0.8)) = 0.6$.
Therefore, putting it all together we get:
$(1 - 2(0.6)^2) \cdot 0.8 - 2(0.6)(0.8) \cdot 0.6$.

-0.352

Ex: 7 Solve $\tan(7x) + \tan(3x) = 0$ for $0^\circ \leq x < 90^\circ$
$\frac{\sin(7x)}{\cos(7x)} + \frac{\sin(3x)}{\cos(3x)} = 0$ Rewrite in term of sin and cos
$\frac{\sin(7x)\cos(3x)+\cos(7x)\sin(3x)}{\cos(7x)\cos(3x)} = 0$ Combining fractions
$\frac{\sin(10x)}{\cos(7x)\cos(3x)} = 0$ Recognizing Angle Sum
$\sin(10x) = 0$ Setting a factor equal to 0. Note that the denominators of the fraction cannot equal 0.
$10x = 0^\circ, 180^\circ, 360^\circ ...$

$x = 0^\circ, 18^\circ, 36^\circ, 54^\circ, 72^\circ$

Ex: 8 Let x and y be positive acute angles such that $3\sin^2 x + 2\sin^2 y = 1, 3\sin 2x - 2\sin 2y = 0$. Find $x + 2y$.
We can expect that problem will allow us to find the value of $\cos(x + 2y)$ or $\sin(x + 2y)$. We then use that to find the value of $x + 2y$.
$3\sin^2 x = 1 - 2\sin^2 y$ Rewriting first equation
$3\sin^2 x = \cos 2y$ Using cos double angle
$3\sin 2x = 2\sin 2y$ Rewriting second equation
$3(2\sin x\cos x) = 2\sin 2y$ Using sin double angle
$3\sin x = \frac{\sin 2y}{\cos x}$ Dividing $2\cos x$ on both sides
Because of what the problem is asking, we want to keep things in terms of x and $2y$.
$\sin x \cdot \frac{\sin 2y}{\cos x} = \cos 2y$ Substituting $3\sin x$
$0 = \cos 2y\cos x - \sin x\sin 2y$ Rewriting expression
$0 = \cos(x + 2y)$ Using cos angle addition identity

$x + 2y = 90^\circ$

Ex: 9 Solve $2\sin(2x) - 3\tan x = \frac{\sin x}{\cos^2 x}$
$4\sin x\cos x - 3\tan x = \frac{\sin x}{\cos^2 x}$ Double Angle Formula
$4\sin x\cos x - \frac{3\sin x}{\cos x} = \frac{\sin x}{\cos^2 x}$ Rewriting tan
$4\sin x\cos^3 x - 3\sin x\cos x = \sin x$ Multiplying $\cos^2 x$
$\sin x(4\cos^3 x - 3\cos x - 1) = 0$ Factoring
$\sin x(\cos x - 1)(4\cos^2 x + 4\cos x + 1) = 0$ Factoring

$\sin x(\cos x - 1)(2\cos x + 1)^2 = 0$ Factoring
$\sin x = 0, \cos x = 1, \cos x = -\frac{1}{2}$ Factor theorem
$x = 180^\circ k, x = 120^\circ + 360^\circ k, x = 240^\circ + 360^\circ k$ Solving

$x = 180^\circ k, x = 120^\circ + 360^\circ k, x = 240^\circ + 360^\circ k$

Ex: 10 Solve $\frac{\sin^2 x - 2\tan x}{\tan x} = -\frac{7}{4}$.
$4\sin^2 x - 8\tan x = -7\tan x$ Cross Multiplying
$4\sin^2 x - \tan x = 0$ Combining like terms
$4\sin^2 x - \frac{\sin x}{\cos x} = 0$ Rewriting $\tan x$
$4\sin^2 x\cos x - \sin x = 0$ Multiplying $\cos x$
$\sin x(4\sin x\cos x - 1) = 0$ Factoring
$\sin x(2\sin(2x) - 1) = 0$ Double Angle Identity
$\sin x = 0, \sin(2x) = \frac{1}{2}$ Factor Theorem
$x = 180^\circ k, 15^\circ + 180^\circ k, 75^\circ + 180^\circ k$ Solving for x

$x = 180^\circ k, 15^\circ + 180^\circ k, 75^\circ + 180^\circ k$

Ex: 11 Solve $\cos(4x) + \sin^2 x + \sin^2(2x) = 0.5$ for $0^\circ \le x < 360^\circ$
$2\cos^2(2x) - 1 + \sin^2 x + \sin^2(2x) = 0.5$ Double Angle
$\cos^2(2x) + \cos^2(2x) + \sin^2(2x) - 1 + \sin^2 x = 0.5$
Splitting $\cos^2(2x)$ to use pythagorean identity
$\cos^2(2x) + \sin^2 x = 0.5$ Pythagorean Identity
$(1 - 2\sin^2 x)^2 + \sin^2 x = 0.5$ Double Angle
$8\sin^4 x - 6\sin^2 x + 1 = 0$ Expanding and simplifying
$(4\sin^2 x - 1)(2\sin^2 x - 1) = 0$ Factoring
$\sin^2 x = \frac{1}{4}, \sin^2 x = \frac{1}{2}$ Solving for $\sin^2 x$
$\sin x = \pm\frac{1}{2}$ Taking square root
$x = 30^\circ, 150^\circ, 210^\circ, 300^\circ$ Solving for x
$\sin x = \pm\frac{\sqrt{2}}{2}$ Taking square root
$x = 45^\circ, 135^\circ, 225^\circ, 315^\circ$ Solving for x

$x = 30^\circ, 150^\circ, 210^\circ, 300^\circ, 45^\circ, 135^\circ, 225^\circ, 315^\circ$

Ex: 12 If $\sin B = \frac{1}{\sqrt{10}}$ and $A + 2B = 45^\circ$, find $\tan A$.
Let $\tan A = x$, therefore, $A = \tan^{-1} x$ and $B = \sin^{-1}\frac{1}{\sqrt{10}}$ by using inverse trig.
$\tan(A + 2B) = \tan 45^\circ$ Taking $\tan$ on both sides
$\frac{\tan A + \tan 2B}{1 - \tan A\tan 2B} = 1$ tan angle sum identity
$\frac{\tan(\tan^{-1} x) + \tan(2\sin^{-1}\frac{1}{\sqrt{10}})}{1 - \tan(\tan^{-1} x)\tan(2\sin^{-1}\frac{1}{\sqrt{10}})} = 1$ Substituting in values
$\frac{x + \tan(2\sin^{-1}\frac{1}{\sqrt{10}})}{1 - x\tan(2\sin^{-1}\frac{1}{\sqrt{10}})} = 1$ Properties of inverse trig
Now let's work on simplifying $\tan(2\sin^{-1}\frac{1}{\sqrt{10}})$.
$\tan(2\sin^{-1}\frac{1}{\sqrt{10}}) = \frac{2\tan(\sin^{-1}\frac{1}{\sqrt{10}})}{1 - \tan^2(\sin^{-1}\frac{1}{\sqrt{10}})}$ tan double angle
In a right triangle, with opposite length 1, hypotenuse length $\sqrt{10}$, the length of the adjacent is 3. Therefore, the $\tan(\sin^{-1}\frac{1}{\sqrt{10}}) = \frac{1}{3}$.
$\frac{2\tan(\sin^{-1}\frac{1}{\sqrt{10}})}{1 - \tan^2(\sin^{-1}\frac{1}{\sqrt{10}})} = \frac{2/3}{1 - (1/3)^2} = \frac{3}{4}$ Simplifying
$\frac{x + \frac{3}{4}}{1 - \frac{3}{4}x} = 1$ Substituting in $\tan(2\sin^{-1}\frac{1}{\sqrt{10}}) = \frac{3}{4}$
$x + \frac{3}{4} = 1 - \frac{3}{4}x$ Simplifying
$x = \frac{1}{7}$

$\frac{1}{7}$

Ex: 13 If $\tan 4x = \cot 3y$ and $\tan 2x = \tan y$ such that x and y are the smallest possible positive degrees, $\frac{2\cos x}{\sin y}$ can be expressed as $\csc n^\circ$. Find n.
$\frac{\sin 4x}{\cos 4x} - \frac{\cos 3y}{\sin 3y} = 0$ Expressing as $\sin$ and $\cos$
$\frac{\sin 4x\sin 3y - \cos 4x\cos 3y}{\cos 4x\sin 3y} = 0$ Combining Fraction
$\frac{-\cos(4x + 3y)}{\cos 4x\sin 3y} = 0$ cos angle sum identity
$4x + 3y = 90$ since $\cos(4x + 3y) = 0$
$\frac{\sin 2x}{\cos 2x} - \frac{\sin y}{\cos y} = 0$ Expressing as $\sin$ and $\cos$
$\frac{\sin 2x\cos y - \sin y\cos 2x}{\cos 2x\cos y} = 0$ Combining fractions
$\frac{\sin(2x - y)}{\cos 2x\cos y} = 0$ sin angle difference identity
$2x - y = 0$ since $\sin(2x - y) = 0$
Solving our system of equations, we get $x = 9^\circ, y = 18^\circ$.
$\frac{2\cos 9^\circ}{\sin 18^\circ} = \frac{2\cos 9^\circ}{2\sin 9^\circ\cos 9^\circ} = \csc 9^\circ$ Simplifying

$n = 9$

The important lesson here is that when in doubt, express things in terms of $\sin$ and $\cos$

Ex: 14 Solve $\sin x - \sin 2x + \sin 3x = 0$ for $0^\circ \le x < 360^\circ$.
$\sin x - 2\sin x\cos x + \sin 3x = 0$ sin double angle
Now let's rewrite $\sin 3x$. $\sin 3x = \sin(2x + x) = \sin 2x\cos x + \cos 2x\sin x$ by angle sum identity.
$\sin 3x = 2\sin x\cos^2 x + (1 - 2\sin^2 x)\sin x$ Double Angle Identities

$\sin 3x = 3\sin x - 4\sin^3 x$ Simplifying

$\sin x - 2\sin x\cos x + 3\sin x - 4\sin^3 x = 0$ Plugging $\sin 3x$

$4\sin x(1 - \sin^2 x) - 2\sin x\cos x = 0$ Factoring

$4\sin x\cos^2 x - 2\sin x\cos x = 0$ Pythagorean Identity

$4\sin x\cos x(\cos x - \frac{1}{2}) = 0$ Factoring

$\sin x = 0, \cos x = 0, \cos x = \frac{1}{2}$ Factor Theorem

$x = 0^\circ, 60^\circ, 90^\circ, 180^\circ, 270^\circ, 300^\circ$ Solving for x

$x = 0^\circ, 60^\circ, 90^\circ, 180^\circ, 270^\circ, 300^\circ$

Ex: 15 Simplify $\sqrt{3}\csc 20^\circ - \sec 20^\circ$.

$\tan 60^\circ \csc 20^\circ - \sec 20^\circ$ Rewriting $\sqrt{3}$

$\frac{\sin 60^\circ}{\cos 60^\circ \sin 20^\circ} - \frac{1}{\cos 20^\circ}$ Expressing as sin and cos

$\frac{\sin 60^\circ \cos 20^\circ - \cos 60^\circ \sin 20^\circ}{\cos 60^\circ \sin 20^\circ \cos 20^\circ}$ Combining fractions

$\frac{\sin 40^\circ}{\cos 60^\circ \sin 20^\circ \cos 20^\circ}$ Angle difference identity

$\frac{\sin 40^\circ}{\frac{1}{4}\sin 40^\circ}$ Double angle identity

4 Simplifying

4

Product to Sum, Sum to Product

Ex: 1 Verify $\sin x + \sin(3x) = 4\sin x \cdot \cos^2 x$

Applying the sum to product on the left side, we get $2\sin(\frac{3x+x}{2})\cos(\frac{3x-x}{2})$ or $2\sin(2x)\cos x$. Using double angle formula, we get $2(2\sin x \cdot \cos x)\cos x$ That simplifies to $4\sin x \cdot \cos^2 x$

Ex: 2 Solve $\frac{\sin x + \sin(3x) + \sin(5x)}{\cos x + \cos(3x) + \cos(5x)} = 1$ for $0^\circ \le x < 90^\circ$

Rewrite the fraction as $\frac{(\sin x + \sin(5x)) + \sin(3x)}{(\cos x + \cos(5x) + \cos(3x)} = 0$

Using the sum to product identities, we get:

$\frac{2\sin(3x)\cos(2x) + \sin(3x)}{2\cos(3x)\cos(2x) + \cos(3x)} = 1.$

We can factor to get: $\frac{\sin(3x)(2\cos(2x)+1)}{\cos(3x)(2\cos(2x)+1)} = 1$

Cancelling out common factors and simplifying we get: $\tan(3x) = 1$. Therefore, $3x = 45^\circ, 225^\circ$

$x = 15^\circ, 75^\circ$

Ex: 3 Solve $\sin(2x)\cos(3x) - \cos(x)\sin(4x) = 0$ for $0^\circ \le x < 360^\circ$.

$\frac{1}{2}[\sin(5x) - \sin x] - \frac{1}{2}[\sin(5x) + \sin(3x)] = 0$

Product to Sum Formulas

$-\frac{1}{2}\sin x - \frac{1}{2}\sin(3x) = 0$ Simplifying

$\sin x + \sin 3x = 0$ Simplifying

$2\sin(2x)\cos x = 0$ Sum to product formula

$\sin(2x) = 0$ so $x = 0^\circ, 90^\circ, 180^\circ, 270^\circ$. $\cos x = 0$ produces overlapped results.

$x = 0^\circ, 90^\circ, 180^\circ, 270^\circ$

Ex: 4 Find the maximum and minimum of $f(x) = \sin(3x + \frac{\pi}{2})\sin(3x - \frac{\pi}{6})$.

We want to express this as one trigonometric function in order to find the max and min.

$f(x) = \frac{1}{2}[\cos(\frac{\pi}{2} + \frac{\pi}{6}) - \cos(6x + \frac{\pi}{3})]$

Using the product to sum identity

$f(x) = \frac{1}{2}[-\frac{1}{2} - \cos(6x + \frac{\pi}{3})]$ Simplifying

$f(x) = -\frac{1}{2}\cos(6x + \frac{\pi}{3}) - \frac{1}{4}$ Simplifying

The max and min of a cos function is -1 and 1 no matter its transformations. If $\cos(6x + \frac{\pi}{3}) = 1$, $6x + \frac{\pi}{3} = 0$. Solving for x, we get $x = -\frac{\pi}{18}$. Evaluating $f(-\frac{\pi}{18})$, we see that the minimum is $-\frac{1}{2}(1) - \frac{1}{4} = -\frac{3}{4}$. If $\cos(6x + \frac{\pi}{3}) = -1$, $6x + \frac{\pi}{3} = -\pi$. Solving for x, we get $x = -\frac{2\pi}{9}$. Evaluating $f(-\frac{2\pi}{9})$, we see that the maximum is $-\frac{1}{2}(-1) - \frac{1}{4} = -\frac{1}{4}$.

Maximum: $-\frac{1}{4}$ when $x = -\frac{2\pi}{9}$
Minimum: $-\frac{3}{4}$ when $x = -\frac{\pi}{18}$

Ex: 5 If $\sin^4 x - \sin^4 y = \frac{3}{16}$ and $\sin(x+y)\sin(x-y) = \frac{1}{4}$, find $\tan^2 x + \tan^2 y$.

$(\sin^2 x + \sin^2 y)(\sin x - \sin y)(\sin x + \sin y) = \frac{3}{16}$

Factoring by difference of Squares

Let's use sum to product identities to simplify.

$\sin x - \sin y = 2\cos(\frac{x+y}{2})\sin(\frac{x-y}{2})$

$\sin x + \sin y = 2\sin(\frac{x+y}{2})\cos(\frac{x-y}{2})$

If we multiply these together and rearrange:

$2\sin(\frac{x-y}{2})\cos(\frac{x-y}{2}) \cdot 2\sin(\frac{x+y}{2})\cos(\frac{x+y}{2})$

This fits nicely with sin double angle identity!

$\sin(x-y)\sin(x+y)$ Using double angle identity

We know from our given information that this equals $\frac{1}{4}$. Therefore, $\sin^2 x - \sin^2 y = \frac{1}{4}$

$(\sin^2 x + \sin^2 y)(\frac{1}{4}) = \frac{3}{16}$ Substituting

$\sin^2 x + \sin^2 y = \frac{3}{4}$ Simplifying

$2\sin^2 x = 1$ Adding two equations together

$\sin^2 x = \frac{1}{2}$ Simplifying

$\cos^2 x = \frac{1}{2}$ Pythagorean Identity

$\sin^2 y = \frac{3}{4} - \frac{1}{2} = \frac{1}{4}$ Solving for $\sin^2 y$

$\cos^2 y = \frac{3}{4}$ Pythagorean Identity

$\tan^2 x + \tan^2 y = \frac{\sin^2 x}{\cos^2 x} + \frac{\sin^2 y}{\cos^2 y}$ Rewriting tan

$\tan^2 x + \tan^2 y = 1 + \frac{1}{3} = \frac{4}{3}$

$\frac{4}{3}$

Ex: 6 Find the value of $\sin^3 285^\circ + \sin^3 165^\circ$ without solving for $\sin 285^\circ$ or $\sin 165^\circ$.

$(\sin 285^\circ + \sin 165^\circ)(\sin^2 285^\circ - \sin 285^\circ \sin 165^\circ + \sin^2 165^\circ)$

Factoring the sum of cubes

$2\sin 225^\circ \cos 60^\circ(\sin^2 285^\circ - \sin 285^\circ \sin 165^\circ + \sin^2 165^\circ)$

Using sin sum to product formula

By power reducing formulas, $\sin^2 285^\circ = \frac{1-\cos 2(285)^\circ}{2}$ and $\sin^2 165^\circ = \frac{1+\sin 2(165)^\circ}{2}$. Power to sum formula tells us that $\sin 285^\circ \sin 165^\circ = \frac{\cos(285-165)^\circ - \cos(285+165)^\circ}{2}$.

Using this information, our expression becomes:

$-\frac{\sqrt{2}}{2}\left(\frac{1-\cos 570^\circ}{2} + \frac{1+\cos 330^\circ}{2} - \frac{\cos 120^\circ - \cos 450^\circ}{2}\right)$

$-\frac{\sqrt{2}}{2}\left(\frac{1-\frac{\sqrt{3}}{2}+1+\frac{\sqrt{3}}{2}+\frac{1}{2}-0}{2}\right)$ Evaluating trig functions

$-\frac{5\sqrt{2}}{8}$ Simplifying

$-\frac{5\sqrt{2}}{8}$

Ex: 7 Find the value of $\sin(x+y) + \sin(x-y)$ if $\sqrt{\sin x} + \sqrt{\sin y} = \frac{\sqrt{2}+1}{2}, \cos(x-y) - \cos(x+y) = \frac{1}{4}$, and $\sin x < \sin y$

Let's first work with $\sqrt{\sin x} + \sqrt{\sin y} = \frac{\sqrt{2}+1}{2}$.

$\sin x + 2\sqrt{\sin x \sin y} + \sin y = \frac{3+2\sqrt{2}}{4}$ Squaring

Now let's simplify $\cos(x-y) - \cos(x+y) = \frac{1}{4}$.

$-2\sin x \sin(-y) = \frac{1}{4}$ Sum to Product Identity

$\sin x \sin y = \frac{1}{8}$ Using even/odd properties

Now let's substitute the value of $\sin x \sin y$ into our previous equation.

$\sin x + 2\sqrt{\frac{1}{8}} + \sin y = \frac{3+2\sqrt{2}}{4}$ Substituting

$\sin x + \sin y = \frac{3+2\sqrt{2}}{4} - \frac{2}{2\sqrt{2}}$ Simplifying

$\sin x + \sin y = \frac{3}{4}$ Simplifying

If we let $\sin x = a, \sin y = b$, we need to solve $ab = \frac{1}{8}, a+b = \frac{3}{4}$. Because $\sin x < \sin y$, we get $\sin y = \frac{1}{2}, \sin x = \frac{1}{4}$. Keeping our end goal in mind, let's simplify $\sin(x+y) + \sin(x-y)$ to be $2\sin x \cos y$ by Sum to Product Identity. We know the value of $\sin x$ already. Because $\sin y = \frac{1}{2}$, we can easily find $\cos y = \frac{\sqrt{3}}{2}$ since $\frac{\sqrt{3}}{2} = \sqrt{1-(\frac{1}{2})^2}$

$2\sin x \cos y = 2(\frac{1}{4})(\frac{\sqrt{3}}{2}) = \frac{\sqrt{3}}{4}$.

$\frac{\sqrt{3}}{4}$

Ex: 8 Find $\sin 12^\circ \sin 48^\circ \sin 54^\circ$.

$\frac{\sin 54^\circ}{2}(\cos 36^\circ - \cos 60^\circ)$ Product to Sum

$\frac{1}{2}(\cos 36^\circ \sin 54^\circ - \frac{1}{2}\sin 54^\circ)$ Simplifying

$\frac{1}{4}(2\cos 36^\circ \sin 54^\circ - \sin 54^\circ)$ Factoring $\frac{1}{2}$

$\frac{1}{4}(\sin 90^\circ + \sin 18^\circ - \sin 54^\circ)$ Product to Sum

$\frac{1}{4}(1 - (\sin 54^\circ - \sin 18^\circ))$ Simplifying

$\frac{1}{4} - \frac{1}{4}(2\cos 36^\circ \sin 18^\circ)$ Difference to Product

$\frac{1}{4} - \frac{1}{4}(\frac{2\sin 18^\circ \cos 18^\circ \cos 36^\circ}{\cos 18^\circ})$ Multiplying $\cos 18^\circ$

$\frac{1}{4} - \frac{1}{4}(\frac{\sin 36^\circ \cos 36^\circ}{\sin 72^\circ})$ sin double angle and complementary angle properties

$\frac{1}{4} - \frac{1}{8}(\frac{\sin 72^\circ}{\sin 72^\circ})$ sin double angle

$\frac{1}{8}$ Simplifying

Ex: 9 Simplify $\frac{8\sin^3 10^\circ - 4\sin 10^\circ + 1}{2\cos 80^\circ}$

$\frac{4\sin 10^\circ(2\sin^2 10 - 1) + 1}{2\cos 80^\circ}$ Factoring $\sin 10^\circ$

$\frac{-4\sin 10^\circ(\cos 20^\circ) + 1}{2\cos 80^\circ}$ cos double angle identity

$\frac{-4(\frac{1}{2})(\sin 30^\circ + \sin 10^\circ) + 1}{2\cos 80^\circ}$ Product to Sum Identity

$\frac{-2(\frac{1}{2} + \sin 10^\circ) + 1}{2\cos 80}$ Simplifying

$\frac{\sin 10^\circ}{\cos 80^\circ}$ Simplifying

1 $\sin x = \cos(90^\circ - x)$ Complementary Angles

1

The lesson here is to look to see how you can form a trig function you know how to evaluate (multiples of 45 or 30 degrees).

Trig Identities/Equations Test 1

#1: (4 points each) Evaluate.

a) $\sin(\frac{\pi}{2} + \arccos\frac{5}{6})$

b) $\sec(\pi + \arctan\frac{2}{5})$

c) $\cos(\frac{1}{2}\arcsin\frac{5}{13})$

#2: (10 points) Simplify

$\frac{\sin 12^\circ + \sin 42^\circ + \sin 48^\circ + \sin 78^\circ}{\sin 27^\circ + \sin 63^\circ}$ **24**

#3: (12 points) Find the $\tan 52.5^\circ$ degrees in exact form.

#4: (10 points each) Solve for values between 0 and π radians.

a) $\frac{9+4\sqrt{3}}{3} + \sec(4x + \frac{3\pi}{2}) = 3 + 3\sec(4x + \frac{3\pi}{2})$

b) $\frac{1+\sin x}{\cos x} + \frac{\cos x}{1+\sin x} = 4$

c) $\cos(4x) - 7\cos(2x) = 8$

d) $\sin(11x)\sin(4x) = \cos(5x)\cos(2x)$

#5: (10 points) If $\tan x - \tan y = 14$ and $\cot y - \cot x = 28$, find $\tan(x - y)$.

#6: (8 points each) Verify

a) $1 - 4\sin^2 x\cos^2 x = (2\cos^2 x - 1)^2$

b) $2\tan x - 2\tan\sin^2 x = \tan(2x) \cdot \cos(2x)$

Trig Identities/Equations Test 2

#1: (5 points each) Evaluate.

a) $\sin(\arccos(x+2))$

b) $\tan(\arccos(\frac{x-2}{2}))$

c) $\sin(\cos^{-1}0.8 - \sin^{-1}0.96)$

#2: (10 points) Simplify

$1 - (\frac{2\sin 4x}{1+\cos 4x} \cdot \cos 2x \cdot \cos x \cdot \sin x)$

#3: (12 points) Find the $\cos 232.5^{\circ}$ in exact form.

#4: (10 points) A trough is 4 meters long and its cross sections are isosceles triangles with two equal sides of 0.5 meter. the angle between the equal sides is θ.

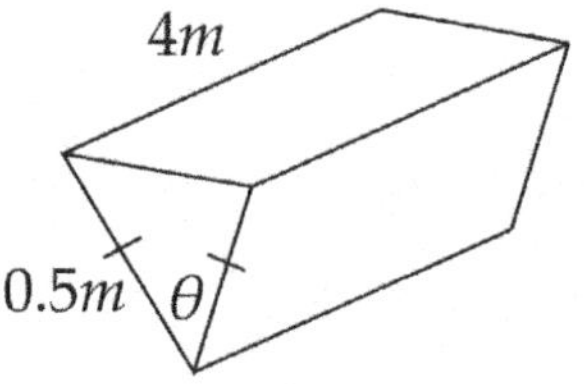

a) Write the volume of the trough as a function of $\frac{\theta}{2}$ and determine the value of θ such that the volume is maximum. What is the maximum?

b) Then write the volume of the trough as a function of θ using the double angle formula.

#5: (10 points) Solve each for all values of x between 0 and 2π radians.

a) $\sin(x + \frac{\pi}{2}) - \sin(x - \frac{\pi}{2}) = \sqrt{2}$

b) $2\tan x \cos 2x + \tan x - \cos^2 x - 2\cos 2x = \sin^2 x$

#6: Verify

a) (12 points) $\frac{1-\cot x}{1+\cot^2 x} = \frac{4\sin^2 x(\sin 2x - 1)}{4\cos 2x - \sin 4x}$ **36**

b) (9 points)
$(\cos 2x - \cos 4x)^2 + (\sin 4x + \sin 2x)^2 = 4\sin^2 3x$

#8: (12 points) If $\sin(2x) = \frac{21}{25}$ and $\cos x > \sin x$ find the value of $\frac{\cos^3 x + \sin^3 x}{\cos^3 x - \sin^3 x}$

Trig Identities/Equations Test 3

#1: (5 points each) Evaluate.

a) $\sin(\arctan(\cos(\arcsin(x + 1))$

b) $\sec(\arcsin(\frac{x-2}{2}))$

c) $\sin(\cos^{-1}0.6 - \sin^{-1}0.28)$

#2: (12 points) Express this strictly as a sum of sines and cosines to the first power.

$32\sin^2 x \cdot \cos^4 x$

#3: (12 points) Find $\sin 142.5^\circ$ in exact form.

#4: (9 points) The Mach number (M) is related to the apex angle x (between 0 and 90 degrees) of a cone by: $\sin(\frac{x}{2}) = \frac{1}{M}$

a) Find the angle that corresponds with a Mach number of 2:

b) Rewrite the equation as a trigonometric equation of x.

#5: (10 points) Solve for all values of x between 0 and 2π radians.
$\sin^2 3x - \sin^2 x = 0$

#6: (12 points) If $45^\circ = \tan^{-1}(\frac{1}{x}) + \tan^{-1}(\frac{1}{x+1})$, find $\sin(2\tan^{-1} x)$.

#7: Verify (9 points each)

a) $\sin^2(\theta + \frac{\pi}{4}) = \frac{1}{2}(1 + \sin 2\theta)$

b) $\frac{\cos 3x}{\cos x} = 1 - 4\sin^2 x$

#8: (12 points) If $\cos x = \frac{\sqrt{5}}{5}, \tan y = -\frac{3}{4}$, find $2x + y$.

Trig Identities/Equations Test 4

#1: (5 points each) Evaluate.

a) $\sec(\arccos(\sin(\arccos(x+1))$

b) $\csc x(\arctan \frac{x-1}{2}))$

c) $\sin(\tan^{-1}0.75 - \sin^{-1}0.28)$

#2: (10 points) Let $\frac{2\sin(6x-\frac{\pi}{3})-1}{4\cos(3x-\frac{\pi}{12})} = \sin(Ax+B)$. Find A and B.

#3: (8 points) If $\sin(2x) = \frac{13}{49}$ and $\sin x > \cos x$ find the value of $\cos x - \sin x$.

#4: (12 points) Find $\sin 277.5^\circ$ in exact form.

#5: (10 points) Let $\sin x + \sin y = \frac{\sqrt{5}}{2}$ and $\cos x + \cos y = \sqrt{2}$. What is $\sin(x-y)$?

#6: (12 points) Solve for all values of x between 0° and 360°. **28**

$\cot^2(\frac{1}{2}x)(2 - 2\cos x - \sin^2 x)(1 + \cos 2x) = \frac{3}{4}(1 - \cos 2x)$

#7: (15 points) Let the quadratic equation $x^2 + 2\cos(4\theta) = 4x\sin(\theta + \frac{\pi}{4})$ have roots r_1 and r_2. If $r_1^2 + r_2^2 = 10$, find the smallest positive θ. **5**

#8: Verify (9 points each)

a) $\cot(3x) = \frac{1-3\tan^2 x}{3\tan x - \tan^3 x}$

b) $2\sin^2 4x - 2\sin^2 2x = \cos 4x - \cos 8x$

Trig Identities/Equations Test 5

#1: (4 points each) Evaluate.

a) $\sin(\frac{\pi}{12})$

b) $\tan(2\sin^{-1}\frac{3}{5})$

#2: If $\csc x + \cot x = \frac{4}{3}$, follow the steps to find $\sec x + \tan x$.

a) (9 points) Verify $\frac{\sec x + \tan x + 1}{\sec x + \tan x - 1} = \csc x + \cot x$

b) (3 points) Find $\sec x + \tan x$.

#3: (12 points) If $\cos x - \sin x = \frac{10}{11}$, find the value of $\tan x$. Don't rationalize!

#4: (12 points) Find $\sin 52.5^{\circ}$ in exact form.

#5: (10 points) Find the value of $\tan^{-1}1 + \tan^{-1}0.5 + \tan^{-1}\frac{\sqrt{3}}{3} + \tan^{-1}1/3$ **49**

#6: (12 points) Solve for all values of x between 0 and 180 degrees. **29**
$(1+\cos 2x)(\sin(2x+30^\circ)-\sin(2x-30^\circ))=\frac{1}{4}\cot x$

#7: Follow the steps to calculate $\cos 36^\circ - \cos 72^\circ$.

a) (9 points) Verify:
$\cos(3\theta)=4\cos^3\theta-3\cos\theta$

b) (3 points) Rewrite $\cos 54^\circ$ using the triple angle formula.

c) (3 points) Rewrite $\sin 36^\circ$ using the double angle formula.

d) (9 points) Use your answer from b) and c) to write a quadratic equation. Then solve for $\sin 18^\circ$.

e) (9 points) Use the answer from part d) to find $\cos 36^\circ$ and $\cos 72^\circ$

f) (1 point) What is $\cos 36^\circ - \cos 72^\circ$?

Trig Identities/Equations Test 6

#1: (5 points each) Evaluate.

a) $\sec(\arctan(x+1))$

b) $\csc x(\arctan(x+2))$

c) $\sin(\tan^{-1}0.75 + \sin^{-1}5/13)$

#2: (12 points) If $\frac{\sin 2^\circ \sin 4^\circ \sin 6^\circ \ldots \sin 176^\circ \sin 178^\circ}{\sin 1^\circ \sin 2^\circ \sin 3^\circ \ldots \sin 178^\circ \sin 179^\circ} = 2^k$, find k.

#3: (12 points) Find $\sin 82.5^\circ$ in exact form.

#4: (10 points) Let $\sin A - \sin B = \sqrt{\frac{5}{3}}$ and $\cos A + \cos B = \sqrt{\frac{5}{4}}$. What is the value of $\cos(A+B)$?

#5: (12 points) Solve for all values of x between 0 and 360°.

$\tan(4x) + \tan(2x) = 0$

#6: Verify (9 points each)

a) $\sin 4x = 4\sin x \cdot \cos x(1 - 2\sin^2 x)$

b) $\dfrac{2\tan(\frac{a+b}{2})\sin(\frac{a+b}{2}) - \sec(\frac{a+b}{2})}{(\sin a + \sin b)\sin(\frac{a-b}{2})} = -\dfrac{2\cot(a+b)}{\sin(a-b)}$ **37**

#7: (12 points) Algebraically solve for x:

$\sin^{-1} x = 2\sin^{-1}\frac{3}{5} + \cos^{-1}\frac{24}{25}$

#8: (9 points) If $\sin(2x) = \frac{24}{25}$, find the value of $\tan x + 1$ without finding $\sin x$.

Chapter 9 Geometry Trig/Complex Numbers

Law of Sines

Ex: 1 Given triangle ABC with $b = 16,\ a = 10,\ and\ \angle A = 30°$ Solve triangle ABC.

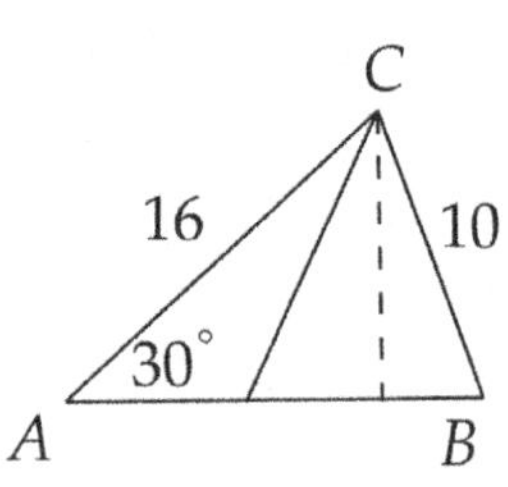

We can apply Law of Sines to solve for $\angle B$: $\frac{\sin 30°}{10} = \frac{\sin B}{16}$ $\sin B = 0.8$. Using inverse sin, $\angle B \approx 53°$. That means $\angle C \approx 97°$. To find side c we solve: $\frac{\sin 97°}{c} = \frac{\sin 30°}{10}$. In a SSA case, we must always look at the angle that we found from applying the Law of Sines. In this case it would be $\angle B$. Looking back to before we applied inverse sin, $\angle B \approx 53°$. Remember, whenever you take the sin of an angle, it has two values. Back to the problem, with this in mind, $\sin B = 0.8$. $B \approx 53°$ or $127°$ since $\sin x = \sin(180 - x)$. $127°$ makes sense in context of the triangle because the $h < a < b$ where $h = 16 \sin 30° = 8$ is the triangle with base c. With $B' = 127°$. $\angle C = 23°$ since the 3 angles need to add up to $180°$. c' can be found through another Law of Sines.

$\angle B \approx 53°, \angle C \approx 97°,\ c \approx 20$, OR
$\angle B' \approx 127°, \angle C' \approx 23°,\ c' \approx 8$,

Ex: 2 Given triangle DEF, with $d = 15,\ e = 7,\ and\ \angle E = 26°$. Solve triangle DEF. Looking at the triangle, it is SSA case, which means we have to watch out for the possibility of two triangles. First step is to use Law of Sines to solve for $\angle D$. $\frac{\sin 26°}{7} = \frac{\sin D}{15}$. We get $\sin D \approx 0.939$. We take inverse sin of both sides to get $\angle D \approx 69.95°$. We also have to check the other possibility of $\angle D$ to see if it makes sense in context of the triangle. $\angle D \approx 110.05°$ (the supplement of $69.95°$) which makes sense because the $h = 15 \sin 26° = 6.57556$ and that's less than e which is less than d. Finding $\angle F'$ is easy because the three angles add up to $180°$, and finding the remaining side f' can be done with Law of Sines.

$\angle D \approx 69.95°, \angle F \approx 84.05°, f \approx 15.88$ OR
$\angle D' \approx 110.05, \angle F' \approx 43.95, f' \approx 11$

Ex: 3 At an amusement park, Jonathan walks 400 meters $N44°W$ from Anaconda to Twisted Timbers. Then, he walks 650 meters to Intimidator 305. Now he is due west of Anaconda. Find the bearing of Jonathan's walk from Twisted Timbers to Intimidator 305.
Using the information, we can create a picture.

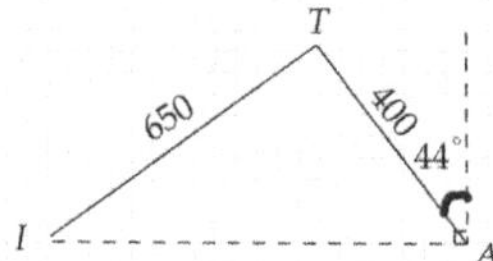

It is clear that $\angle IAT = 90 - 44 = 46°$. Using Law of Sines, we can set up this equation:
$\frac{\sin 46°}{650} = \frac{\sin \angle I}{400}$
$\sin I = \frac{400 \sin 46°}{650}$ Isolating
$\angle I \approx 26.2744°$
Because the angles of a triangle add up to $180°$, $\angle T = 180° - 46° - 26.2744° \approx 107.7255°$. Because of alternate interior angles, we can find the bearing from T to I.

$S(107.7255 - 44)°W = S\ 63.72559°W$

Law of Cosines

Ex: 1 Two ships leave a port at 10 am. One travels with a bearing of $N34°W$ at 18 mph while the other travels with a bearing of $S48°W$ at 16 mph. At 12pm, how far apart are the two ships?

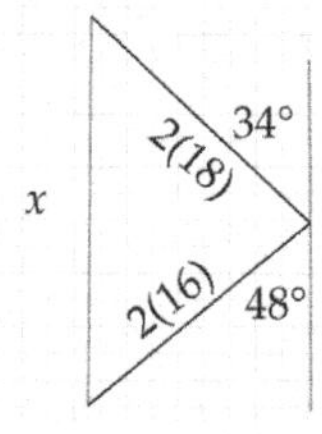

Taking in this information, we are able to draw this diagram. Because of distance equals speed times time, we know the ships travel 36 and 32 miles respectively. The angle between the 36 and 32 would then be $180 - 34 - 48 = 98°$. Now we can apply the Law of Cosines and set up this equation:
$x^2 = 32^2 + 36^2 - 2(32)(36)\cos 98°$.

$x = 51.3873$ miles by solving the equation

Ex: 2 If BD is a median, find BD.

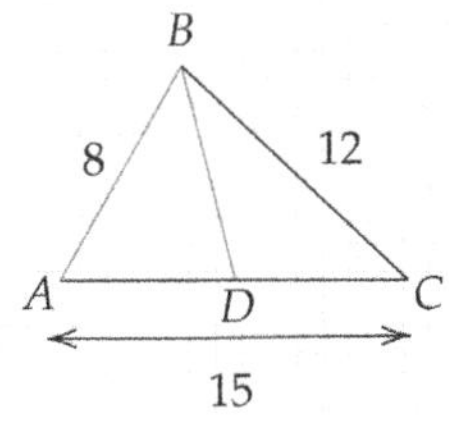

By the definition of a median, AD=7.5. We can use Law of Cosines to find angle A. Then use Law of Cosines again to find the length of BD.

$12^2 = 8^2 + 15^2 - 2(8)(15)\cos A$ Law of Cosines
$240\cos A = 145$ Simplifying
$\cos A = \frac{145}{240} = \frac{29}{48}$ Solving for A
$BD^2 = 8^2 + (7.5)^2 - 2(8)(7.5)\cos A$ Law of Cosines
$BD^2 = 64 + 56.25 - 120(\frac{29}{48})$ Substituting $\cos A$
$BD^2 = 47.75$ Simplifying
$BD \approx 6.91$

$BD \approx 6.91$

Ex: 3 A man on an observation deck of a 1000 foot tower sees two landmarks on the ground below. He observes that the angle formed by the lines of sight to these two landmarks is 41°. The angle of depression to one of the landmarks is 65° while the angle of depression to the other is 55°. What is the distance between the landmarks?

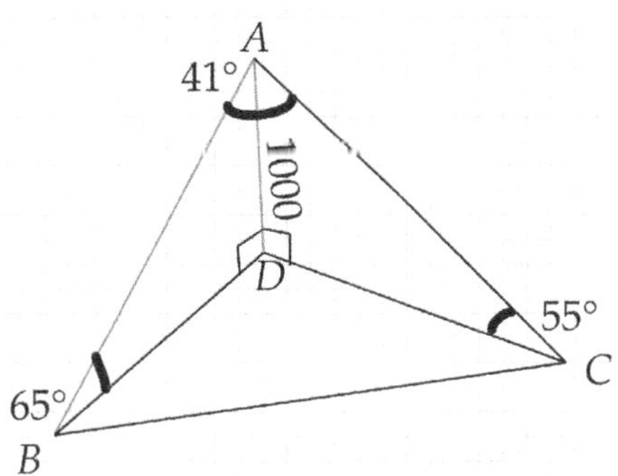

It may be a bit to understand the problem, but here's the 3D drawing of the situation. AB and AC are the lines of sight. We're trying to find BC here. First, let's find AB and AC so we can use the Law of Cosines. Since the tower is standing perpendicular to the ground, $\sin 65^\circ = \frac{1000}{AB}$ and $\sin 55^\circ = \frac{1000}{AC}$. Solving this we get, $AB \approx 1103.38$ and $AC \approx 1220.78$. Now, we can using Law of Cosines to set up the equation: $BC^2 =$
$(1103.38)^2 + (1220.78)^2 - 2(1103.38)(1220.78)(\cos 43^\circ)$

858.78 feet by solving the equation

Ex: 4 A triangle has side lengths $7, 6, 11$. Find the angle measures of the triangle.
For the angle opposite of 7, we can set up the equation: $7^2 = 6^2 + 11^2 - 2(6)(11)\cos\alpha$
$\cos\alpha = \frac{108}{132}$ so $\alpha \approx 35.097^\circ$. Using the angle opposite the side with length 6, we set up:
$6^2 = 7^2 + 11^2 - 2(7)(11)\cos\beta$
$\cos\beta = \frac{134}{154}$ so $\beta \approx 29.526^\circ$. Now, since the angles must add up to 180°, the third angle is approximately 115.377°.

$35.097^\circ, 29.526^\circ, 115.377^\circ$

Ex: 5 Using the diagram, solve for x.

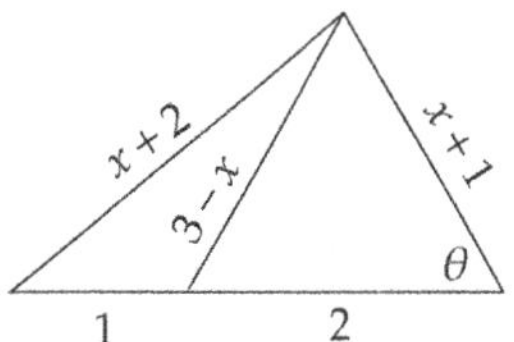

We can use LOC on angle θ to get two equations.
$(3-x)^2 = 2^2 + (x+1)^2 - 2(2)(x+1)\cos\theta$
This Law of Cosines on the smaller triangle.
$x^2 - 6x + 9 = x^2 + 2x + 5 - (4x+4)\cos\theta$ Expand
$(4x+4)\cos\theta = 8x - 4$ More Simplifying
$\cos\theta = \frac{2x-1}{x+1}$ Cancelling out common factor of 4
Now for the bigger triangle, we can set up this:
$(x+2)^2 = (x+1)^2 + 3^2 - 2(x+1)(3)\cos\theta$
$x^2 + 4x + 4 = x^2 + 2x + 10 - (6x+6)\cos\theta$ Expand
$(6x+6)\cos\theta = -2x + 6$ Simplifying
$\cos\theta = \frac{3-x}{3x+3}$ Cancelling out common factor of 2
$\frac{3-x}{3x+3} = \frac{2x-1}{x+1}$ Equating the $\cos\theta$ together
$(3-x)(x+1) = (3x+3)(2x-1)$ Cross multiply
$3x + 3 - x^2 - x = 6x^2 - 3x + 6x - 3$ Expand
$7x^2 + x - 6 = 0$ Combining like terms
$(7x-6)(x+1) = 0$ Factoring
$x = \frac{6}{7}$ Solving for x, $x = -1$ is extraneous

$x = \frac{6}{7}$

Ex: 6 A ship sails at 30 miles per hour from its starting spot due south for 60 miles. Then it

begins sailing with a bearing of $N30^{\circ}E$. How many miles can the ship sail at this bearing so that the ship can turn and get back to its starting point in 5 hours?
Since the ship sailed 60 miles south at 30 miles per hour, that took up 2 hours of its time. With 3 hours, the ship can sail another 90 miles.

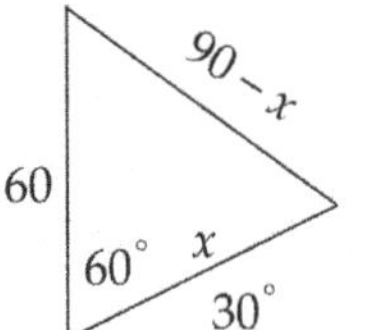

Because the bearing is $N30^{\circ}E$, the angle between the ship's paths is 60 degrees.
$(90-x)^2 = 60^2 + x^2 - 2(60)(x)\cos 60^{\circ}$ LOC
$8100x - 180x = 3600 - 60x$ Simplifying
$4500 = 120x$ Combining like terms
$x = 37.5$ miles Solving for x

$x = 37.5$ miles

Triangle Areas

Ex: 1 Let quadrilateral $ABCD$ be inscribed in a circle. If $AB = 1,\ BC = 2,\ CD = 3,\ DA = 4$, what is the area of $ABCD$?
We know from geometry that the sum of opposite angles is supplementary. So let $A = x^{\circ}$ and $C = (180-x)^{\circ}$. Using Law of Cosines, we get $BD^2 = 4^2 + 1^2 - 2(4)(1)\cos x$ and $BD^2 = 2^2 + 3^2 + 2(2)(3)\cos x$. Note that we used angle difference to get: $\cos(180-x) = -\cos x$. Solving this system we get that $\cos x = \frac{1}{5}$. So, $x \approx 78.463^{\circ}$ and $BD = \sqrt{2^2 + 3^2 + 12(\frac{1}{5})} \approx 3.924$.
Now the area of the quadrilateral is:
$\frac{1}{2}(1)(4)\sin 78.463^{\circ} + \frac{1}{2}(2)(3)\sin(180 - 78.463)$

4.899 Simplifying

Ex: 2 Find the area of $ABCDE$:

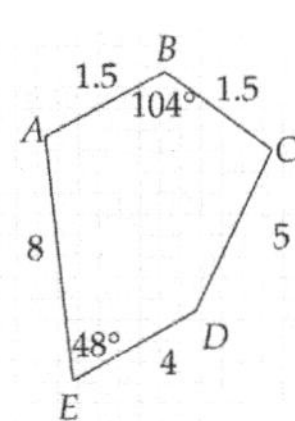

First the area of triangle AED is $\frac{1}{2}(8)(4)(\sin 48^{\circ}) \approx 11.89$. Using Law of Cosines, you can find the length of AD by solving $AD^2 = 8^2 + 4^2 - 2(4)(8)\cos 48^{\circ}$. This gets $AD \approx 6.0972$. For the triangle ABC, the area is $\frac{1}{2}(1.5)^2 \sin 104^{\circ} \approx 1.09158$. The length of AC can be found: $AC^2 = 2(1.5)^2 - 2(1.5)^2\cos 104^{\circ}$. This leads to $AC \approx 2.364$. Now using the lengths of AC and AD, we can find out the area of the "inner" triangle. The triangle has side lengths, $6.0972, 2.364$, and 5 so $s = 6.7306$. Using Heron's Formula, we get the area equals 5.6759.

18.6575 Summing the areas up

Ex: 3 A right triangle ABC has leg lengths $AB = 15$ and $AC = 8$. If $BD = DE = 2$, $AF = \frac{393}{289}$ $GC = 7$, using the diagram below, what is the area of $DFEG$?

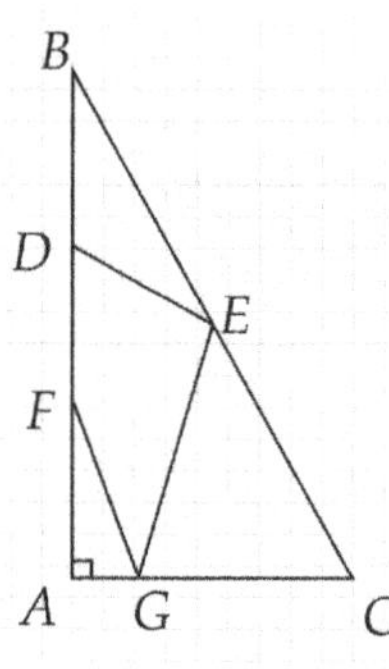

By the pythagorean theorem, we know that $BC = 17$. Let $BE = x$. Using the LOC on DBE, we can set up the equation:
$2^2 = 2^2 + x^2 - 2(2)(x)(\cos B)$
Based on right triangle trigonometry, we know that $\cos B = \frac{15}{17}$. Therefore, we can simplify the equation:
$0 = x^2 - \frac{60}{17}x$. Solving, we get that $x = \frac{60}{17}$. Now we can find the area of BDE to be $\frac{1}{2}(2)(\frac{60}{17})\sin B$
That's equal to $\frac{60}{17} \cdot \frac{8}{17} = \frac{480}{289}$ since we know $\sin B$ by right triangle trig. Since we know $BE = \frac{60}{17}$, we can find $EC = 17 - \frac{60}{17} = \frac{229}{17}$. Now for the area of EGC, that's equal to $\frac{1}{2}(\frac{229}{17})(7)(\frac{15}{17}) = \frac{24045}{578}$. Now the length of AG would equal to $8 - 7 = 1$. We can also find the area of triangle AFG which is $\frac{1}{2}(1)(\frac{393}{289}) = \frac{393}{578}$.
Now adding the areas of the triangles together, we get: $\frac{393}{578} + \frac{24045}{578} + \frac{480}{289} = \frac{747}{17}$.
The total area of the triangle is $\frac{1}{2}(8)(15) = 60$.
Subtracting to get the area of $DFEG$:

$\frac{273}{17}$

Complex Arithmetic

Ex: 1 Simplify $\sqrt[4]{16(\cos\frac{\pi}{2} + i\sin\frac{\pi}{2})}$

$\sqrt[4]{16} \cdot (\cos\frac{\pi}{2} + i\sin\frac{\pi}{2})^{\frac{1}{4}}$ Simplifying

$2(\cos\frac{\pi}{8} + i\sin\frac{\pi}{8})$ De Moivre's

$2(\frac{\sqrt{2+\sqrt{2}}+i\sqrt{2-\sqrt{2}}}{2})$ Using Half Angle Identities

$\sqrt{2+\sqrt{2}} + i\sqrt{2-\sqrt{2}}$

Ex: 2 Simplify $\frac{(-3\sqrt{3}-3i)^{12}}{(4+4i)^4}$

Let's first rewrite the numerator in cis form. $r = \sqrt{(-3\sqrt{3})^2 + (-3)^2} = 6$. $\tan\theta = \frac{-3}{-3\sqrt{3}}, \theta = \frac{7\pi}{6}$. Thus the numerator is equal to $(6cis\frac{7\pi}{6})^{12}$. For the denominator, $r = \sqrt{4^2 + 4^2} = 4\sqrt{2}$. Because $\tan\theta = \frac{4}{4} = 1, \theta = \frac{\pi}{4}$. So the denominator can be written as $(4\sqrt{2}cis\frac{\pi}{4})^4$. Using De Moivre's, the fraction is now, $\frac{6^{12}cis14\pi}{(4\sqrt{2})^4 cis\pi}$. Then simplifying and using complex division rules, we get $2125764cis13\pi$. Because $cis13\pi = cis\pi = -1$:

-2125764

Complex Roots

Ex: 1 Find the roots of $x^5 + 2 = -2i$

$x^5 = -2i - 2$ Isolate the x^5

With $r = \sqrt{(-2)^2 + (-2)^2}$ and $\tan\theta = \frac{-2}{-2}$, we get $x^5 = 2\sqrt{2}(cis\frac{5\pi}{4})$. Therefore the roots can be generalized as: $x_k = \sqrt[5]{2\sqrt{2}cis(\frac{\frac{5\pi}{4}+2\pi k}{5})}$

$\sqrt[5]{2\sqrt{2}(cis\frac{\pi}{4})}$ $\sqrt[5]{2\sqrt{2}(cis\frac{13\pi}{20})}$ $\sqrt[5]{2\sqrt{2}(cis\frac{21\pi}{20})}$ $\sqrt[5]{2\sqrt{2}(cis\frac{29\pi}{20})}$ $\sqrt[5]{2\sqrt{2}(cis\frac{37\pi}{20})}$

Ex: 2 Find the roots of $x^3 = 2\sqrt{3} + 6i$

For $2\sqrt{3} + 6i$, $r = \sqrt{(2\sqrt{3})^2 + 6^2} = \sqrt{48} = 4\sqrt{3}$ and $\tan\theta = \frac{6}{2\sqrt{3}} = \sqrt{3}$ so the $\theta = \frac{\pi}{3}$. Therefore, the roots can be generalized as: $x_k = \sqrt[3]{4\sqrt{3}cis(\frac{\frac{\pi}{3}+2\pi k}{3})}$.

$\sqrt[3]{4\sqrt{3}cis(\frac{\pi}{9})}, \sqrt[3]{4\sqrt{3}cis(\frac{7\pi}{9})}, \sqrt[3]{4\sqrt{3}cis(\frac{13\pi}{9})}$

Ex: 3 Find the roots of $x^6 + 2x^3 + 4 = 0$

$x^6 + 2x^3 + 1 = -3$ Manipulation

$(x^3 + 1)^2 = -3$ Completing the square

$x^3 + 1 = \pm i\sqrt{3}$ Taking the square root, two cases: $x^3 = -1 + i\sqrt{3}$ and $x^3 = -1 - i\sqrt{3}$. For the first case: $-1 + i\sqrt{3}$ can be rewritten as $2cis(\frac{2\pi}{3})$. The roots of the first case could then be generalized as $x_k = \sqrt[3]{2}cis\frac{\frac{2\pi}{3}+2\pi k}{3}$. For the second case, we get $x^3 = 2cis\frac{4\pi}{3}$. The roots could then be generalized as $x_k = \sqrt[3]{2}cis\frac{\frac{4\pi}{3}+2\pi k}{3}$. Plugging in values of k:

$x = \sqrt[3]{2}cis\frac{2\pi}{9}, \sqrt[3]{2}cis\frac{8\pi}{9}, \sqrt[3]{2}cis\frac{14\pi}{9}, \sqrt[3]{2}cis\frac{4\pi}{9}$ $\sqrt[3]{2}cis\frac{10\pi}{9}, \sqrt[3]{2}cis\frac{16\pi}{9}$

Ex: 4 For complex numbers x and y if $x^{30} = -1, y^{20} = 1$, how many ordered pairs of x and y exist such that xy is real?

$-1 = cis180^\circ$ Therefore, x can be expressed as $x_k = cis\frac{180^\circ+360^\circ k}{30}$ or $x_k = cis(6 + 12k)^\circ$ for k from $0 - 17$. For the second equation, we can easily write $y^{20} = cis(0^\circ)$ so $y_n = cis(18n)^\circ$ for n from $0 - 19$. If we multiply x and y together, we get that the product equals $cis(6 + 12k + 18n)^\circ$. In order for xy to be real, the angle of this complex number must be a multiple of 180°.

$6 + 12k + 18n = 0$ is obviously not possible since k and n are positive integers. $6 + 12k + 18n = 180$ simplifies to $2k + 3n = 29$. The greatest possible value of n is 9 which corresponds to $k = 1$. In fact any odd n allow for an integer value of k. There are 5 odd n values (1,3,5,7,9) for this case. For $6 + 12k + 18n = 360$ that simplifies to $2k + 3n = 59$. The greatest possible value of n is 19 which corresponds to $k = 1$. Like before, all odd n values work. Remember the greatest possible value of k is 17 from our restriction above. Therefore, the smallest possible n value is 9 which corresponds to $k = 16$. Therefore, all odd n from $9 - 19$ will allow for integer k values and fulfill the degree requirements. This is 6 values.

11 pairs total

Geometry Trig/Complex Numbers Test 1

#1: (12 points) A plane flies from New York City with bearing of $N84^\circ E$. It then turns and flies with a bearing of $S22^\circ W$ for 140 miles. If the plane is 190 miles from its starting point now, how far did the plane fly from NYC before it turned?

#2: (12 points) Evaluate

$\frac{(-3\sqrt{3}-3i)^8}{(1+\sqrt{3}i)^6}$

#3: (12 points) Find all solutions to $z^3 = -4\sqrt{2} + 4\sqrt{2}i$ in trig form.

#4: (10 points each) Solve each triangle.

a) $a = 25,\ b = 28,\ A = 34^\circ$

b) $A = 39^\circ, B = 71^\circ, C = 70^\circ, s = 23$

#5: (10 points) Use the Law of cosines to a) solve for length AB. b) If $PC = \sqrt{\frac{76}{3}}$, what is the area of ACBP?

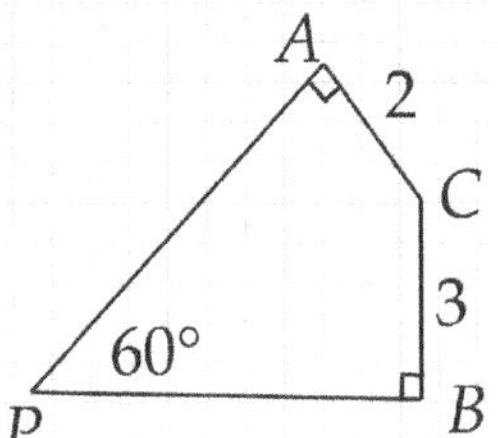

#7: (10 points) Three ships leave a port at 10 am. One travels with a bearing of $N34^{\circ}W$ at 18 mph while the other travels with a bearing of $S48^{\circ}W$ at 16 mph. The last ship travels due W at 24 mph. At 12 pm, what is the area formed by the three ships and the port?

#6: (12 points) After an earthquake, a wooden post leans 8° from the vertical towards the base of the slope it has been constructed on. This slope has an angle of elevation of 13°. If the sun casts a 14 foot shadow onto to the slope in the direction the post leans, the angle of elevation to the sun is 40°. a) Find the height of the post. After another earthquake, the post leans towards the base another θ degrees. Now the shadow cast is 15 feet long. Assuming the Sun didn't move, what is θ?

#8: (12 points) A pilot, who was supposed to fly 120 miles at a bearing of $N20^{\circ}W$ to mistakenly flies 80 miles at a bearing of $N40^{\circ}E$, before realizing her mistake. a) How far is she from her original destination? b) At what bearing should she fly to head directly to her original destination?

Geometry Trig/Complex Numbers Test 2

#1: (12 points) A plane flies from New York City with bearing of $N73^\circ E$. It then turns and flies with a bearing of $S32^\circ W$ for 120 miles. If the plane is 150 miles from its starting point now, how far did the plane fly from NYC before it turned?

#2: (12 points) Evaluate

$$\frac{(-4\sqrt{3}-4i)^6}{(-1+\sqrt{3}i)^4}$$

#3: (12 points) Find all solutions to $z^4 = -8\sqrt{2}+8\sqrt{2}i$ in trig form.

#4: (10 points each) Solve each triangle.

a) $a = 15,\ b = 19,\ A = 43^\circ$

b) $A = 39^\circ, B = 65^\circ, C = 76^\circ$, Area $= 47$

#5: (12 points) Points D and E are the mid points of sides BC and CA, respectively of Triangle ABC. If $AD = 5$ and $BC = BE = 4$, what is the length of CA?

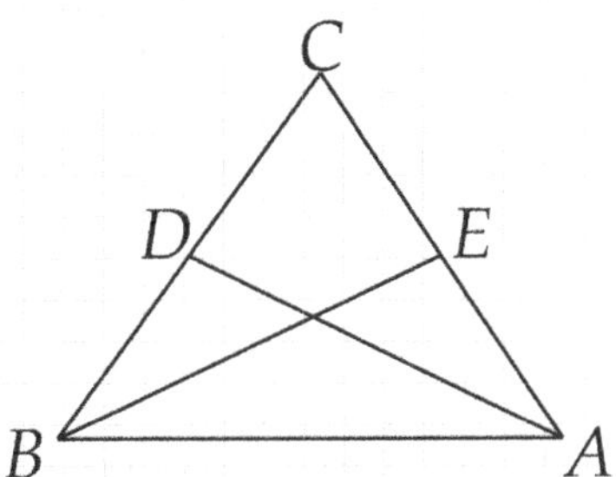

#6: (14 points) In the figure, $AC = 4, EC = 3$, $DC = 3.5$, $ED = 1$. If AD is an angle bisector of Angle BAC, find AB and BE.

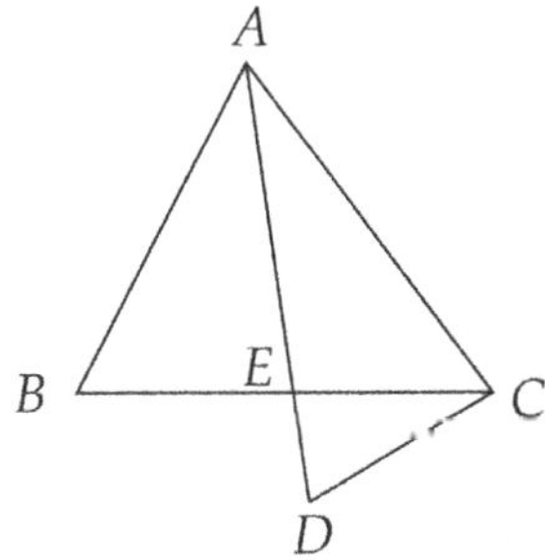

#7: A child walks due North for 120 meters on cement alongside a grass field. Then she steps onto the grass field and walks $N25^{\circ}E$ for 230 meters across the grass.

a) (6 points) How far is she now from where she started?

b) (6 points) If her walking speed on grass is $\frac{3}{4}$ her walking speed on cement, will the child take less time to go back to her starting spot along the original route or walk directly across the grass?

c) (6 points) If she decides to walk across the grass, what is the "area" bounded by her path?

Geometry Trig/Complex Numbers Test 3

#1: (12 points) In quadrilateral $ABCD$, BD bisects angle ABC and AC bisects angle BAD. If $AB = 7, BC = 8, BE = 5, AD = 6$, find the length of DC. **21**

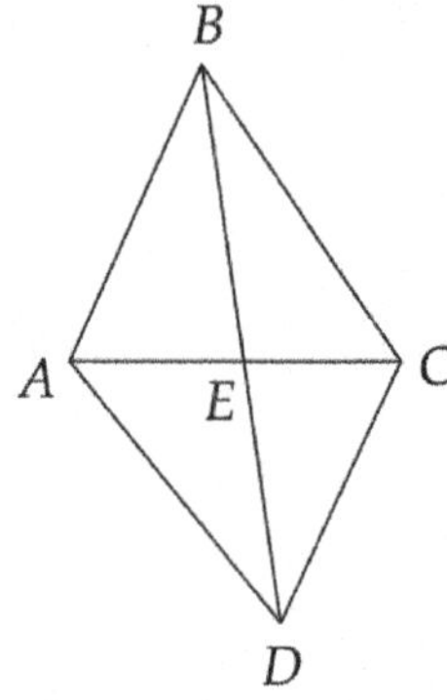

#2: (12 points) Evaluate $\frac{(-2\sqrt{3}-2i)^9}{(\sqrt{5}+\sqrt{15}i)^6}$

#3: (12 points) Find all solutions to $z^3 = -3\sqrt{6} + 9\sqrt{2}i$ in trig form.

4: (10 points each) Solve each triangle.

a) $a = 19,\ b = 25,\ A = 37^\circ$

b) $A = 54^\circ, B = 100^\circ, C = 26^\circ, s = 34$

#5: (12 points) An airplane leaves an aircraft carrier and flies due south at 360 km/h. The carrier continues $N60^{\circ}E$ at 30km/h. What is the maximum south the pilot can travel, so that the aircraft can get back to the carrier in 5 hours?

#6: (10 points) In triangle ABC, $AB = 8$, $BC = 15$, $CA = 17$. Let point D be on AB so that $DA = 2$, point E be on BC so that $EC = 1$, and point F be on CA so that $CF = 3$. What is the area of triangle DEF?

#7: (12 points) In quadrilateral $ABCD$, $DC = 7$, $AB = 10$, $AD = 2$, and $\angle A = \angle B = 60^{\circ}$. All sides of the quadrilateral have different lengths. Find AC. **26**

#8: (10 points) In a parallelogram, the two sides are of length 8 and 9. The length of the smaller diagonal is 12. What is the measure of the largest angle?

Geometry Trig/Complex Numbers Test 4

#1: (12 points) A plane flies and takes off North for 240 miles. Then it flies with a bearing of $N23^{\circ}\ E$ for another 2 hours before landing at an airport that is 760 miles away from where the plane took off. How long did the whole flight take if the plane flew at a constant speed throughout the flight?

#2: (12 points) Evaluate $\frac{(-3\sqrt{3}-3i)^{8}}{(-1-i)^{4}}$

#3: (12 points) Find all solutions to $z^{6} = 4\sqrt{3} + 4i$ in trig form.

#4: (10 points each) Solve each triangle.

a) $a = 10,\ b = 13,\ A = 39^{\circ}$

b) $A = 71^{\circ}, B = 32^{\circ}, C = 77^{\circ}, \text{Area} = 54$

#5: (12 points) Quadrilateral $ABCD$ has $AB = 4$, $BC = 9$, $CD = 10$, and $DA = 6$. Angle $C = 55^\circ$. a) Find the angle measures of $ABCD$. b) Find the area of $ABCD$.

6: (14 points) The equilateral triangle ABC has been folded so that vertex A now rests on A' on BC as shown, decreasing the area by $\frac{169\sqrt{3}}{48}$. If $PQ = \frac{13\sqrt{13}}{12}$, $BA' < A'C$, find BA' and $A'C$. **9**

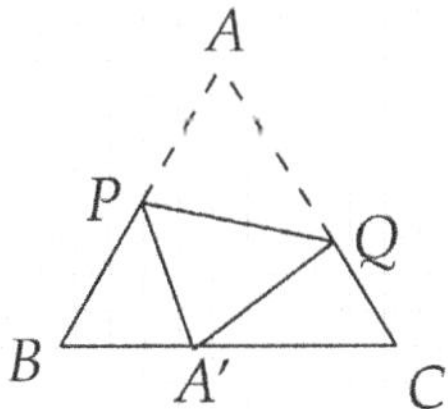

#7: A whale is sighted from boats A and B. The bearing of the whale from boat A is $N33^\circ E$ and the bearing of the whale from boat B is $N54^\circ W$. Boat A is 1.3 miles directly west of Boat B.

a) (6 points) How far is the fire from Boat A?

b) (6 points) At Boat C, which is 1.5 miles from A, there is a zoologist, eager to see the whale. If the bearing of C from A is $S40^\circ E$. Find the distance from C to the whale.

c) (6 points) Find the bearing from C to the whale.

Geometry Trig/Complex Numbers Test 5

#1: (12 points) A plane flies 770 miles from A to B with a bearing of $N57^\circ E$. Then it flies 508 miles from B to C with a bearing of $S41^\circ W$. Find the distance and bearing if the plane were to fly directly from A to C.

#2: (12 points) Evaluate $\frac{(-2\sqrt{3}-2i)^{16}}{(-2-2i)^{8}}$

#3: (12 points) Find all solutions to $z^6 = 32\sqrt{2} + 32\sqrt{2}i$ in trig form.

#4: (10 points each) Solve each triangle.

a) $a = 17,\ b = 21,\ A = 52^\circ$

b) $A = 34^\circ, B = 100^\circ, C = 46^\circ,\ s = 100$

#5: (12 points) A quadrilateral consists of two right triangles. The side lengths for AB, BC, BC are consecutive integers. $< EDC = 30^{\circ}, AE = \frac{10}{3}$, $AD = \frac{10\sqrt{3}}{3}$. Find $< DBC$.

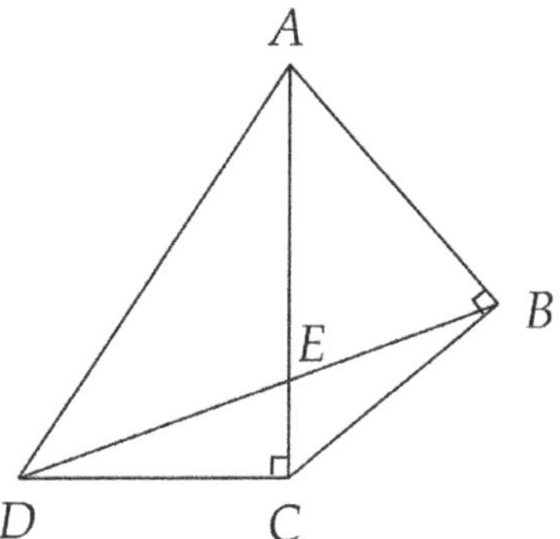

#6: (12 points) Pentagon $ABCDE$ has $AB = 9$, $BC = 6$, $DE = 10$, and $EA = 8$. Angle A is 137°. Angle B is 92°. Angle E is 124°. Find the area of the pentagon.

#7: El Toro can be spotted from tower A and tower B. The bearing of El Toro from A is $S53^{\circ}E$ and the bearing of the El Toro from B is $S24^{\circ}W$. B is 1.4 miles directly east of A.

a) (4 points) How far is El Toro from tower B?

b) (4 points) At Kingda Ka, which is 0.8 miles from B, you can spot tower B with a bearing of $N40^{\circ}W$. Find the distance from Kingda Ka to El Toro.

c) (12 points) There is a gondola ride connecting A and B that travels from tower B to A at a rate of 8 feet per second. Suppose that a rider boards a gondola and after leaving tower B for 2.5 minutes, the gondola stops. What is the bearing from the rider to El Toro? What is the distance to El Toro?

Chapter 10 Matrices

Nobody likes Matrices for a reason. They are incredibly tedious to do by hand. However, they have lots of applications so it's important to know the basics.

Gaussian Elimination

Ex: 1 Solve the matrix using the Gaussian Elimination method

$x+y+z=3$

$4x+3y+4z=8$

$9x+3y+4z=7$

First let's set up a matrix of coefficients:

$$\begin{bmatrix} 1 & 1 & 1 & 3 \\ 4 & 3 & 4 & 8 \\ 9 & 3 & 4 & 7 \end{bmatrix}$$

$$\begin{bmatrix} 1 & 1 & 1 & 3 \\ 0 & -1 & 0 & -4 \\ 0 & -6 & -5 & -20 \end{bmatrix} \begin{matrix} \\ -4R_1+R_2 \\ -9R_1+R_3 \end{matrix}$$

$$\begin{bmatrix} 1 & 1 & 1 & 3 \\ 0 & -1 & 0 & -4 \\ 0 & 0 & -5 & 4 \end{bmatrix} \begin{matrix} \\ \\ -6R_2+R_3 \end{matrix}$$

$$\begin{bmatrix} 1 & 1 & 1 & 3 \\ 0 & 1 & 0 & 4 \\ 0 & 0 & 1 & -\frac{4}{5} \end{bmatrix} \begin{matrix} \\ -R_2 \\ -\frac{1}{5}R_3 \end{matrix}$$

Now, we can see that $z=\frac{-1}{5}$ and $y=4$. Plugging this in to the first equation, we get $x=-\frac{1}{5}$.

$(-\frac{1}{5}, 4, \frac{-4}{5})$

Matrix Operations

Ex: 1 Multiply the matrices:

$$\begin{bmatrix} -1 & 2 & 0 \\ -3 & 5 & 2 \\ 7 & -2 & 1 \end{bmatrix} \begin{bmatrix} 3 \\ 2 \\ -9 \end{bmatrix}$$

This matrix multiplication is possible because the number of rows in the first is equivalent to the number of columns in the second. Remember multiplication is row by column.

$$\begin{bmatrix} -1 & 2 & 0 \\ -3 & 5 & 2 \\ 7 & -2 & 1 \end{bmatrix} \begin{bmatrix} 3 \\ 2 \\ -9 \end{bmatrix} = \begin{bmatrix} -1(3)+2(2)+0(-9) \\ -3(3)+5(2)+2(-9) \\ 7(3)-2(2)+1(-9) \end{bmatrix}$$

Simplify to get:

$$\begin{bmatrix} 1 \\ -17 \\ 8 \end{bmatrix}$$

All the operations like multiplying by a scalar multiple and adding/subtracting matrices of the same dimensions should be easy and intuitive. Remember that multiplication isn't commutative.

Ex: 2 Solve the matrix equation below.

$$\begin{bmatrix} a & b \\ c & d \end{bmatrix} \begin{bmatrix} 2 & 3 \\ -1 & 1 \end{bmatrix} = \begin{bmatrix} 5 & 5 \\ 0 & 5 \end{bmatrix}$$

If you multiply out the matrices, you get:

$$\begin{bmatrix} 2a-b & 3a+b \\ 2c-d & 3c+d \end{bmatrix} = \begin{bmatrix} 5 & 5 \\ 0 & 5 \end{bmatrix}$$

Now we can match up corresponding entries.

$2a-b=5, 3a+b=5$ Row 1

We can add up the two equations to get $5a=10$. Therefore, $a=2$ and $b=-1$.

$2c-d=0, 3c+d=5$ Row 2

We can add up the two equations to get $5c=5$. Therefore, $c=1, d=2$.

$$\begin{bmatrix} 2 & -1 \\ 1 & 2 \end{bmatrix}$$

This problem could have been solved with inverse matrices but sometimes it's easier to multiply things out to get systems of equations.

Inverse Matrices

Ex: 1 Find the inverse of the matrix:

$$\begin{bmatrix} -2 & 4 \\ -1 & 5 \end{bmatrix}$$

This is easy to solve. Just use the formula: Swap the spots of $a =-2$ and $d = 5$. Negate $b =-1$ and $c = 4$. Then divide by $ad - bc$ or determinant. $ad - bc =-2(5) - (-1)(4) =-6$.

$$\begin{bmatrix} -5/6 & 2/3 \\ -1/6 & 1/3 \end{bmatrix}$$

Ex: 2 Solve the system using inverse matrices:

$x - 4y - 2z = 5$

$-3y - 2z = 2$

$-3x + 4y + z =-9$

Let's set up a matrix equation to represent this.

$$\begin{bmatrix} 1 & -4 & -2 \\ 0 & -3 & -2 \\ -3 & 4 & 1 \end{bmatrix}\begin{bmatrix} x \\ y \\ z \end{bmatrix} = \begin{bmatrix} 5 \\ 2 \\ -9 \end{bmatrix}$$

We need to find the inverse of the coefficient matrix. Then multiply the inverse to isolate the matrix for solving x, y, z.

$$\begin{bmatrix} 1 & -4 & -2 \\ 0 & -3 & -2 \\ -3 & 4 & 1 \end{bmatrix}$$

Adjoin an identity matrix.

$$\begin{bmatrix} 1 & -4 & -2 & 1 & 0 & 0 \\ 0 & -3 & -2 & 0 & 1 & 0 \\ -3 & 4 & 1 & 0 & 0 & 1 \end{bmatrix}$$

$$\begin{bmatrix} 1 & -4 & -2 & 1 & 0 & 0 \\ 0 & -3 & -2 & 0 & 1 & 0 \\ 0 & -8 & -5 & 3 & 0 & 1 \end{bmatrix} \quad 3R_1 + R_3$$

$$\begin{bmatrix} 1 & -4 & -2 & 1 & 0 & 0 \\ 0 & -3 & -2 & 0 & 1 & 0 \\ 0 & 0 & \frac{1}{3} & 3 & \frac{-8}{3} & 1 \end{bmatrix} \quad -\frac{8}{3}R_2 + R_3$$

$$\begin{bmatrix} 1 & -4 & -2 & 1 & 0 & 0 \\ 0 & 1 & \frac{2}{3} & 0 & \frac{-1}{3} & 0 \\ 0 & 0 & 1 & 9 & -8 & 3 \end{bmatrix} \quad \begin{matrix} \\ \frac{-1}{3}R_2 \\ 3R_3 \end{matrix}$$

$$\begin{bmatrix} 1 & -4 & 0 & 19 & -16 & 6 \\ 0 & 1 & 0 & -6 & 5 & -2 \\ 0 & 0 & 1 & 9 & -8 & 3 \end{bmatrix} \quad \begin{matrix} 3R_3 + R_1 \\ \frac{-2}{3}R_3 + R_2 \\ \end{matrix}$$

$$\begin{bmatrix} 1 & 0 & 0 & -5 & 4 & -2 \\ 0 & 1 & 0 & -6 & 5 & -2 \\ 0 & 0 & 1 & 9 & -8 & 3 \end{bmatrix} \quad 4R_2 + R_1$$

Now after we have gotten the inverse, multiply the inverse on both sides to get:

$$\begin{bmatrix} x \\ y \\ z \end{bmatrix} = \begin{bmatrix} -5 & 4 & -2 \\ -6 & 5 & -2 \\ 9 & -8 & 3 \end{bmatrix}\begin{bmatrix} 5 \\ 2 \\ -9 \end{bmatrix} = \begin{bmatrix} 1 \\ -2 \\ 2 \end{bmatrix}$$

$(1,-2,2)$

Ex: 3 Solve the matrix equation using inverses.

$$\begin{bmatrix} a & b \\ c & d \end{bmatrix}\begin{bmatrix} 2 & 3 \\ -1 & 1 \end{bmatrix} = \begin{bmatrix} 5 & 5 \\ 0 & 5 \end{bmatrix}$$

In order to isolate our matrix, we need to divide out the matrix on the right. However, matrix division isn't a thing. Instead, we must multiply by an inverse. Let's first find the inverse:

$$\begin{bmatrix} 2 & 3 \\ -1 & 1 \end{bmatrix}^{-1} = \frac{1}{2+3}\begin{bmatrix} 1 & -3 \\ 1 & 2 \end{bmatrix} = \begin{bmatrix} 1/5 & -3/5 \\ 1/5 & 2/5 \end{bmatrix}$$

Since we multiply the inverse on the right side to "cancel" out with the matrix factor, we must multiply the inverse of the right side of the product matrix as well.

$$\begin{bmatrix} 5 & 5 \\ 0 & 5 \end{bmatrix}\begin{bmatrix} 1/5 & -3/5 \\ 1/5 & 2/5 \end{bmatrix} = \begin{bmatrix} 1+1 & -3+2 \\ 0+1 & 0+2 \end{bmatrix}$$

$$\begin{bmatrix} 2 & -1 \\ 1 & 2 \end{bmatrix}$$

Finding Determinants

Ex: 1 Find the determinant of the matrix

$$\begin{vmatrix} 7 & 9 \\ 6 & -1 \end{vmatrix}$$

By definition, the determinant is $-1(7) - 6(9)$.

-61

Ex: 2 Find the determinant of the matrix

$$\begin{vmatrix} 6 & 1 & 1 \\ 4 & -2 & 5 \\ 2 & 8 & 7 \end{vmatrix}$$

Using the first row for a matrix of minors:

$$6\begin{vmatrix} -2 & 5 \\ 8 & 7 \end{vmatrix} - 1\begin{vmatrix} 4 & 5 \\ 2 & 7 \end{vmatrix} + 1\begin{vmatrix} 4 & -2 \\ 2 & 8 \end{vmatrix}$$

$6(-14-40) - 1(28-10) + 1(32+4)$ Simplifying
$6(-54) - 1(18) + 1(36)$ Simplifying

-306 Simplifying

Ex: 3 Find the determinant of the matrix

$$\begin{bmatrix} -1 & 2 & 0 & 0 \\ -3 & 5 & 2 & 1 \\ 7 & -2 & 1 & 2 \\ 1 & -2 & 9 & 3 \end{bmatrix}$$

Obviously, we should use the matrix of minors on the first row since it has two zeroes.

$$-1\begin{vmatrix} 5 & 2 & 1 \\ -2 & 1 & 2 \\ -2 & 9 & 3 \end{vmatrix} - 2\begin{vmatrix} -3 & 2 & 1 \\ 7 & 1 & 2 \\ 1 & 9 & 3 \end{vmatrix}$$

Now find the determinant of the 3 by 3s to get:

$-1(-87) - 2(69)$

-51

Ex: 4 Find the determinant of the matrix.

$$\begin{vmatrix} 1 & -1 & 2 & 3 \\ -1 & 4 & 2 & 3 \\ 2 & 1 & 4 & 0 \\ 1 & 4 & 2 & 2 \end{vmatrix}$$

You may be tempted to begin the normal determinant process. However, this matrix can be simplified using some row operations. Remember that row operations do not change the "value" of the matrix.

$$\begin{vmatrix} 1 & -1 & 2 & 3 \\ 0 & 3 & 4 & 6 \\ 0 & 3 & 0 & -6 \\ 0 & 5 & 0 & -1 \end{vmatrix} \begin{matrix} \\ R_1 + R_2 \\ -2R_1 + R_2 \\ R_3 - R_1 \end{matrix}$$

Now, we can use the matrix of minors on our first column to evaluate our determinant.

$$1\begin{vmatrix} 3 & 4 & 6 \\ 3 & 0 & -6 \\ 5 & 0 & -1 \end{vmatrix} = -4\begin{vmatrix} 3 & -6 \\ 5 & -1 \end{vmatrix}$$

$-4(-3+30) = -4(27) = -108$

-108

Application of Determinants

Ex: 1 Solve the system of equations using Cramer's Rule:

$-3x + 2y - 6z = 6$
$5x + 7y - 5z = 6$
$x + 4y - 2z = 8$

First take the coefficients of the variables and find the determinant of this coefficient matrix:

$$\begin{vmatrix} -3 & 2 & -6 \\ 5 & 7 & -5 \\ 1 & 4 & -2 \end{vmatrix}$$

$-3(-14+20)-2(-10+5)-6(20-7)$ We get that the coefficient determinant equals -86. Now, we replace the column of the x coefficients with the constant values to get a new matrix:

$$\begin{vmatrix} 6 & 2 & -6 \\ 6 & 7 & -5 \\ 8 & 4 & -2 \end{vmatrix}$$

$6(-14+20)-2(-12+40)-6(24-56)$
We get that this determinant equals 172. Divide this x column determinant by the coefficient determinant to get $x=-2$.
Now, we replace the column of the y coefficients with the constant values to get a new matrix:

$$\begin{vmatrix} -3 & 6 & -6 \\ 5 & 6 & -5 \\ 1 & 8 & -2 \end{vmatrix}$$

$-3(-12+40)-6(-10+5)-6(-10+5)$
We calculate that this equals -258. Divide this y column determinant by the coefficient determinant to get $y=3$. Finally we replace the column of the z coefficients with the constant values and repeat the process. The determinant of this z column determinant is -86 so $z=1$.

$(-2,3,1)$

Ex: 2 Find the area of the triangle with coordinates $(-2,2)$, $(6,-1)$, $(1,5)$ using matrices.

$$\begin{vmatrix} -2 & 2 & 1 \\ 6 & -1 & 1 \\ 1 & 5 & 1 \end{vmatrix}$$

Using the coordinates, we set up this determinant. Remember the third column is always 1's. Using the first row of matrix of minors to evaluate this determinant we get:
$-2(-1-5)-2(6-1)+1(30+1)=33$. Since it's an area of a triangle, you have to divide by 2:

Area $=\frac{33}{2}$

Ex: 3 Find x such that the points $(1,3x)$, $(-1,-2)$, $(3,x)$ are collinear.
If the points are collinear, the "area" of the triangle formed between them must be 0.

$$\begin{vmatrix} 1 & 3x & 1 \\ -1 & -2 & 1 \\ 3 & x & 1 \end{vmatrix} = 0$$

Using the first row for the matrix of minors:
$1(-2-x)-3x(-1-3)+1(-x+6)=0$
$-2-x+3x+9x-x+6=0$ Simplifying
$10x=-4$ Combining like terms

$x=\frac{-2}{5}$

Ex: 4 Use the information below to find positive x and y if the matrix does not have an inverse.

$$M=\begin{bmatrix} 2 & x & y \\ -2 & 3 & x-3 \\ 4 & x-3 & y \end{bmatrix} \qquad M^2=\begin{bmatrix} 2 & 15 & 3 \\ -10 & 3 & -2 \\ 12 & 12 & 5 \end{bmatrix}$$

If the matrix does not have inverse, its determinant must equal 0. Remember in the formula for solving an inverse for a 2 by 2, we had to divide each term by its determinant at the end. That's not possible if the determinant is 0.

$$|M|=2\begin{vmatrix} 3 & x-3 \\ x-3 & y \end{vmatrix}-x\begin{vmatrix} -2 & x-3 \\ 4 & y \end{vmatrix}+y\begin{vmatrix} -2 & 3 \\ 4 & x-3 \end{vmatrix}$$

$0=2x^2-18$ Evaluating and simplifying
$x=3$ x must be positive
To find y, we must multiply out $M \times M$.
In fact, we only need to multiply out the first entry of our matrix to get the information we need to find y.

$$\begin{bmatrix} 2 & x & y \\ -2 & 3 & x-3 \\ 4 & x-3 & y \end{bmatrix}\begin{bmatrix} 2 & x & y \\ -2 & 3 & x-3 \\ 4 & x-3 & y \end{bmatrix}=\begin{bmatrix} 4-2x+4y & \cdots & \cdots \\ \cdots & \cdots & \cdots \\ \cdots & \cdots & \cdots \end{bmatrix}$$

We know that the entry in our first and first column should equal 2.
$4-2x+4y=2$ Setting entries equal to each other
$4-2(3)+4y=2$ Substituting $x=3$
$y=1$ Solving for y

$x=3, y=1$

Matrices Test 1

#1: (14 points) Find the value(s) of x such that the following determinant equals -8:

$$\begin{vmatrix} 2 & 1 & 0 & -1 \\ 0 & -2 & 4 & 0 \\ 0 & 1 & x & x-2 \\ 0 & 0 & 0 & 2x \end{vmatrix}$$

#2: (14 points) Find matrix X if the following equals the 2 by 2 identity matrix: **31**

$$X\begin{bmatrix} 2 & 5 \\ 1 & 3 \end{bmatrix} + 3\begin{bmatrix} 2 & 1 \\ -4 & -3 \end{bmatrix} - 2X$$

#3: (14 points each) Solve each using the listed method:

a) Cramer's Rule:

$2x + 4y + 3z = 17$

$x - 2y - 4z = 2$

$-x + 8y + 2z = 18$

b) Gaussian Elimination:

$x + 2y + z = -1$

$3x - y + 2z = -9$

$3y + 4z = -1$

c) Inverse Matrices:

$x - y + z = 1$
$2x + 2y - z = 10$
$-x + y + 2z = -1$

#4: (10 points) Using determinants, what is the area formed by the quadrilateral with vertices $(-1,2)$, $(-3,4)$, $(0,3)$, $(1,-1)$ in clockwise direction?

#5: (20 points) The following points satisfy a cubic function $f(x) = ax^3 + bx^2 + cx + d$: $(2,10)$, $(1,-2)$, $(-1,-8)$, $(-2,-26)$. Using any matrix method, find a, b, c, and d.

Matrices Test 2

#1: (14 points) Find the determinant of the following matrix:

$$\begin{vmatrix} -1 & 0 & 0 & 4 \\ 2 & 3 & 4 & 1 \\ 4 & -1 & -2 & 0 \\ 1 & 2 & 1 & 1 \end{vmatrix}$$

#2: (14 points) Solve for matrix X: **3**

$$\begin{bmatrix} 2 & 0 \\ 5 & 4 \end{bmatrix} X \begin{bmatrix} 2 & 4 \\ 5 & 6 \end{bmatrix} - 2\begin{bmatrix} 15 & 12 \\ 70 & 80 \end{bmatrix} = \begin{bmatrix} 4 & 20 \\ 9 & 14 \end{bmatrix}$$

#3: (14 points) Solve each using the listed method:

a) Cramer's Rule

$3x + 2y + z = 13$

$x - y + z = 6$

$2x + y - 2z = -5$

b) Gaussian Elimination:

$x + 2y + 3z = 12$

$-x + y + 2z = 9$

$-x + 3y + z = 10$

c) Inverse Matrices:

$x + y + z = 0$

$-x + y + z = -2$

$2x + 2y - z = 9$

#4: (10 points) Find x if $(1, -2), (x, 2), (5, 6)$ are collinear.

#5: (20 points) Jessie, Tenny, Jonathan, and Jerry each have a bunch of marbles. The total amount of marbles they own is 360 marbles. If Jessie doubles the number of marbles she owns and Tenny loses 20 marbles, they will have the same number of marbles. If Jessie and Tenny have $\frac{3}{4}$ of the number of marbles while Jonathan and Jerry double the number of marbles, their total will now be 515. If Jerry gets 20 more marbles, he will own as many marbles as Tenny and Jessie combined. Using any matrix method, how many marbles does each person own?

Matrices Test 3

#1: (14 points) Find the determinant of the following matrix:

$$\begin{vmatrix} 1 & 4 & 2 & -1 \\ 2 & 3 & 4 & 1 \\ 4 & 5 & 2 & 2 \\ 3 & 2 & 1 & -1 \end{vmatrix}$$

#2: (14 points) Solve for matrix X if the determinant of X is 2. **19**

$$X^2 + 2X + 2\begin{bmatrix} 1 & 3 \\ -5 & -6 \end{bmatrix} = \begin{bmatrix} 0 & 1 \\ 0 & 1 \end{bmatrix}$$

#3: (14 points) Solve each with the listed method.

a) Gaussian-Elimination:

$x + 3y - 2z = 10$

$-2x + 5y - 3z = -1$

$3x - 2y + z = 12$

b) Inverse Matrices:

$x + y + z = 0$

$3x - 2y - z = 4$

$x + 4y + 2z = 3$

c) Cramer's Rule:

$$2x + 3y - 3z = -2$$
$$x - y + z = 4$$
$$3x - 2y + 3z = 11$$

#5: (20 points) In the table below is the reading rate in pages per hour for Alex, Bob, Cathy, and Daniel. The rate depends on the type of book.

	Classics	Comics	Fantasy	Science
Alex	40	90	60	45
Bob	30	72	60	40
Cathy	45	72	80	90
Dan	30	180	48	60

All four students are assigned to read the same 4 classic, comic, fantasy, and science fiction books. Alex takes a total of 27 hours. Bob takes 32.5 hours. Cathy takes 22.5 hours. Dan takes 26 hours. Using any matrix method, find the length of each book.

#4: (10 points) Find the area of the quadrilateral with coordinates $(4,0),(2,-1),(-1,4),(3,3)$.

Chapter 11 Conics

Conics is one of the hardest chapters just because there's so many different types of applications to these problems. This problem is so heavy in both algebra and geometry.

Parabolas

Ex: 1 Find all characteristics of $y = x^2 + 8x + 6$.

$y = x^2 + 8x + 16 - 10$ Setting up the square

$y = (x + 4)^2 - 10$ Complete the square

Vertex is at $(-4, -10)$. Looking at the coefficient of the x^2 term, we see $1 = \frac{1}{4p}$. So $p = 1/4$.

The focus is $1/4$ above the vertex and the directrix is $1/4$ below. Solving $0 = (x + 4)^2 - 10$ we get the x-intercepts to be $(-4 \pm \sqrt{10}, 0)$.

Vertex: $(-4, -10)$ Focus: $(-4, -\frac{39}{4})$ Directrix: $y = \frac{-41}{4}$ x-intercepts: $(-4 \pm \sqrt{10}, 0)$, y-intercept: $(0, 6)$

Ex: 2 Find the equation of the line that is tangent to $y = x^2 + 8x + 6$ at $(-1, -1)$.

From example 1, we see that the focus is at $(-4, -\frac{39}{4})$. The distance from the focus to the point of tangency must be equal to the distance from the focus to the point where the tangent line intersects the axis of symmetry $(x = -4)$. The distance from $(-1, -1)$ to $(-4, -\frac{39}{4})$ is $\sqrt{3^2 + (\frac{35}{4})^2} = \frac{37}{4}$. Therefore, the point where the tangent line intersects $x = -4$ is $\frac{37}{4}$ below the focus. This point is at $(-4, -19)$. The slope between this point at $(-1, -1)$ would be 6. Using point slope form and simplifying, we get:

$y = 6x + 5$

Ex: 3 What is the equation of the rotated parabola with vertex $(3, 4)$ and foci $(0, 0)$?

Let's first find the directrix. The vertex is halfway between the foci and the point where the axis of symmetry intersects the directrix. The point where the axis of symmetry intersects the directrix would be $(2(3) - 0, 2(4) - 0) = (6, 8)$. The axis of symmetry goes through the vertex and foci. The slope of this line would be $\frac{4}{3}$. Since it goes through the origin, the line is $y = \frac{4}{3}x$. The directrix must be perpendicular to this line so the directrix has slope $\frac{-3}{4}$. Since it goes through $(6, 8)$ the directrix has equation: $y = -\frac{3}{4}x + \frac{25}{2}$ or $3x + 4y - 50 = 0$. The definition of a parabola is the set of all points that has a constant difference from focus to directrix. Use the point to line formula. The difference from (a, b) to $Ax + By + C = 0$ is $\frac{|Aa+Bb+C|}{\sqrt{A^2+B^2}}$. The distance from the points (x, y) to the focus $(0, 0)$ must be constant. Therefore, $\frac{3x+4y-50}{\sqrt{3^2+4^2}} = \sqrt{x^2 + y^2}$ since the distance from origin (focus) is constant.

$3x + 4y - 50 = 5\sqrt{x^2 + y^2}$ Multiply 5

$9x^2 + 24xy - 300x + 16y^2 - 400y + 2500 = 25(x^2 + y^2)$ Squaring both sides

$-16x^2 + 24xy - 300x - 9y^2 - 400y + 2500 = 0$

Ex: 4 A tunnel is in the shape of a parabola. The tunnel is 20 feet wide and is 12 feet high at its highest point. If a truck is 6 feet wide, at most how tall can the truck be to safely pass under the tunnel?

If we model this situation on a coordinate plane, we can have this parabola have vertex $(0, 12)$ and have x intercepts $(10, 0)$ $(-10, 0)$. Since the parabola has form $y = ax^2 + 12$, plugging in a point gets $a = \frac{-3}{25}$. Now if the truck is 6 feet wide, we want to see the height of the tunnel at $x = 3$ or $x = -3$. Plugging in $x = 3$ for $y = \frac{-3}{25}x^2 + 12$ gets $y = 10.92$.

The truck can be at most 10.92 ft

Circles

Ex: 1 Find all applicable characteristics of:

$x^2 + y^2 + 8x - 12y + 27 = 0$

$x^2 + 8x + 16 + y^2 - 12y + 36 = -27 + 16 + 36$

$(x + 4)^2 + (y - 6)^2 = 25$ Completing the square

Center $(-4, 6)$ Radius: 5

Ex: 2 A circle has center on the line with equation $y = 2x - 11$. It passes through $(8,0)$ and has a radius of 5. Find the possible equation(s) of the circle.
Let the center be at (h,k). Therefore, $k = 2h - 11$. The circle can be written as $(x-h)^2 + (y-k)^2 = 25$. Plugging in $k = 2h - 11$, we get $(x-h)^2 + (y - 2h + 11)^2 = 25$. Since we know the circle passes through $(8,0)$, plug that point in to solve for h :
$(8-h)^2 + (0 - 2h + 11)^2 = 25$
$64 - 16h + h^2 + 4h^2 - 44h + 121 = 25$ Expanding
$5h^2 - 50h + 160 = 0$ Simplifying
$h^2 - 12h + 32 = 0$ Dividing 5
$(h-8)(h-4) = 0$ Factoring
Therefore, $h = 8, 4$. The respective values of k would $k = 5, k = -3$.

$(x-8)^2 + (y-5)^2 = 25$ $(x-4)^2 + (y+3)^2 = 25$

Ex: 3 Find the equation(s) of lines tangent to the circle $x^2 + 4x + y^2 + 6y + 8 = 0$ that pass through $(-5,1)$.
We know a line tangent to a point on the circle must be perpendicular to the radius through that point. Let's first complete the square to get the radius: $x^2 + 4x + 4 + y^2 + 6y + 9 = 9 + 4 - 8$. Simplifying we get, $(x+2)^2 + (y+3)^2 = 5$. Therefore the center is at $(-2,-3)$. Let the point of tangency be (a,b). We know that the slope to the center would then be $\frac{b+3}{a+2}$. For the slope of the line to our point $(-5,1)$, that would be $\frac{b-1}{a+5}$. Because the two lines are perpendicular, their must be -1. $(\frac{b+3}{a+2})(\frac{b-1}{a+5}) = -1$. Multiplying $(a+2)(a+5)$ on both sides and simplifying we get, $b^2 + 2b + a^2 + 7a + 7 = 0$. Now because our point must to through our circle, it must also fulfil the equation $a^2 + 4a + b^2 + 6b + 8 = 0$. If you subtract this equation from the first equation:
$3a - 4b = 1$. Solving for a, we get $a = \frac{4b+1}{3}$. Now if we plug this back into one of our original equations: $(\frac{4b+1}{3})^2 + 4(\frac{4b+1}{3}) + b^2 + 6b + 8 = 0$
After expanding and multiplying 9 on both sides: $5b^2 + 22b + 17 = 0$. We can factor this to get $(b+1)(5b+17) = 0$. So $b = -1, -\frac{17}{5}$. The respective a values would be $-1, \frac{-21}{5}$. The slope of the that goes through $(-5,1)$ and $(-1,-1)$ is $\frac{-1}{2}$. Using point slope form: we get that the equation is $(y-1) = \frac{-1}{2}(x+5)$. The slope for the other point would be $-\frac{11}{2}$. We can use point slope form again: $(y-1) = \frac{-11}{2}(x+5)$.

$y = \frac{-1}{2}x - \frac{3}{2}$ and $y = \frac{-11}{2}x - \frac{53}{2}$.

Ex: 4 Find the value of a and b such that the circle $(x-a)^2 + (y-b)^2 = 4$ is tangent to $y = x$ and $y = -x$ if a is positive.
Let's plug in each of the y values into the equation of this circle. Because the lines are tangent to this circle, they only intersect at one point so the discriminant $(b^2 - 4ac)$ must equal 0.
$x^2 - 2ax + a^2 + (x-b)^2 = 4$. Using first line
$x^2 - 2ax + a^2 + x^2 - 2bx + b^2 - 4 = 0$ Expanding
$2x^2 + (-2a - 2b)x + a^2 + b^2 - 4 = 0$ Quadratic form
$(-2a - 2b)^2 - 4(2)(a^2 + 4 - 4) = 0$ Discriminant
$4a^2 + 8ab + 4b^2 - 8a^2 - 8b^2 + 32 = 0$ Expanding
$a^2 - 2ab + b^2 = 8$ Simplifying
Now plugging in $y = -x$.
$x^2 - 2ax + a^2 + (-x - b)^2 = 4$ Using second line
$x^2 - 2ax + a^2 + x^2 + 2bx + b^2 = 4$ Expanding
$2x^2 + (-2a + 2b)x + a^2 + b^2 - 4 = 0$ Quadratic form
$(-2a + 2b)^2 - 4(2)(a^2 + b^2 - 4) = 0$ Discriminant
$4a^2 - 8ab + 4b^2 - 8a^2 - 8b^2 + 32 = 0$ Expanding
$a^2 + 2ab + b^2 = 8$ Simplifying
Subtract this equation from the first:
$4ab = 0$ so either a or b is zero. Since we're given a is positive, $b = 0$. Plugging this in to any equation, we get $a^2 = 8$ or $a = 2\sqrt{2}$.

$(x - 2\sqrt{2})^2 + y^2 = 4$

Ellipses

Ex:1 Find applicable characteristics of
$9x^2 + 16y^2 + 18x - 64y - 71 = 0$
$9(x^2 + 2x) + 16(y^2 - 4y) = 71$ Factoring
$9(x^2 + 2x + 1) + 16(y^2 - 4y + 4) = 71 + 9(1) + 16(4)$
Completing the square
$9(x+1)^2 + 16(y-2)^2 = 144$ Simplifying

$\frac{(x+1)^2}{16} + \frac{(y-2)^2}{9} = 1$ Dividing 144

Therefore, the center is at $(-1,2)$. $a = \sqrt{16} = 4$ and $b = \sqrt{9} = 3$. Therefore, the vertices are 4 units left and right of the center at $(-5,2)$ and $(3,2)$. The covertices would be 3 units up and down of the center at $(-1,5)$ and $(-1,-1)$. Because $a^2 = b^2 + c^2$, plugging in what we know gets $c^2 = 7$ or $c = \sqrt{7}$. Therefore we know that the foci are $\sqrt{7}$ left and right of the center. We get eccentricity by dividing c over a.

Center: $(-1,2)$ Vertices: $(-5,2)$ and $(3,2)$ Covertices: $(-1,5)$ and $(-1,-1)$ Foci $(-1 \pm \sqrt{7},2)$ Eccentricity: $\frac{\sqrt{7}}{4}$

Ex: 2 Given an ellipse $\frac{x^2}{a^2} + \frac{y^2}{b^2} = 1$ where $a > b$. The distance from the center to a focus is $\sqrt{3}$. The line $y = \frac{b}{2}x$ intersects the ellipse at a point X such that a right angle is formed between the center, X, and one of the vertices. Find the equation of the ellipse.

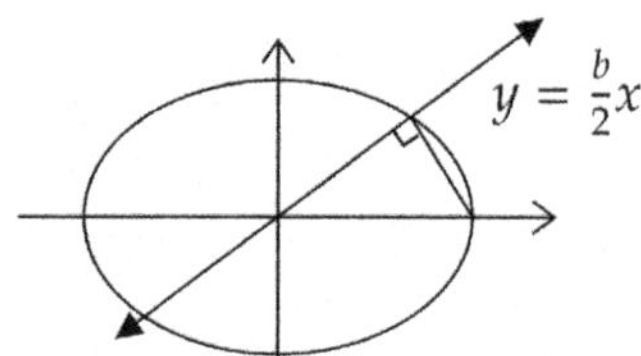

Let's find where this line intersects our ellipse.

$\frac{x^2}{a^2} + \frac{\frac{b^2x^2}{4}}{b^2} = 1$ Plugging in $y = \frac{b}{2}x$

$\frac{x^2}{a^2} + \frac{x^2}{4} = 1$ Simplifying

$x^2(\frac{1}{a^2} + \frac{1}{4}) = 1$ Factoring

$x = \frac{2a}{\sqrt{4+a^2}}$ Solving for x

$y = \frac{ab}{\sqrt{4+a^2}}$ Solving for y

By the pythagorean theorem, we can set up an equation to represent the lengths of the triangle.

Hypotenuse: a, $(0,0)$ to $(a,0)$

Leg 1: $\sqrt{\frac{4a^2}{4+a^2} + \frac{a^2b^2}{4+a^2}}$ $(0,0)$ to $(\frac{2a}{\sqrt{4+a^2}}, \frac{ab}{\sqrt{4+a^2}})$

Leg 2: $\sqrt{(\frac{2a}{\sqrt{4+a^2}} - a)^2 + \frac{a^2b^2}{4+a^2}}$ $(a,0)$ to $(\frac{2a}{\sqrt{4+a^2}}, \frac{ab}{\sqrt{4+a^2}})$

Setting up an equation:

$a^2 = \frac{4a^2}{4+a^2} + \frac{a^2b^2}{4+a^2} + \frac{4a^2}{4+a^2} - \frac{4a^2}{\sqrt{4+a^2}} + a^2 + \frac{a^2b^2}{4+a^2}$

$\frac{4a^2}{\sqrt{4+a^2}} = \frac{8a^2+2a^2b^2}{4+a^2}$ Combining like terms

$\frac{2}{\sqrt{4+a^2}} = \frac{4+b^2}{4+a^2}$ Simplifying

Now because the distance from the center to a focus is $\sqrt{3}, c = \sqrt{3}$. Remember that $a^2 = b^2 + c^2$ in an ellipse. Using this, we can let $b^2 = a^2 - 3$.

$\frac{2}{\sqrt{4+a^2}} = \frac{a^2+1}{a^2+4}$ Substituting $b^2 = a^2 - 3$

Let $a^2 = x$.

$\frac{4}{4+x} = \frac{x^2+2x+1}{x^2+8x+16}$ Substituting and squaring

$4(x^2 + 8x + 16) = (x+4)(x^2 + 2x + 1)$ Cross Multiply

$x^3 + 2x^2 - 23x - 60 = 0$ Expanding and simplifying

$(x-5)(x+4)(x+3) = 0$ Factoring

$x = 5$, since a^2 must be positive

Because $a^2 = 5, b^2 = 2$.

$\frac{x^2}{5} + \frac{y^2}{2} = 1$

Ex: 3 What is the general equation of the rotated ellipse that has (co)vertices at $(\frac{\sqrt{3}}{2}, \frac{1}{2})$ $(\frac{\sqrt{3}}{2}, -\frac{1}{2})$ $(1, -\sqrt{3})$ $(-1, \sqrt{3})$?

It is obvious that the center of this conic must be at the origin. The distance $(1, -\sqrt{3})$ $(-1, \sqrt{3})$ are from the origin is 2 while the distance from $(\frac{\sqrt{3}}{2}, \frac{1}{2})$ $(\frac{\sqrt{3}}{2}, -\frac{1}{2})$ to the origin is 1. This tells us $a = 2, b = 1$. Using $a^2 = b^2 + c^2$, we get that $c = \sqrt{3}$. Now if we can find where the foci are, we can use the definition of an ellipse to find it's equation. We know the foci are $\sqrt{3}$ from the origin and lie along the same line as the vertices. Since the vertices are $(1, -\sqrt{3})$ and $(-1, \sqrt{3})$, the foci must lie on $y = -\sqrt{3}x$. The foci must also lie on $x^2 + y^2 = 3$ by the distance formula. Solving this system, we get that the foci are at $(\frac{\sqrt{3}}{2}, -\frac{3}{2})$ and $(-\frac{\sqrt{3}}{2}, \frac{3}{2})$. By the definition of an ellipse, the distance from a point to these foci must be constant. This constant is the "length of the string" or $2a = 2(2) = 4$. Using the distance formula, we can set up an equation.

$$\sqrt{(x - \frac{\sqrt{3}}{2})^2 + (y + \frac{3}{2})^2} + \sqrt{(x + \frac{\sqrt{3}}{2})^2 + (y - \frac{3}{2})^2} = 4$$

Subtracting one radical and squaring both sides

$$(x - \frac{\sqrt{3}}{2})^2 + (y + \frac{3}{2})^2 =$$
$$16 - 2\sqrt{(x + \frac{\sqrt{3}}{2})^2 + (y - \frac{3}{2})^2} + (x + \frac{\sqrt{3}}{2})^2 + (y - \frac{3}{2})^2$$

After more expanding and cancelling out terms:

$$-\sqrt{3}x + 3y - 8 = -4\sqrt{x^2 + \sqrt{3}x + y^2 - 3y + 3}$$

Square both sides and cancel out more terms:

$$13x^2 + 6\sqrt{3}xy + 7y^2 - 16 = 0$$

Ex: 4 In the ellipse centered at origin, $AB = 10, AC = 17, BC = 21$. If the perpendicular from A to BC intersects a foci of the ellipse, find the equation of the ellipse.

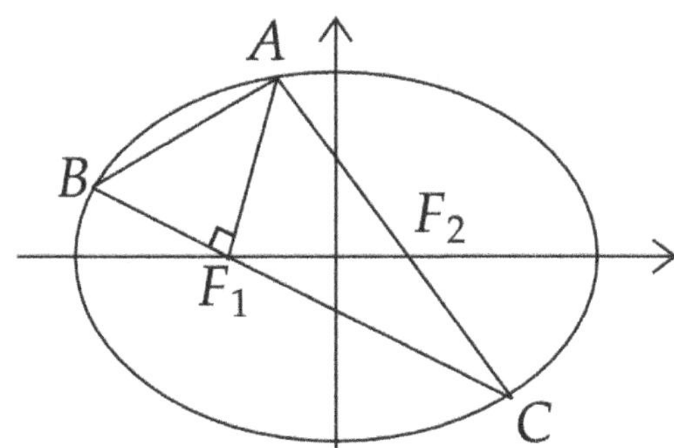

Let's first work to solve some side lengths. Suppose $BF_1 = n, F_1C = m,$ we can say $n + m = 21$ and $AF_1 = \sqrt{100 - n^2} = \sqrt{289 - m^2}$ by using the pythagorean theorem.

$100 - (21 - m)^2 = 289 - m^2$ Plugging in $a = 21 - b$

$100 - 441 + 42m - m^2 = 289 - m^2$ Expanding

$42m = 630$ Combining like terms

$m = 15$ Solving for b

Therefore, $n = 6$ and $AF_1 = 8$.

Now, remember that by foci properties that the sum of the distances from the foci is constant and that this sum is the length of the major axis $(2a)$.

$AF_1 + AF_2 = F_1C + F_2C$ Foci property

$8 + AF_2 = 15 + F_2C$ Plugging in known values

$AF_2 = 7 + F_2C$ Simplifying

Remember that $AF_2 + F_2C = AC = 17$. By solving these equations, we get $AF_2 = 12, F_2C = 5$.

The constant foci distance sum would be $12 + 8 = 20$. Therefore, $a = 10$ and $a^2 = 100$.

Now we need to find the distance between the two foci in order to find the length of the minor axis. Suppose Angle $F_1AF_2 = \theta$ and $F_1F_2 = x$. By the Law of Cosines, $x^2 = 64 + 144 - 2(8)(12)\cos\theta$

$x^2 = 208 - 192\cos\theta$ Simplifying

Because AF_1C is a right angle, $\cos\theta = \frac{8}{17}$.

$x^2 = 208 - 192 \cdot \frac{8}{17} = \frac{2000}{17}$

x is the total distance between the foci so $c = \frac{x}{2}$.

Using this, we can find that $c^2 = \frac{1}{4}(\frac{2000}{17}) = \frac{500}{17}$.

Remember that in an ellipse, $a^2 = b^2 + c^2$. Since $a^2 = 100$, we can solve that $b^2 = \frac{1200}{7}$.

$$\frac{x^2}{100} + \frac{y^2}{1200/7} = 1 \text{ Putting the information together}$$

Hyperbolas

Ex: 1 Find all applicable characteristics of

$9x^2 - 25y^2 - 36x - 150y - 414 = 0.$

$9(x^2 - 4x) - 25(y^2 + 6y) = 414$

$9(x^2 - 4x + 4) - 25(y^2 + 6y + 9) = 414 + 36 - 225$

$9(x - 2)^2 - 25(y + 3)^2 = 225$

$\frac{(x-2)^2}{25} - \frac{(y+3)^2}{9} = 1$

Follow the process of completing the square to get this standard form.

The center therefore is $(2, -3)$. Since $a = \sqrt{25}$, the vertices are 5 units left and right of the center at $(-3, -3)$ and $(7, -3)$. The covertices would be 3 units up and down of the center at $(2, 0)$ and $(2, -6)$. Using $a^2 + b^2 = c^2$, we get that $c^2 = 25 + 9$. So the foci are $\sqrt{34}$ left and right of the center at $(2 \pm \sqrt{34}, -3)$. By the formula the asymptotes would be at $y + 3 = \pm \frac{3}{5}(x - 2)$. The eccentricity would be $\frac{\sqrt{34}}{5}$.

Center: $(2, -3)$ Vertices: $(-3, -3)$ and $(7, -3)$
Covertices: $(2, 0)$ and $(2, -6)$ Eccentricity: $\frac{\sqrt{34}}{5}$
Foci: $(2 \pm \sqrt{34}, -3)$ Asymptotes:
$y + 3 = \pm \frac{3}{5}(x - 2)$

Ex: 2 If a hyperbola has vertices at $(-1, -1)$ and $(7, -1)$ and has asymptotes $y = \frac{1}{2}x - \frac{5}{2}$ and $y = -\frac{1}{2}x + \frac{1}{2}$, find the equation of this hyperbola?

The midpoint of the vertices is the center of the hyperbola, which is at $(3, -1)$. Because this hyperbola has a horizontal transverse axis and the slope of the asymptotes is $\frac{1}{2}$, $\frac{b}{a}$ must equal $\frac{1}{2}$. The two vertices are 4 away from the center so $a = 4$. Therefore, $b = 2$. Putting these together we get:

$$\frac{(x-3)^2}{16} - \frac{(y+1)^2}{4} = 1$$

Ex: 3 Find the general equation of the rotated hyperbola with vertices $(\frac{8}{5},\frac{6}{5})$ and $(\frac{-8}{5},\frac{-6}{5})$ and foci $(\frac{4\sqrt{10}}{5},\frac{3\sqrt{10}}{5})$ and $(\frac{-4\sqrt{10}}{5},\frac{-3\sqrt{10}}{5})$.

By the definition of a hyperbola, the difference in distances between any point to the foci must be constant. Let's take $(\frac{8}{5},\frac{6}{5})$ and calculate the distances to the two foci.

$D_1 = \sqrt{(\frac{8-4\sqrt{10}}{5})^2 + (\frac{6-3\sqrt{10}}{5})^2}$ Distance Formula

$D_1 = \sqrt{\frac{64-64\sqrt{10}+160+36-36\sqrt{10}+90}{25}}$ Expanding

$D_1 = \sqrt{14-4\sqrt{10}}$ Simplifying

$D_2 = \sqrt{14+4\sqrt{10}}$ Repeating the process

Let $x = \sqrt{14+4\sqrt{10}} - \sqrt{14-4\sqrt{10}}$.

$x^2 = 28 - 2\sqrt{14^2 - (4\sqrt{10})^2}$ Squaring Both Sides

$x^2 = 16$ Simplifying

$x = 4$ Solving for x

Now the set of all points (x,y) such that the difference in the distances to the foci is always 4 represents this hyperbola:

$$\sqrt{(x-\frac{4\sqrt{10}}{5})^2 + (y-\frac{3\sqrt{10}}{5})^2} = \sqrt{(x+\frac{4\sqrt{10}}{5})^2 + (y+\frac{3\sqrt{10}}{5})^2} + 4$$

It doesn't matter if we do $D_1 - D_2$ or the other way because we square both sides anyways.

If we square both sides and do a bunch of cancellation, we get:

$$-(\frac{4\sqrt{10}}{5}x + \frac{3\sqrt{10}}{5}y + 4) = 2\sqrt{(x+\frac{4\sqrt{10}}{5})^2 + (y+\frac{3\sqrt{10}}{5})^2}$$

If we square both sides again (I'm sorry for this):

$$\frac{2(4x+3y)^2+8\sqrt{10}(4x+3y)+80}{5} = 4(x^2 + \frac{8\sqrt{10}}{5}x + y^2 + \frac{6\sqrt{10}}{5}y + 10)$$

Luckily the square roots cancel out and after a bunch of simplification we get:

$6x^2 + 24xy - y^2 = 60$

$6x^2 + 24xy - y^2 = 60$

Rotating Conics

Ex: 1 Use a rotation of axes to eliminate the xy term for $3x^2 - 2\sqrt{3}xy + y^2 + 2x + 2\sqrt{3}y = 0$.

First we need to find the angle of rotation. The angle of rotation can be found by solving $\cot(2\theta) = \frac{3-1}{-2\sqrt{3}} = \frac{-1}{\sqrt{3}}$. $2\theta = 120^\circ$ so $\theta = 60^\circ$. Now, we can find the x and y coordinates in terms of the rotated x' and y' coordinates.

$x = x'\cos 60^\circ - y'\sin 60^\circ$, $y = x'\sin 60^\circ + y'\cos 60^\circ$

$x = \frac{x'-\sqrt{3}y'}{2}$, $y = \frac{\sqrt{3}x'+y'}{2}$

Now let's plug this in to our original equation.

$$3(\frac{x'-\sqrt{3}y'}{2})^2 - 2\sqrt{3}(\frac{x'-\sqrt{3}y'}{2})(\frac{\sqrt{3}x'+y'}{2}) + (\frac{\sqrt{3}x'+y'}{2})^2 + 2(\frac{x'-\sqrt{3}y'}{2}) + 2\sqrt{3}(\frac{\sqrt{3}x'+y'}{2}) = 0$$

$$\frac{3}{4}x'^2 - \frac{3\sqrt{3}}{2}x'y' + \frac{9}{4}y'^2 - \frac{3}{2}x'^2 + \sqrt{3}x'y' + \frac{3}{2}y'^2 + \frac{3}{4}x'^2 + \frac{\sqrt{3}}{2}x'y' + \frac{1}{4}y'^2 + x' - \sqrt{3}y' + 3x + '\sqrt{3}y' = 0$$

Before you expand, check that the $x'y'$ term is eliminated. It must be gone. Don't commit to something and realize you've done it wrong.

$4y'^2 + 4x' = 0$ Combining like terms

$x' = -(y')^2$ Expanding and simplifying

Ex: 2 Use a rotation of axes to eliminate the xy term for $9x^2 + 24xy + 16y^2 + 90x - 130y = 0$. Find all applicable characteristics in xy and $x'y'$ form.

The angle of rotation can be found by solving $\cot(2\theta) = \frac{9-16}{24} = \frac{-7}{24}$. It's not obvious what the angle is. If we draw a right triangle that has a point at $(-7, 24)$ we see that this forms a $7-24-25$ right triangle. Therefore, $\cos(2\theta) = \frac{-7}{25}$ and. By half angle identities, $\cos\theta = \sqrt{\frac{1+\cos(2\theta)}{2}}$ and $\sin\theta = \sqrt{\frac{1-\cos(2\theta)}{2}}$. Plugging in $\cos(2\theta)$ for each, we get that $\cos\theta = \frac{3}{5}$ and $\sin\theta = \frac{4}{5}$. The formulas show that $x = \frac{3x'-4y'}{5}$ and $y = \frac{4x'+3y'}{5}$. Plugging this into our equation:

$$9(\frac{3x'-4y'}{5})^2 + 24(\frac{3x'-4y'}{5})(\frac{4x'+3y'}{5}) + 16(\frac{4x'+3y'}{5})^2 + 90(\frac{3x'-4y'}{5}) - 130(\frac{4x'+3y'}{5}) = 0$$

$$\frac{81x'^2-216xy+144y^2+288x^2-168xy-288y^2+256x^2+384xy+144y^2}{25} = 50x' + 150y'$$

After checking that $x'y'$ has been eliminated

$25x'^2 - 50x - 150y' = 0$ Simplifying

$x'^2 - 2x = 6y'$

$y' = \frac{1}{6}(x'^2 - 2x')$

$\frac{1}{6}(x'^2 - 2x + 1) - \frac{1}{6} = y'$ Completing the square

Now finding characteristics in $x'y'$ form:

The vertex is obviously at $(1, \frac{-1}{6})$. The coefficient of x'^2 is 1. Since $\frac{1}{4p} = \frac{1}{6}, p = \frac{3}{2}$. Therefore, the focus is $\frac{3}{2}$ above the vertex at $(1, \frac{4}{3})$. The directrix would be $\frac{3}{2}$ below at $y' = -\frac{5}{3}$. Now what we can do is take these points and use the conversion formulas above that relate $x'y'$ to xy terms in order to get

the characteristics in xy form. The vertex would be $(\frac{11}{15},\frac{7}{10})$ because
$x = \frac{3(1)-4(\frac{-1}{6})}{5} = \frac{11}{15}$ and $y = \frac{4(1)+3(\frac{-1}{6})}{5} = \frac{7}{10}$.
The focus would be $(\frac{-7}{15},\frac{17}{20})$ because
$x = \frac{3(1)-4(\frac{4}{3})}{5} = \frac{-7}{15}$ and $y = \frac{4(1)+3(\frac{4}{3})}{5} = \frac{8}{5}$
For the directrix plug in $y' = \frac{-5}{3}$ into both formulas and solve a system.
$x = \frac{3x'-4(-\frac{5}{3})}{5} = \frac{3}{5}x' + \frac{4}{3}$. Solving for x' we get, $x' = \frac{5}{3}x - \frac{20}{9}$. Now for y. $y = \frac{4x'+3(-\frac{5}{3})}{5} = \frac{4}{5}x' - 1$.
Solving for x' we get, $x' = \frac{5}{4}y + \frac{5}{4}$. Now equating these two equations for x', we get:
$\frac{5}{3}x - \frac{20}{9} = \frac{5}{4}y + \frac{5}{4}$
$\frac{5}{4}y = \frac{5}{3}x - \frac{125}{36}$ Isolating y
$y = \frac{4}{3}x - \frac{25}{9}$.

$y' = \frac{1}{6}(x'-1)^2 - \frac{1}{6}$
$x'y'$: Vertex $(1,\frac{-1}{6})$ Focus $(1,\frac{4}{3})$ Directrix $y' = -\frac{5}{3}$
xy : Vertex $(\frac{11}{15},\frac{7}{10})$ Focus $(\frac{-7}{15},\frac{8}{5})$ Directrix $y = \frac{4}{3}x - \frac{25}{9}$

Potpourri

Ex: 1 The foci of an ellipse are at $A(-1,1)$ and $B(5,1)$, with the length of the minor axis being 4. If A is the focus and B is the vertex of a parabola, what are the points of intersection between the ellipse and the parabola?
The midpoint of the two foci would be the center of the ellipse. Because $\frac{-1+5}{2} = 2$, the center is at $(2,1)$. Because the distance between the two foci is 6, $c = 3$. Since the length of the minor axis is 4, $b = 2$. Using the formula, $a^2 = b^2 + c^2$, $a = \sqrt{13}$.
Putting this together, the formula for the ellipse is $\frac{(x-2)^2}{13} + \frac{(y-1)^2}{4} = 1$. For the parabola, the distance between the foci and vertex is the p value, which in this case is -6. Therefore, the equation of the parabola is $-24(x-5) = (y-1)^2$. Now substituting in $(y-1)^2$ for the ellipse equation, we get $\frac{(x-2)^2}{13} + \frac{-24(x-5)}{4} = 1$.
$\frac{x^2-4x+4}{13} - 6(x-5) = 1$ Simplifying
$x^2 - 4x + 4 - 78x + 390 = 13$ Multiplying by 13
$x^2 - 82x + 381 = 0$ Combining like terms
$x = \frac{82 \pm \sqrt{5200}}{2} = 41 \pm 10\sqrt{13}$ Quadratic formula
Just base on intuition, you can tell the negative version of this x value is way too small. So we only use the positive $\sqrt{13}$ version which is approximately equal to 4.9445. Plugging this into the parabola equation, we get $1.3323 = (y-1)^2$.
This yields $y \approx 2.154, -0.1543$.

$(4,9445, 2.154)$ $(4.9445, -0.1543)$

Ex: 2 The parabola $y = x^2 - 14x$ intersects the foci of an ellipse with a horizontal major axis of 28. If this ellipse passes through $(5,12)$ find the equation of the ellipse.
We know the parabola has an axis of symmetry at $x = 7$. Any two points that intersect the parabola at the same y coordinate (the foci) will be equidistant from $x = 7$. Therefore, the center has x coordinate 7 because the center is also the midpoint of the two foci. Since the ellipse has major axis 28, $a^2 = 196$.
$\frac{(x-7)^2}{196} + \frac{(y-k)^2}{b^2} = 1$ General Structure of Ellipse
$\frac{(5-7)^2}{196} + \frac{(12-k)^2}{b^2} = 1$ Intersects $(5,12)$
$\frac{(12-k)^2}{b^2} = \frac{48}{49}$ Simplifying
Remember that the foci lie on the line $y = k$.
Using the quadratic formula, the points (the foci) where this line intersects $y = x^2 - 14x$ has x coordinate $7 \pm \sqrt{49+k}$. The distance between the foci is $2\sqrt{49+k}$ so $c = \sqrt{49+k}$. Remember that in an ellipse $a^2 = b^2 + c^2$.
$196 = b^2 + (\sqrt{49+k})^2$ Plugging in a and c
$b^2 = 147 - k$ Simplifying
$\frac{(12-k)^2}{147-k} = \frac{48}{49}$ Substituting $b^2 = 147 - k$
$7056 - 1176k + 49k^2 = 7056 - 48k$ Cross Multiply
$49k^2 - 1128k = 0$ Simplifying
$49k(k - \frac{1128}{49}) = 0$
$k = 0, \frac{1128}{49}$
$b^2 = 147, \frac{6075}{49}$

$\frac{(x-7)^2}{196} + \frac{y^2}{147} = 1$ OR $\frac{(x-7)^2}{196} + \frac{(y-1128/49)^2}{6075/49} = 1$

Ex: 3 The ellipse given below has foci at A and B and center at the origin. If C is a covertex of the ellipse but is also the vertex of a parabola that goes through points A and B, what is the equation of this parabola?

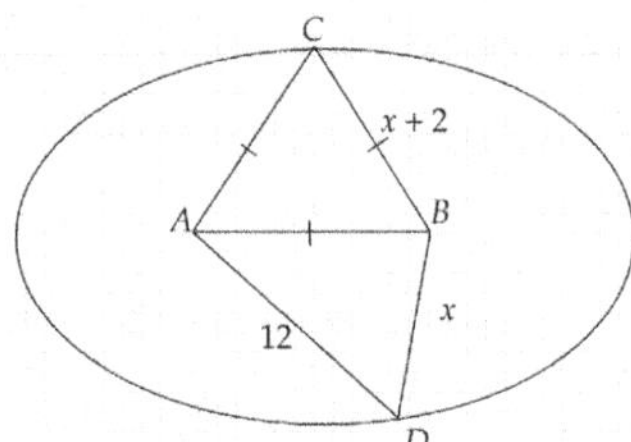

We must use the fact that the sum of the distances from any point to the foci are constant. Therefore, $AD + BD = AC + BC$.

$12 + x = 2(x + 2)$ In terms of x

$x = 8$ Solving the linear equation

Since the equilateral triangle ABC has side length 10, the height from C to AB is $5\sqrt{3}$. So point C would be at $(0, 5\sqrt{3})$ since it is a covertex of the ellipse. The foci would also therefore, be 5 left and right of the center (origin) at $(5,0)$ and $(-5,0)$. This parabola that has vertex at C and goes through $(5,0)$ and $(-5,0)$ can be modeled by $y = ax^2 + 5\sqrt{3}$. Plug in $(5,0)$ to get $a = \frac{-\sqrt{3}}{5}$.

$$y = \frac{-\sqrt{3}}{5}x^2 + 5\sqrt{3}$$

Ex: 4 What is the radius of a circle with center $(1,3)$ that is inscribed within the parabola $y = x^2 - 2x - 1$?

The equation of the circle can be represented by $(x-1)^2 + (y-3)^2 = r^2$. If you complete the square for the parabola, we get $y = x^2 - 2x + 1 - 2$ or $y + 2 = (x-1)^2$. Plug in $(x-1)^2$ for $y + 2$ into the circle's equation to get $y + 2 + (y-3)^2 = r^2$.

Expand to get,

$y + 2 + y^2 - 6y + 9 = r^2$. Combine like terms to get, $y^2 - 5y + 11 - r^2 = 0$. Think about it geometrically. In order for a circle to be inscribed within a parabola, it only makes sense for the points of intersection to be at the same y value. Therefore, use the discriminant on this equation since there's only one y value.

$5^2 - 4(1)(11 - r^2) = 0$

$25 - 44 + 4r^2 = 0$

$r^2 = \frac{19}{4}$

$$r = \frac{\sqrt{19}}{2}$$

Ex: 5 A hyperbola has equation $4x^2 - 32x - y^2 - 2y = 133$. An ellipse can be drawn by a string of length $8\sqrt{3}$ whose ends are at $(1, 1 \pm 2\sqrt{11})$. The hyperbola's asymptote with positive slope intersects the ellipse at what point(s)?

Let's first complete the square for the hyperbola to find its asymptote.

$4(x^2 - 8x) - (y^2 + 2y) = 133$

$4(x^2 - 8x + 16) - (y^2 + 2y + 1) = 133 + 64 - 1$

$4(x-4)^2 - (y+1)^2 = 196$

$\frac{(x-4)^2}{49} - \frac{(y+1)^2}{196} = 1$

Therefore, the asymptote would be $y + 1 = \frac{14}{7}(x - 4)$ since the slope is positive. Simplifying, we get $y = 2x - 9$. Now for the ellipse, because the distance from the two foci is constant (length of the string) $2a = 8\sqrt{3}$ and so $a = 4\sqrt{3}$. The two points where the ends of the string are fixed are the foci, which are clearly $c = 2\sqrt{11}$ from the center at $(1,1)$. Using $a^2 = b^2 + c^2$, we get that $b^2 = 4$. Therefore, the equation of the ellipse is: $\frac{(x-1)^2}{4} + \frac{(y-1)^2}{48} = 1$. Now solve this system to find the intersection by substituting $y = 2x - 9$.

$\frac{(x-1)^2}{4} + \frac{(2x-10)^2}{48} = 1$

$12(x-1)^2 + (2x-10)^2 = 48$

$12(x^2 - 2x + 1) + 4x^2 - 40x + 100 - 48 = 0$

$16x^2 - 64x + 64 = 0$

$x^2 - 4x + 4 = 0$

$(x-2)^2 = 0$ so $x = 2$

Solving for y we get $y = 2(2) - 9 = -5$.

Point of Intersection $(2, -5)$

Ex: 6 In the figure, a kite is tangent to an ellipse at three points. Two of those points are directly above the foci of the ellipse. A circle, whose center is a foci of the ellipse, is inscribed within the kite. The circle also intersects the center of the ellipse at a point. If the distance between F_1 and F_2 is 6. Find the equation of the ellipse and the circle.

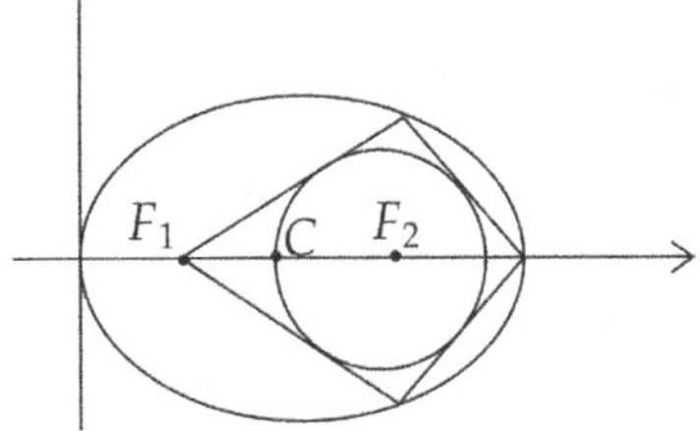

Because the distances between the two foci is 6, the distance from one foci to the center is $c = 3$. The radius of the circle would also be 3. Because the circle is inscribed within the kite, we can draw a line to form a right triangle.

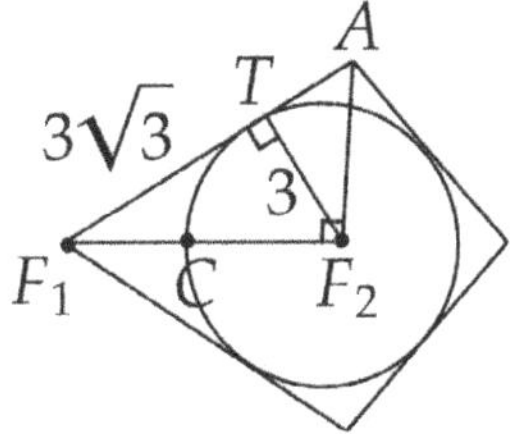

Looking at the triangle side lengths, we see that F_1F_2T is a $30-60-90$ triangle. Because Angle TF_1F_2 is 30°, we can find that $AF_1 = 4\sqrt{3}$ and that $AF_2 = 2\sqrt{3}$. Remembering that the sum of the distances from any point to the foci must be constant, we know that the "string" length is $AF_1 + AF_2 = 6\sqrt{3}$ so $a = 3\sqrt{3}$. Therefore, the center of the ellipse is $(3\sqrt{3}, 0)$. Because $a^2 = b^2 + c^2$ in an ellipse, we plug in a and c to find that $b^2 = 18$. Therefore, the equation of the ellipse is $\frac{(x-3\sqrt{3})^2}{27} + \frac{y^2}{18} = 1$

The circle's radius is 3 and its center is 3 units right of $(3\sqrt{3}, 0)$. Therefore, the equation is:

> Circle: $(x - 3\sqrt{3} - 3)^2 + y^2 = 9$
> Ellipse: $\frac{(x-3\sqrt{3})^2}{27} + \frac{y^2}{18} = 1$

Ex: 7 The directrix of a rotated parabola with vertex $(2,0)$ and foci $(4,2)$ is tangent to a circle with center at $(-5, 1)$. What is the circle's equation and the point of tangency?

Remember that the vertex is equidistant between the foci and the directrix. Therefore, half way between where the axis of symmetry intersects the directrix and the foci is the vertex. This point would be $(0,-2)$ since $(\frac{4+0}{2}, \frac{2-2}{2}) = (2,0)$. Because the axis of symmetry has slope $\frac{2-0}{4-2} = 1$, the directrix has slope -1.

Since it goes through $(0,-2)$, the directrix is $y = -x - 2$.

$(x+5)^2 + (y-1)^2 = r^2$ Setting up circle's equation

$(x+5)^2 + (-x-3)^2 = r^2$ Plugging in $y = -x - 2$ since the line intersects the circle

$x^2 + 10x + 25 + x^2 + 6x + 9 = r^2$ Expanding

$2x^2 + 16x + 34 - r^2 = 0$ Combining like terms

Because the circle is tangent to this directrix, there is only one valid x value.

$16^2 - 4(2)(34 - r^2) = 0$ Discriminant

$256 - 272 + 8r^2 = 0$ Expanding

$r^2 = 2$ Solving

To find point of tangency, simply solve

$2x^2 + 16x + 34 - 2 = 0$ Plugging in $r^2 = 2$

$x^2 + 8x + 16 = 0$ Simplifying

$(x+4)^2 = 0$ Factoring

$x = -4$ Solving for x

$y = -(-4) - 2 = 2$ Substituting x into $y = -x - 2$

> Circle's Equation: $(x+5)^2 + (y-1)^2 = 2$
> Point of Tangency: $(-4, 2)$

Ex: 8 A line with slope $-\frac{1}{2}$ is tangent both to a circle with center $(\frac{1}{2}, 2)$ and to an ellipse with equation $\frac{(x-3)^2}{12} + \frac{(y+1)^2}{6} = 1$ at two different points. The circle and the ellipse are also tangent to each other. What is the point of tangency between the circle and the ellipse?

Let the line be $y = -\frac{1}{2}x + b$. We can plug this into the equation of the ellipse.

$\frac{(x-3)^2}{12} + \frac{(-\frac{1}{2}x+b+1)^2}{6} = 1$ Substituting in $y = -\frac{1}{2}x + b$.

$(x-3)^2 + 2(-\frac{1}{2}x + b + 1)^2 = 12$ Multiplying by 12

$2b^2 + 4b + \frac{3x^2-4bx-16x}{2} + 11 = 12$ Expanding

$4b^2 + 8b + 3x^2 - 4bx - 16x = 2$ Multiplying 4

$3x^2 + x(-4b - 16) + 4b^2 + 8b - 2 = 0$ Simplifying

There must only be one valid x value so we use the discriminant.

$(-4b-16)^2 - 4(3)(4b^2 + 8b - 2) = 0$ Discriminant

$-8b^2 + 8b + 70 = 0$ Combining like terms

$(2b-7)(2b+5) = 0$ Factoring

$b = \frac{7}{2}, b = -\frac{5}{2}$

$y = -\frac{1}{2}x + \frac{7}{2}, y = -\frac{1}{2}x - \frac{5}{2}$

Now which line is the valid one? If you draw a sketch, you see that $y =-\frac{1}{2}x+\frac{7}{2}$ must be the line because $(\frac{1}{2},2)$ is in the "top left" section of the ellipse while $y =-\frac{1}{2}x-\frac{5}{2}$ passes beneath the "bottom left" part of the ellipse. The circle with center $(\frac{1}{2},2)$ would intersect the ellipse at 2 points instead of one if the line was $y =-\frac{1}{2}x-\frac{5}{2}$.

The circle's equation is $(x-\frac{1}{2})^2+(y-2)^2=r^2$

$(x-\frac{1}{2})^2+(-\frac{1}{2}x+\frac{3}{2})^2=r^2$ Substituting for y

$x^2-x+\frac{1}{4}+\frac{1}{4}x^2-\frac{3}{2}x+\frac{9}{4}=r^2$ Expanding

$5x^2-10x+10-4r^2=0$ Combining like terms

$100-4(5)(10-4r^2)=0$ Using discriminant

$r^2=\frac{5}{4}$ Solving for r^2

Circle's Equation: $(x-\frac{1}{2})^2+(y-2)^2=\frac{5}{4}$

$x^2-x+y^2-4y+3=0$ Expanded form

Ellipse's Equation Equation: $\frac{(x-3)^2}{12}+\frac{(y+1)^2}{6}=1$

$x^2-6x+2y^2+4y-1=0$ Expanded form

Let's subtract one equation from the other to cancel out x^2 term.

$y^2-5x+8y-4=0$ Subtracting the equations

$(y+4)^2=5x+20$ Completing the square

$y=-4\pm\sqrt{5x+20}$ Solving for y

If you subtract two times the circle's equation from the ellipse's, we can cancel out the y^2 term.

$x^2+4x-12y+7=0$ Subtracting the equations

$x=-2\pm\sqrt{12y-3}$ Completing the square

$x+2=\pm\sqrt{12(-4\pm\sqrt{5x+20})-3}$ Substituting

$x^2+4x+4=-51\pm12\sqrt{5x+20}$ Squaring

$x^2+4x+55=\pm12\sqrt{5x+20}$ Simplifying

$x^4+8x^3+126x^2-280x+145=0$ Squaring both sides and simplifying a lot.

$(x-1)^2(x^2+10x+145)=0$ Factoring

$x=1$ since $x^2+10x+145$ has no real solutions

$1=-2\pm\sqrt{12y-3}$ Plugging $x=1$

$9=12y-3$ Squaring both sides

$y=1$

$(1,1)$

The key here is to remember that tangency implies using the discriminant.

Ex: 9 The focus of a parabola is a vertex of an ellipse, whose equation is $\frac{x^2}{9/14}+\frac{y^2}{a^2}=1$ where $a>b>0$. The major axis of the ellipse coincides with the directrix of the parabola. If the distance of the points of intersection between the parabola and ellipse is $\frac{4}{3}$, find the equation of the ellipse and the point of intersection.

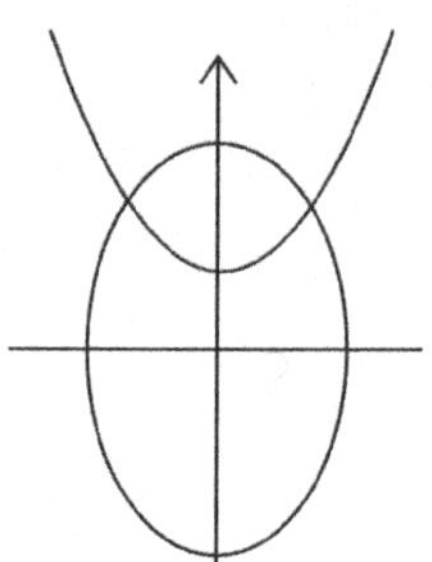

Remember that the vertex of a parabola is halfway between the foci and the directrix. The total distance from directrix to the ellipse's vertex is a (half the ellipse's major axis). Therefore, the distance from the parabola's vertex to foci is $\frac{a}{2}$.

The parabola's vertex would be at $(0,\frac{a}{2})$.

$y=\frac{1}{2a}x^2+\frac{a}{2}$ Setting up parabola's equation

When we solve for the point of intersection between this parabola and the ellipse, we'll get two x values that are opposites of each other, by symmetry. Since the distance between the points is $\frac{4}{3}$, the x coordinates must be $\pm\frac{2}{3}$.

$y=\frac{1}{2a}(\frac{4}{9})+\frac{a}{2}=\frac{4+9a^2}{18a}$ Finding y coordinate.

For the ellipse, if you plug in $x=\pm\frac{2}{3}$ we get:

$\frac{4/9}{9/14}+\frac{y^2}{a^2}=1$ Substituting

$\frac{y^2}{a^2}=\frac{25}{81}$ Subtracting

$y=\frac{5a}{9}$ $\frac{y^2}{a^2}$ is always positive

$\frac{4+9a^2}{18a}=\frac{5a}{9}$ Equating the two y equations

$90a^2=81a^2+36$ Cross multiplying

$a^2=4$ Solving for a

Therefore, $a=2$ (must be positive)

$y=\frac{4+9(4)}{18(2)}=\frac{10}{9}$ Solving for y coordinate

Ellipse's Equation: $\frac{x^2}{9/14}+\frac{y^2}{4}=1$ Points of Intersection: $(\pm\frac{2}{3},\frac{10}{9})$

Conics Test 1

#1: (15 points) Find the center, vertices, co-vertices, foci, eccentricity, etc. of $9y^2 - x^2 + 2x + 54y + 62 = 0$.

#2: (15 points) Given the parabola $y^2 + 6y + 8x + 25 = 0$. Find the line that is tangent to the parabola at $(-20, 9)$.

#3: (25 points) Let the equation of the line that has a negative slope and is tangent to $(x+3)^2 + (y-4)^2 = 13$ at one of its y-intercepts be Line A. Let the equation of the line that has a positive slope and is tangent to one of its y-intercepts be Line B. What is the point of intersection of Line A and B?

#4: (20 points) A circle, centered at the origin, is inscribed within the parabola with equation $y = x^2 - 100$. What is the area of the circle?

#5: (25 points) Use a rotation of axes to eliminate the xy term in $8x^2 - 12xy + 17y^2 = 20$. Then find applicable characteristics in xy form.

Conics Test 2

#1: (15 points) Find the center, vertices, co-vertices, foci, eccentricity, etc of $7x^2 - 42x + 25y^2 + 50y - 87 = 0$.

#2: (20 points) The parabolic door is 70 in. wide at the bottom of the door and 110 in. high. a) If you are 72 inches tall, how far must you stand from the edge of the door so that your head does not hit the top of the door? b) If you try to pass a 30 inch wide statue through, at most how tall can the statue be?

#3: (25 points) An isosceles trapezoid is drawn within an ellipse that is centered at origin such that two of the vertices lie on the ellipse's foci. The area of the trapezoid is $\frac{192}{25}$. If the ellipse has minor axis length of $2\sqrt{6}$, find the equation of the ellipse. <u>**15**</u>

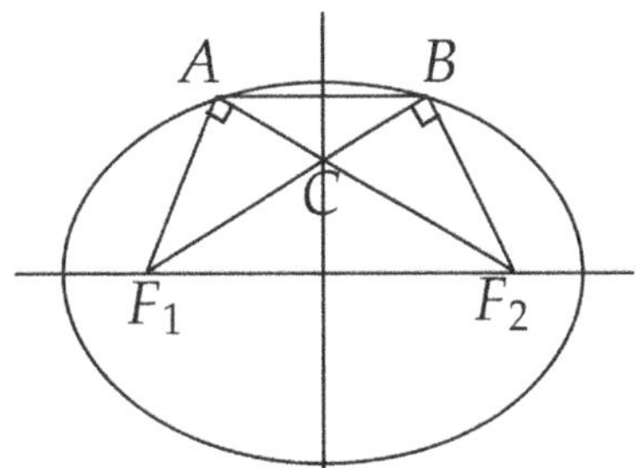

#4: (20 points) The center of $x^2 + y^2 - 4x + 8y - 29 = 0$ is 17 units away from the center a circle with radius 5 that goes through $(-9, 7)$. What are the possible equations of this circle?

#5: (20 points) Use rotation of axes to eliminate the xy term in $11x^2 + 10\sqrt{3}xy + y^2 - 64 = 0$.

Conics Test 3

#1: (15 points) Find the center, vertices, co-vertices, foci, eccentricity, etc. of $36x^2 + 9y^2 + 48x - 36y + 43 = 0$.

#2: (15 points) For the parabola $x^2 + 2x + 8y + 9 = 0$, find the equation of the line that is tangent to this parabola at $(3, -3)$.

#3: (25 points) Find the equations of the possible circles with radius 5 that are tangent to the line $y = 2x + 4$ at $(2, 8)$.

#4: (20 points) Let there be an oblique ellipse with eccentricity 0.8, minor axis (which is vertical) length of 12, one focus at $(-8,3)$. It is also tangent to the line $x = 6$. Find the equation of this ellipse.

#5: (25 points) Use a rotation of axes to eliminate the xy term in $7x^2 + 6\sqrt{3}xy + y^2 - 20 = 0$. Then find the equation of the smallest circle inscribed between the two branches of the hyperbola. **22**

Conics Test 4

#1: (15 points) Find the center, vertices, co-vertices, foci, eccentricity, etc. of $4x^2+32x-36y^2+288y-521=0$.

#2: (20 points) Find the equation of the parabola whose vertex is the point $(2,3)$ and whose focus is $(5,6)$.

#3: (25 points) In the ellipse $\frac{x^2}{9}+\frac{y^2}{b^2}=1$, where $b<3$, the line $y=\frac{b}{2}$ intersects the ellipse at two points X and Y. Let F be one of the foci. If XFY is a right angle, find the points of intersection between this ellipse and $x^2+y^2=4$. **38**

#4: (20 points) The line tangent to the circle $(x+2)^2+(y-4)^2=2$ at the point $(-1,5)$ intersects $(x-4)^2+(y+1)^2=9$ at two points. What is the distance between these two points?

#5: (20 points) Use a rotation of axes to eliminate the xy term in $6x^2+4xy+3y^2-20=0$.

Conics Test 5

#1: (15 points) Find the center, vertices, co-vertices, foci, eccentricity, etc. of $2x^2 - 12x - 17y^2 - 102y - 169 = 0$.

#2: (20 points) An ellipse with eccentricity $\frac{\sqrt{57}}{11}$ and co-vertices $(10,9)$ and $(10,-7)$ has foci at point A and B. Within the ellipse lies a smaller ellipse that intersects A and B, has center $(10,0)$, and horizontal major axis length $2\sqrt{114}$. What is the equation of the second ellipse?

#3: (20 points) Given a parabola with focus $(3,2)$ and directrix $y=0$. Let A be the y intercept, B be a point on the parabola and C be the vertex. If angle BAC is a right angle, what are the coordinates of B?

#4: (25 points) Find the equations of all possible circles with radius $\sqrt{5}$ that are tangent to the lines $y = 2x - 4$ and $y = \frac{1}{2}x + \frac{1}{2}$. **1**

#5: (20 points) Use a rotation of axes to eliminate the xy term in $17x^2 + 48xy + 3y^2 - 24 = 0$.

Conics Test 6

#1: (15 points) Find the center, vertices, co-vertices, foci, eccentricity, etc. of $25x^2 - 250x - 9y^2 - 126y - 41 = 0$.

#2: (20 points) A circle has 2 endpoints of a diameter with coordinates $(-2,4)$ and $(-8,12)$. The line tangent to the circle at $(-9,11)$ will intersect the line tangent to the circle at $(-2,12)$ at what point?

#3: (20 points) Points A and B are on the parabola $y = 4x^2 + 2x - 3$ with their midpoint being $(2,18)$. What are points A and B? **12**

#4: (25 points) Given a hyperbola with equation $16x^2 + 96x - 25y^2 - 100y - 356 = 0$. What is the area of the triangle enclosed by the two asymptotes of this hyperbola and the directrix of the parabola $5x^2 + 30x + 28y - 39 = 0$?

#5: (20 points) Use a rotation of axes to eliminate the xy term in $9x^2 + 8xy + 3y^2 - 24 = 0$.

Conics Test 7

#1: (15 points) Find the center, vertices, co-vertices, foci, eccentricity, etc. of $6x^2 - 60x + 36y^2 + 216y + 258 = 0$.

#2: (20 points) A circle has its center on the line with equation $y = -2x + 1$. It passes through $(5, -3)$ and has a radius of $2\sqrt{2}$. If you extend the diameter that passes through $(5, -3)$ to form a line, the line is the directrix of a parabola that has a vertex of $(-2, -6)$. What is the general form of this rotated parabola?

#3: (20 points) Suppose the line whose equation $x + y = r$ is tangent to the circle $x^2 + y^2 = r$. If r is the eccentricity of a hyperbola that happens to intersect the circle $x^2 + y^2 = 3r$ at exactly two points which both have y-coordinate -1 and has conjugate axis of length $2\sqrt{6}$, what is the equation of this hyperbola? **50**

#4: (25 points) The lactus rectum BC (a line parallel to the minor axis that passes through a foci) of an ellipse is drawn below. If triangle ABC is equilateral, find the eccentricity of the ellipse. **45**

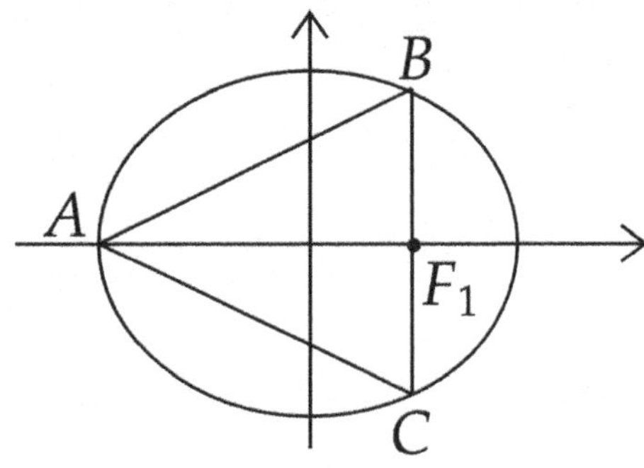

#5: (20 points) Use a rotation of axes to eliminate the xy term in $37x^2 + 32xy + 13y^2 - 225 = 0$.

Chapter 12 Parametric/Polar Equations

Parametric Equations

Ex: 1 Eliminate the parameter for
$x = 2t + 1,\ y = t^2 - t$

We want to express t in terms of x and y.

$x = 2t + 1$ First equation

$x - 1 = 2t$ Isolating

$t = \frac{x-1}{2}$

$y = t^2 - t$ Second equation

$y + \frac{1}{4} = t^2 - t + \frac{1}{4}$ Completing the square

$y + \frac{1}{4} = (t - \frac{1}{2})^2$ Factoring

$t = \frac{1}{2} \pm \sqrt{y + \frac{1}{4}}$ Isolating

Equating the two equations for t together

$\frac{x-1}{2} = \frac{1}{2} \pm \sqrt{y + \frac{1}{4}}$

Subtracting $\frac{1}{2}$ we get: $\frac{x-2}{2} = \pm \sqrt{y + \frac{1}{4}}$

$\frac{(x-2)^2}{4} = y + \frac{1}{4}$ Squaring both sides

$y = \frac{1}{4}(x - 2)^2 - \frac{1}{4}$ Simplifying

In this case we don't have to modify the domain and range since nothing is changed.

Ex: 2 Eliminate the parameter for $x = 4\cos\theta$, $y = -3\sin\theta$. Does the domain/range need to be restricted?

We can use the trig identity $\cos^2\theta + \sin^2\theta = 1$ to eliminate the parameter (theta).

$\cos\theta = \frac{x}{4}$ and $\sin\theta = \frac{y}{-3}$ Rewriting our equations

$(\frac{x}{4})^2 + (\frac{y}{-3})^2 = 1$ Substituting into identity

$\frac{x^2}{16} + \frac{y^2}{9} = 1$ Expanding

Because both sin and cos range from -1 to 1, x ranges from -4 to 4 while y ranges from -3 to 3. This fits exactly with the constraints of an ellipse since the vertices are at $(\pm 4, 0)$ and co vertices are at $(0, \pm 3)$.

$\frac{x^2}{16} + \frac{y^2}{9} = 1$

Ex: 3 Eliminate the parameter for $x = 2 + 3\cos 2\theta$ and $y = \sin\theta - 1$. Does the domain/range need to be restricted?

$\cos 2\theta = \frac{x-2}{3}$ Solving for $\cos 2\theta$

$\sin\theta = y + 1$ Solving for $\sin\theta$

Remember that from the $\cos 2\theta$ identity,
$\cos 2\theta = 1 - 2\sin^2\theta$

We can rearrange this into $\cos 2\theta + 2\sin^2\theta = 1$.

$\frac{x-2}{3} + 2(y + 1)^2 = 1$ Substituting $\cos 2\theta$ and $\sin\theta$

$x - 2 + 6(y + 1)^2 = 3$ Multiplying by 3

$x = -6(y + 1)^2 + 5$ Expressing in vertex form

From this equation it may seem like the maximum x value is 5 and there is no restriction on y. Given our parametric equation, the maximum of x occurs when $\cos 2\theta = 1$ and the minimum when $\cos 2\theta = -1$. Therefore, x ranges from -1 to 5. Similarly, y ranges from -2 to 0.

$x = -6(y + 1)^2 - 5$, Domain: $-1 \le x \le 5$, Range: $-2 \le y \le 0$

Ex: 4 If a projectile is fired with an initial speed of v_0 ft/s above the horizontal, then its position after t seconds is given by the parametric equations $x = (v_0\cos\theta)t$ and $y = (v_0\sin\theta)t - 16t^2$, where x and y are measured in feet. Suppose a man shoots an arrow with initial speed 50 ft/s at an angle of 35° above the horizontal.

a) How long is the arrow in flight?

The arrow lands on the ground at $y = 0$ so we need to solve $y = 0 = (50\sin 35^\circ)t - 16t^2$.

$0 = 28.6788t - 16t^2$ Simplifying

$0 = -16t(t - 1.7924)$ Factoring

The arrow flies $t \approx 1.7924$ seconds

b) What is the total horizontal distance traveled by the ball before it lands?

Plug in the value of time into the x parametric equation: $x = 50\cos 35^\circ(1.792426)$

$x \approx 73.41347$ feet

c) What is the maximum height attained by the ball?

The maximum height occurs at the halfway point between the two zeroes because the vertex is where the axis of symmetry is at. $\frac{0+1.7924}{2} = 0.896$ Therefore, the maximum occurs at $t = 0.896$. Plugging this into the y parametric equation:

$$50 \sin 35^\circ \cdot 0.896 - 16(0.896)^2 \approx 12.8512 \text{ ft}$$

Ex: 5 Particle A's motion in the coordinate plane can be modelled parametrically by $x_1(t) = 2t + 3, y_1(t) = t - 1$. Particle B's motion in the coordinate plane can be modelled parametrically by $x_2(t) = 9 - 2t, y_2(t) = 10 - 3t$. At what time t, is the distance between two particle's minimized? What is this minimum distance?
Using the distance formula, the distance between the two particles at a given time would be:

$D = \sqrt{(x_1 - x_2)^2 + (y_1 - y_2)^2}$

$D = \sqrt{(4t - 6)^2 + (4t - 11)^2}$ Simplifying

$D = \sqrt{16t^2 - 48t + 36 + 16t^2 - 88t + 121}$ Expanding

$D = \sqrt{32t^2 - 136t + 157}$ Combining like terms

$D = \sqrt{32(t^2 - \frac{17}{4}t + \frac{289}{64}) - 32(\frac{289}{64}) + 157}$ Completing the square

$D = \sqrt{32(t - \frac{17}{8})^2 + \frac{25}{2}}$ Simplifying

The maximum distance would be $\sqrt{\frac{25}{2}} = \frac{5\sqrt{2}}{2}$ which is achieved at $t = \frac{17}{8}$.

$$t = \frac{17}{8}, \frac{5\sqrt{2}}{2} \text{ units}$$

Polar Coordinates

Ex: 1 Convert $(2, \frac{5\pi}{6})$ into rectangular form. Then, find the three additional polar representations of $(2, \frac{5\pi}{6})$, using $-2\pi < \theta < 2\pi$.
By the definition of polar coordinates, $x = 2\cos\frac{5\pi}{6}$ and $y = 2\sin\frac{5\pi}{6}$. This gets us $(-\sqrt{3}, 1)$. Now polar coordinates, similar to the unit circle, repeats itself every 2π. So you can subtract 2π to get a coordinate. That gets $(2, \frac{-7\pi}{6})$. Whenever we add or subtract by π we've gone half way in the circle, so negating the r value would also get the same value. So we also write $(-2, -\frac{7\pi}{6} + \pi) = (-2, \frac{-\pi}{6})$.

Similar to above, we can add 2π to get another point: $(-2, \frac{11\pi}{6})$.

Rectangular form: $(-\sqrt{3}, 1)$ Polar form: $(2, \frac{-7\pi}{6})$ $(-2, \frac{-\pi}{6})$ $(-2, \frac{11\pi}{6})$

Ex: 2 Find the area of the region enclosed by the graph of the polar curve $r = \frac{12}{3\sin\theta + 4\cos\theta}$ and the axes.
Let's first convert this to rectangular form:
$r(3\sin\theta + 4\cos\theta) = 12$
Since $r\sin\theta = y$ and $r\cos\theta = x$:
$3y + 4x = 12$. Now let's see where this line intersects the axes. It's y intercept is at $(0, 4)$ while the x intercept is at $(3, 0)$. This line creates a right triangle with the axes.

$$A = \frac{1}{2}(3)(4) = 6 \text{ units squared}$$

Ex: 3 Convert $r = \sin(2\theta)$ into rectangular form.
$r = 2\sin\theta\cos\theta$ Using trig identities
$r^3 = 2 \cdot r\sin\theta \cdot r\cos\theta$ Multiply by r^2 on both sides
$r^3 = 2xy$ Substituting in x and y
$r^6 = 4x^2y^2$ Squaring both sides

$(x^2 + y^2)^3 = 4x^2y^2$ Substituting in $x^2 + y^2 = r^2$

Ex: 4 Find the point(s) of intersection in polar form between the graphs of $r = \frac{6}{3\cos\theta - 2\sin\theta}$ and $r = \frac{6}{2 - \cos\theta}$.
Let's equate the two r values together.
$\frac{6}{2-\cos\theta} = \frac{6}{3\cos\theta - 2\sin\theta}$. Setting up an equation
$2 - \cos\theta = 3\cos\theta - 2\sin\theta$ Simplifying
$2\cos\theta = 1 + \sin\theta$ Combining like terms
From the pythagorean identity, $\sin^2\theta + \cos^2\theta = 1$, therefore, $\cos\theta = \sqrt{1 - \sin^2\theta}$.
$2\sqrt{1 - \sin^2\theta} = 1 + \sin\theta$ Using pythagorean identity
$4(1 - \sin^2\theta) = \sin^2\theta - 2\sin\theta + 1$ Squaring
$0 = 5\sin^2\theta + 2\sin\theta - 3$ Combining like terms
$0 = (5\sin\theta - 3)(\sin\theta + 1)$ Factoring
$\sin\theta = \frac{3}{5}, \sin\theta = -1$ Solving for $\sin\theta$
$\cos\theta = \frac{4}{5}, \cos\theta = 0$ Solving for respective $\cos\theta$
$\theta \approx 36.87^\circ$ and $\theta = -90^\circ$

Now we plug these values back into any of our original equations to find r.
$r = \frac{6}{2-\frac{4}{5}} = 5$ and $r = \frac{6}{2-0} = 3$.
$(5, 36.87^\circ)$ and $(3, -90^\circ)$

$(5, 36.87^\circ)$ and $(3, -90^\circ)$

Graphing Polar Equations

Ex: 1 For $r = 1 - 2\sin\theta$:

a) Test for symmetry.

For symmetry with respect to the line $\theta = \frac{\pi}{2}$ we can replace θ with $\pi - \theta$.
$r = 1 - 2\sin(\pi - \theta)$ Testing for symmetry
$r = 1 - 2(\sin\pi\cos\theta - \sin\theta\cos\pi)$ Angle Difference
$r = 1 - 2(0 \cdot \cos\theta - \sin\theta(-1))$ Evaluating
$r = 1 - 2\sin\theta$ Simplifying
Since the equation is the same, we can conclude this graph is symmetrical to $\theta = \frac{\pi}{2}$.
For symmetry about the polar axis, replace θ with $-\theta$. Because sin is not an even function, we can immediately tell that this will lead to the same equation. This doesn't mean that the graph isn't symmetrical about the polar axis; it's just inconclusive. Symmetry rules do not have valid converses. Finally for symmetry about the pole, replace r with $-r$. This obviously does not get the same equation so it's inconclusive again.

$\theta = \frac{\pi}{2}$: Yes, Polar Axis and Pole: Inconclusive

b) Find the maximum r values and zeroes as well as the angles to get them.
Maximum occurs when $\sin\theta$ is minimized (-1). This is when $\theta = \frac{3\pi}{2}$ and that causes $r = 3$. Finding the zeros, we solve $0 = 1 - 2\sin\theta$ to get $\theta = \frac{\pi}{6}, \frac{5\pi}{6}$.

Max: $(3, \frac{3\pi}{2})$ Zeros: $(0, \frac{\pi}{6})(0, \frac{5\pi}{6})$

c) Then graph.
Plot some values and use symmetry.

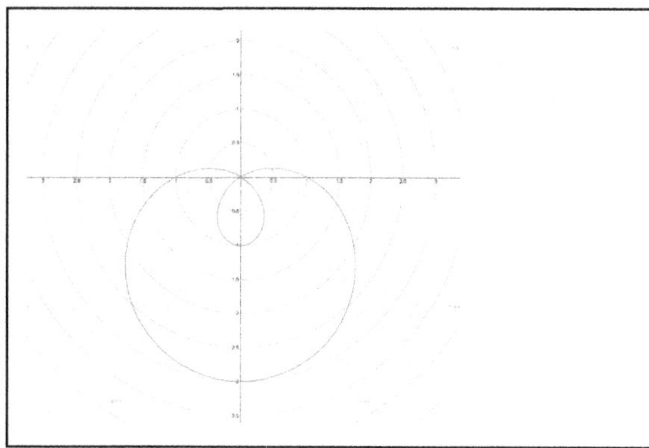

Ex: 2 For $r^2 = 4\cos(2\theta)$

a) Test for symmetry

$\theta = \frac{\pi}{2}$: $r^2 = 4\cos(2(\pi - \theta))$
$r^2 = 4\cos(2\pi - 2\theta)$
$r^2 = 4(\cos 2\pi \cos 2\theta + \sin 2\pi \sin 2\theta)$
$r^2 = 4\cos 2\theta$ Symmetrical
Polar Axis: $r^2 = 4\cos(2(-\theta))$ $r^2 = 4\cos(2\theta)$ cos is an even function, Symmetrical
The Pole: $(-r)^2 = 4\cos(2\theta)$
$r^2 = 4\cos(2\theta)$ Symmetrical

Symmetrical to $\theta = \frac{\pi}{2}$, polar axis, and pole

b) Find the maximum r values and zeros as well as the angles to get them.

The maximum occurs when $\cos(2\theta) = 1$ which is when $\theta = 0$. Find zeros by solving $0 = 4\cos(2\theta)$.
$\theta = \frac{\pi}{4}, \frac{3\pi}{4}, \frac{5\pi}{4}, \frac{7\pi}{4}$

Maximum: $(1, 0)$ Zeros: $(0, \frac{\pi}{4}), (0, \frac{3\pi}{4}), (0, \frac{5\pi}{4}), (0, \frac{7\pi}{4})$

c) Then graph.

Symmetry will greatly help for this one.

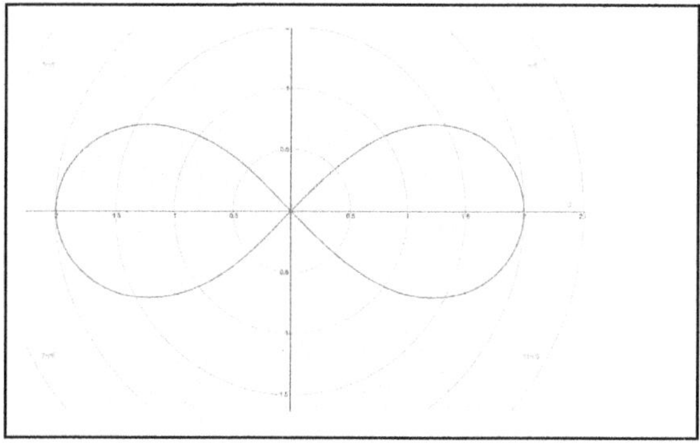

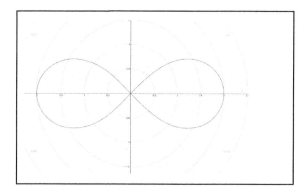

Polar Equations of Conics

Remember that the directrix of a polar conic is always on the side of the vertex closer to the focus.

Ex: 1 Find the polar equation of the parabola with directrix $y = 4$ and focus at the pole.

Looking at where the directrix is, it's a horizontal line above the pole. Therefore, the way we can represent this conic is in the form:

$r = \frac{ep}{1+e \sin \theta}$

We know that a parabola always has eccentricity 1 and that since the directrix is 4 away from the pole, $p = 4$.

$r = \frac{4}{1+4 \sin \theta}$

Ex: 2 Find the polar equation of the ellipse with vertices $(1, \frac{\pi}{2})$ and $(5, \frac{3\pi}{2})$ and focus at the pole. Then find all applicable characteristics in polar coordinates.

The distance between the two vertices is 6 so $a = 3$. The center would be at $(2, \frac{3\pi}{2})$ since $\frac{1-5}{2} = -2$. The distance from center to focus is 2 so $c = 2$. Since $a^2 = b^2 + c^2$, $b = \sqrt{5}$. Now the eccentricity would be $e = \frac{c}{a} = \frac{2}{3}$. Now to find the distance from pole to directrix, we let the distance from the closest vertex to the directrix be m.

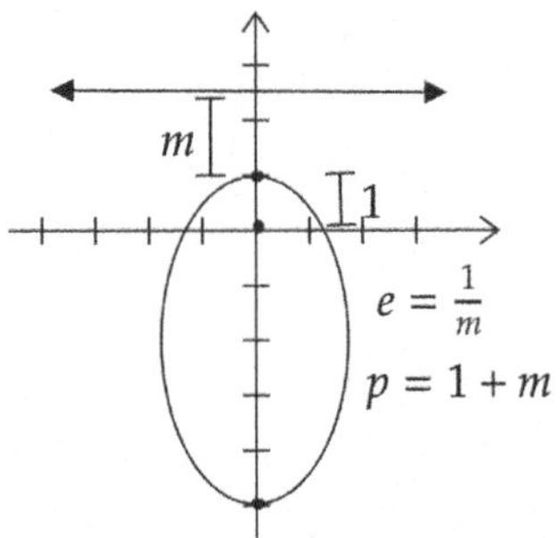

Since the constant ratio of the ellipse from the pole to the directrix is e and we know the distance from foci to the pole is 1 we set up: $\frac{2}{3} = \frac{1}{m}$. Therefore, $m = \frac{3}{2}$ and the distance (p) from pole to directrix would be $y = \frac{5}{2}$. The directrix would then be $r = \frac{5}{2 \sin \theta}$. Since the directrix is a horizontal line above the pole, the equation is $r = \frac{(\frac{2}{3})(\frac{5}{2})}{1-\frac{2}{3} \sin \theta}$. Multiply 3 on both sides to get $r = \frac{5}{3-2 \sin \theta}$. The other foci would be at $(4, \frac{3\pi}{2})$ since the foci is 2 away from the center. Now the co-vertices in rectangular coordinates would be at $(\pm \sqrt{5}, -2)$. Converting to polar form, we would get $(3, -48.189^\circ)$ and $(3, 228.189^\circ)$.

$r = \frac{5}{3-2 \sin \theta}$ Center: $(2, \frac{3\pi}{2})$, Foci: $(4, \frac{3\pi}{2})$, Covertices: $(3, -48.189^\circ)$ and $(3, 228.189^\circ)$ Directrix: $r = \frac{5}{2 \sin \theta}$

Ex: 3 Find the polar equation of the hyperbola with vertices $(-2, \frac{\pi}{2})$ and $(6, \frac{3\pi}{2})$ and focus at the pole. Then find all applicable characteristics in polar coordinates.

The center is at $(4, \frac{3\pi}{2})$. The distance between the two vertices is 4 so $a = 2$. The distance between the center and the pole (focus) is $c = 4$. The other foci would be 4 units below the center at $(8, \frac{3\pi}{2})$. Therefore the eccentricity is $e = \frac{4}{2} = 2$. Let the distance between the directrix and the closest vertex be m. Therefore, $2 = \frac{2}{m}$ since the distance from the pole to this closest vertex is 2. $m = 1$ so the directrix is at $y = -3$ or $r = \frac{-3}{\sin \theta}$. Since the directrix is 3 below from the pole, we get the equation, $r = \frac{2(3)}{1-2 \sin \theta} = \frac{6}{1-2 \sin \theta}$. Since $a = 2, c = 4$, and $a^2 + b^2 = c^2$, we can solve that $b = 2\sqrt{3}$. The co-vertices in rectangular form would be at $(\pm 2\sqrt{3}, -4)$. For the covertices, $r = \sqrt{12 + 16} = 2\sqrt{7}$. Use the rectangular to polar conversion formulas to get $(2\sqrt{7}, -49.1066^\circ)$ and $(2\sqrt{7}, 229.1066^\circ)$. To find the asymptotes, first find them in rectangular form. The "rise" of the asymptotes would be the a value or 2. The "run" would be the b value or $2\sqrt{3}$. Therefore, asymptotes in rectangular form: $y - 4 = \pm \frac{2}{2\sqrt{3}}x$. Converting this to polar form and isolating the r gets $r = \frac{4}{\sin \theta \pm \frac{\sqrt{3}}{3} \cos \theta}$.

$r = \frac{6}{1-2 \sin \theta}$ Center: $(4, \frac{3\pi}{2})$ Foci: $(8, \frac{3\pi}{2})$ Co-vertices: $(2\sqrt{7}, -49.1066^\circ)$ and $(2\sqrt{7}, 229.1066^\circ)$ Asymptotes: $r = \frac{4}{\sin \theta \pm \frac{\sqrt{3}}{3} \cos \theta}$ Directrix: $r = \frac{-3}{\sin \theta}$

Parametric/Polar Equations Test 1

#1: (15 points) Graph the following set of parametric equations by eliminating the parameter. Adjust the domain if necessary.
$x = \sin(\theta)$ $y = 3 - \cos(2\theta)$

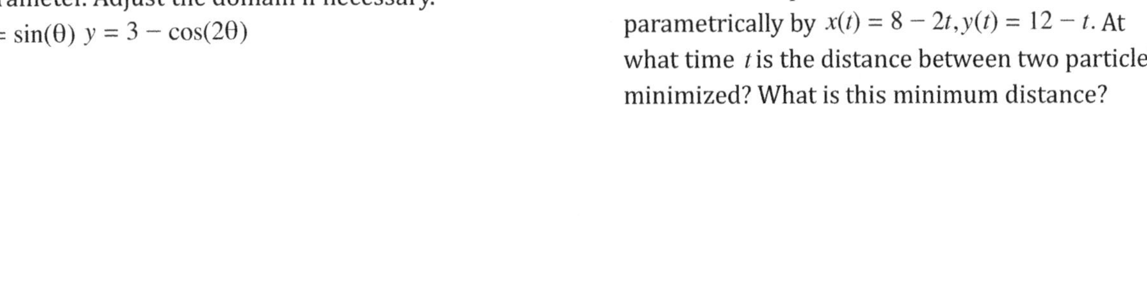

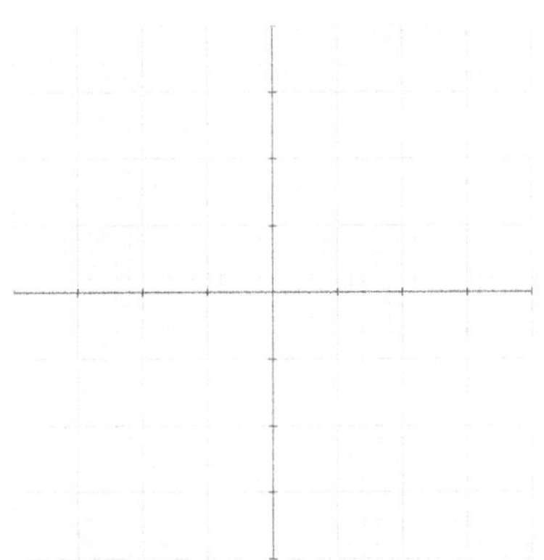

#2: (15 points) Find the distance between $(3, \frac{\pi}{6})$ and $(5, \frac{5\pi}{6})$ and the equation of the line that goes through them in polar form.

#3: (15 points) Particle A's motion in the coordinate plane can be modelled parametrically by $x(t) = t + 1, y(t) = 2t + 1$. Particle B's motion in the coordinate plane can be modelled parametrically by $x(t) = 8 - 2t, y(t) = 12 - t$. At what time t is the distance between two particle's minimized? What is this minimum distance?

#4: (15 points) Write $r^2 = \sin 3\theta$ in rectangular form.

#5: Given the equation $r^2 = 4\sin(2\theta)$:

a) (10 points) Test for symmetry with respect to the line $\theta = \frac{\pi}{2}$ and the pole.

b) (5 points) Find the max r values and zeroes, along with their respective angles.

c) (5 points) Find at least two additional points and graph the equation.

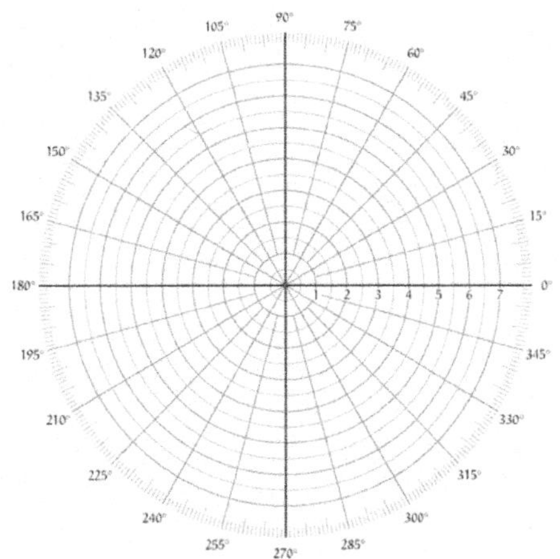

#6: Given the rotated ellipse with vertices at $(1, \frac{\pi}{4})$ and $(3, \frac{5\pi}{4})$, and focus at the pole:

a) (10 points) Find the equation of the ellipse in polar form.

b) (10 points) Find the center, co-vertices, foci, and directrix of the ellipse, all in polar form. Then graph.

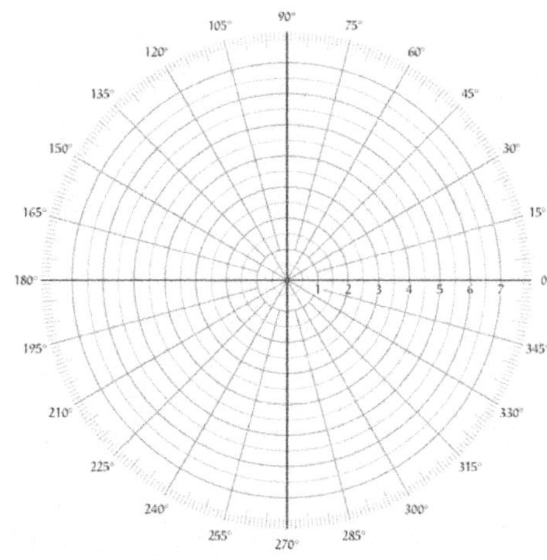

Parametric/Polar Equations Test 2

#1: (15 points) Graph the following set of parametric equations. Then find the rectangular equation by eliminating the parameter. Adjust domain if necessary. $x = t^2 + 2t$
$y = t^2 - t$

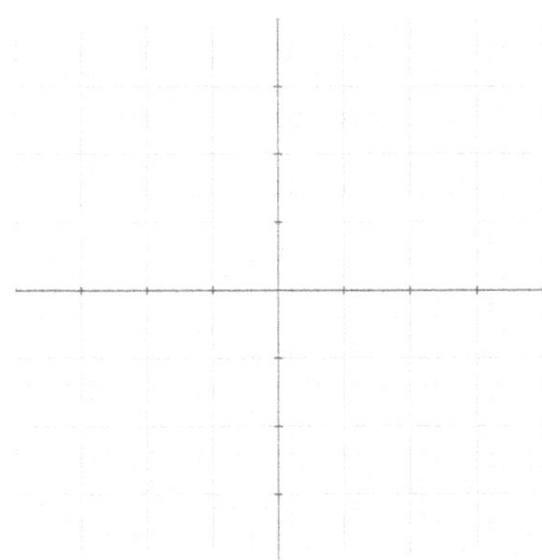

#2: (15 points) Let a particle's motion in space be represented by $x = \sqrt{t} + 2, y = 3\sqrt{t} - 1, z = t + 2$. For what t value is the distance between $(-1, 0, 4)$ and the particle minimized? What is the minimized distance?

#3: (15 points) Max throws a ball at Aaron who is 400 cm away. Max's ball can be modeled by the parametric equations: $x_m = 80t,\ y_m = 100t - 16t^2$ where t is in seconds. Two seconds later, Aaron throws a ball which is modeled by:
$x_a = 400 - 400(t-2),\ y_a = K(t-2) - 16(t-2)^2$.
Find the value of K such that Aaron's ball will intercept Max's ball.

#4: (15 points) Find the equation in polar form that represents the set of all points that is equidistant from the pole and the graph of $r = \frac{4}{4\cos\theta + 4\sin\theta - r}$. **44**

#5: Given the equation $r = 1 + 2\sin(\theta)$:

a) (10 points) Test for symmetry with respect to the line $\theta = \frac{\pi}{2}$ and the pole.

b) (5 points) Find the max r values and zeroes, along with their respective angles.

c) (5 points) Graph the equation.

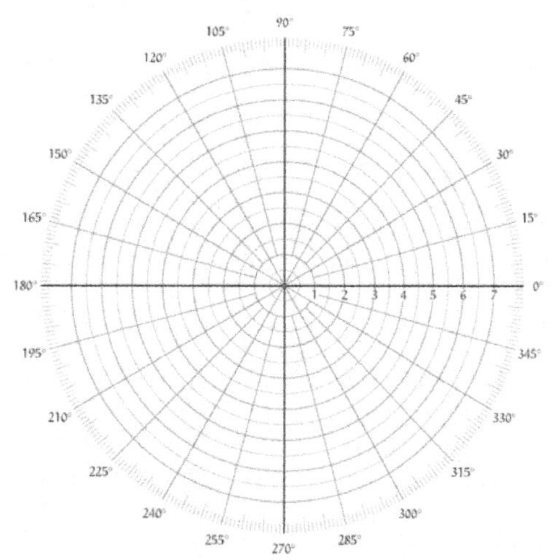

#6: Given the hyperbola with asymptotes $r = \frac{2}{\pm\frac{\sqrt{3}}{3}\cos\theta - \sin\theta}$ and focus at the pole.

a) (10 points) Find the equation of the hyperbola in polar form.

b) (10 points) Find the center, vertices, co-vertices, foci, and directrix of the hyperbola in polar form. Then graph.

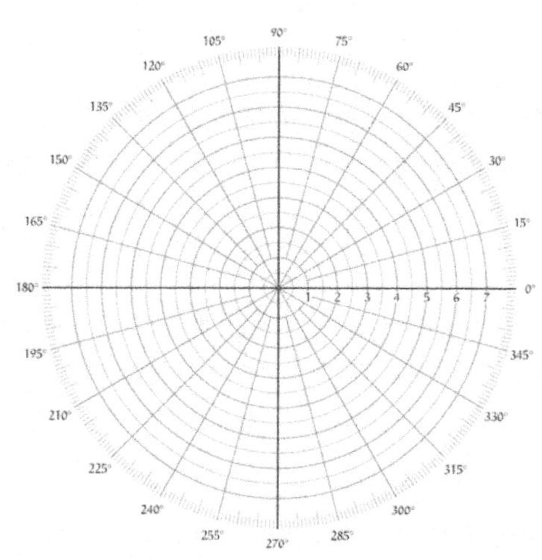

Chapter 13 Vectors and Planes

2D Vectors

Ex: 1 Find the component form and length of the vector V that has initial point of $(-4,3)$ and terminal point of $(5,-9)$.

To get the component form, subtract the initial values from the terminal point values.

$< 5-(-4),-9-3 >=< 9,-12 >$

To find the magnitude, you're finding the "length". The magnitude is $\sqrt{9^2+12^2}$ which is intuitive from the pythagorean theorem.

Component Form: $<9,-12>$ Magnitude: 15

Ex: 2 Two ropes are supporting a load of 150 pounds. If Angle 1 is 30° and Angle 2 is 40°, what is the tension of each rope?

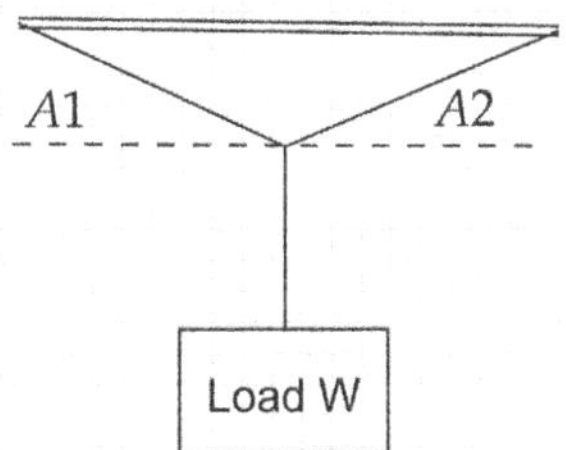

In order for the load to be at rest, the three vectors (two ropes and the load) must equal 0 when added together. Let the point where the three meet be the origin. The load's vector would be $150 < \cos 270^\circ, \sin 270^\circ >$ by the trigonometric definition of a vector. The first rope would be represented by $a < \cos 150^\circ, \sin 150^\circ >$ where a is the tension or "magnitude" of each rope. The second rope would be represented by $b < \cos 40^\circ, \sin 40^\circ >$ where b is the tension.

$150 < \cos 270^\circ, \sin 270^\circ > + a < \cos 150^\circ, \sin 150^\circ > + b < \cos 40^\circ, \sin 40^\circ > = 0$ Adding them together

$< b\cos 40^\circ, b\sin 40^\circ > + < a\cos 150^\circ + a\sin 150^\circ > = < 0, 150 >$

By adding up the respective parts of the vectors:

$b \cdot \cos 40^\circ + a \cdot \cos 150^\circ = 0$

$b \cdot \sin 40^\circ + a \cdot \sin 150^\circ = 150$

This a system of equations that you can solve.

$a = 0.88455b$ by manipulating the first equation

Then substitute this into the second equation:

$(0.6428b) + 0.5(0.88455b) = 150$. Solving we get, $b \approx 138.241\ lbs$. Plug this in to get: $a \approx 122.281\ lbs$.

$122.281,\ 138.241$ pounds

Ex: 3 An boat is sailing $N50^\circ E$ with a speed of 300 km/h. If there is a 20 km/h current with a bearing of $N70^\circ W$, find the direction and speed that the boat is actually moving in.

The vector represented by the boat is $300 < \cos 40^\circ, \sin 40^\circ >$ since the speed is 300 km/h. The vector represented by the wind would be $20 < \cos 160^\circ, \sin 160^\circ >$. Remember from the unit circle that we count angles starting from the positive x axis and moving clockwise. Now let's add these two vectors together:

$300 < \cos 40^\circ, \sin 40^\circ > + 20 < \cos 160^\circ, \sin 160^\circ > =$
$< 229.8133, 192.836 > + < -18.7938, 6.8404 > =$
$< 211.0195, 199.676 >$. The speed would be the magnitude of this vector.

Speed $= \sqrt{(211.0195)^2 + (199.676)^2} \approx 290.516$ kmh

Now, if we factor out this magnitude from our true vector, we can find the magnitude.

$< 211.0195, 199.676 > = 290.516 < 0.72636, 0.6873 >$

Solving $\cos\theta = 0.72626$, we get $\theta \approx 43.426^\circ$. Since are bearing starts from the y axis, the bearing would be $N(90-43.426)^\circ E$

Speed: 290.516 kmh, Bearing: $N46.573^\circ E$

Dot Product

Ex: 1 Find the angle between vector $U < -5,4 >$ and vector $V < 3,9 >$.

By the formula, the angle between two vectors can be found be solving:

$\cos\theta = \frac{U \cdot V}{\|U\| \cdot \|V\|}$

The dot product of these two vectors would be equal to $-5(3) + 9(4) = -15 + 36 = 21$. The magnitude of $U = \sqrt{5^2+4^2} = \sqrt{41}$. The magnitude of $V = \sqrt{3^2+9^2} = 3\sqrt{10}$. Now plugging this into the formula, we get $\cos\theta = \frac{21}{\sqrt{41} \cdot 3\sqrt{10}}$

$\theta \approx 69.775^\circ$

Ex: 2 If the two vectors U $< \frac{1}{4}a, 4b >$ and V $<-18, 2b>$ are orthogonal and vector $< a, b >$ has magnitude $\sqrt{265}$, what is a and b?

If two vectors are orthogonal, their dot product must equal 0 since $\cos 90^{\circ} = 0$. Therefore the dot product of U and V is $-\frac{9}{2}a + 4b(2b) = 0$

Simplify to get $-\frac{9}{2}a + 8b^2 = 0$. Since the magnitude is 265, we know that $a^2 + b^2 = 265$. This means $b^2 = 265 - a^2$. Plugging this in:

$-\frac{9}{2}a + 8(265 - a^2) = 0$

$-\frac{9}{2}a + 2120 - 8a^2 = 0$

$16a^2 + 9a - 4240 = 0$

$(a - 16)(16a + 265) = 0$ So $a = 16, \frac{-265}{16}$.

However, a cannot be negative. This is because that would make $-\frac{9}{2}a$ positive. Since $8b^2$ will always be positive, if a is negative, the dot product will never be 0. Plugging $a = 16$ in to $b^2 = 265 - a^2$, we get $b = \pm 3$.

$a = 3, b = \pm 3$

Ex: 4 Find the projection of $< 1, 2 >$ onto $< 2, 3 >$.

$proj_u v = \frac{<1,2>\cdot<2,3>}{\sqrt{2^2+3^2}} \cdot < 2, 3 >$ By formula

$\frac{8}{\sqrt{13}} < 2, 3 >$ Evaluating Dot Product

$(\frac{16}{\sqrt{13}}, \frac{24}{\sqrt{13}})$

Ex: 5 A force of 30 pounds in the direction of 30° above the horizontal is required to slide a table across a floor. Find the work done if the table is dragged 15 feet.

For work problems, remember $W = F \cdot PQ$. where F is force (magnitude) and PQ is the distance vector.

$F = 30 < \cos 30^{\circ}, \sin 30^{\circ} > = < 15\sqrt{3}, 15 >$

$PQ = < 0, 15 >$ since the table is dragged 15 feet

$W = 0(15\sqrt{3}) + 15(15) = 225$

225 foot pounds

3D Vectors and the Cross Product

Ex: 1 Find the magnitude and the component form for the vector V with initial point at $(-3, 4, 9)$ and terminal point at $(5, 6, -1)$.

To find the component form, simplify subtract the coordinates of the initial point from the terminal point to get: $< 8, 2, -10 >$. It's the same as 2D vectors. For magnitude, it would be the "distance" from origin or $\sqrt{8^2 + 2^2 + 10^2} = 2\sqrt{42}$.

Component Form: $(8, 2, -10)$, Magnitude: $2\sqrt{42}$

Ex: 2 Let vector V be $<-6, 0, 8>$. Let a vector U be $<-4, -8, 10>$. Determine the angle between the two vectors.

We can use the same formula that uses the dot product: $\cos\theta = \frac{U \cdot V}{\|U\| \cdot \|V\|}$

$\cos\theta = \frac{(-6(-4)+0+8(10))}{\sqrt{36+64} \cdot \sqrt{16+64+100}}$

$\cos\theta = \frac{104}{10 \cdot 6\sqrt{5}}$

$\theta \approx 39.1795°$

Ex: 3 Find the vector of magnitude 6 that is orthogonal to both $< 4, 3, 5 >$ and $<-1, 2, 3>$.

To find the vector that is orthogonal to both of these, we must take the cross product.

$< 4, 3, 5 > \times <-1, 2, 3> =$

$$i\begin{vmatrix} 3 & 5 \\ 2 & 3 \end{vmatrix} - j\begin{vmatrix} 4 & 5 \\ -1 & 3 \end{vmatrix} + k\begin{vmatrix} 4 & 3 \\ -1 & 2 \end{vmatrix}$$

$\mathbf{i}(9 - 10) - \mathbf{j}(12 + 5) + \mathbf{k}(8 + 3) =$

$-\mathbf{i} - 17\mathbf{j} + 11\mathbf{k}$

We got a vector that's the same direction as the vector we want. Now just gotta change the magnitude of the vector. First let's find the unit vector of $-\mathbf{i} - 17\mathbf{j} + 11\mathbf{k}$. Then, we multiply by 6 since we want a vector of magnitude 6.

$\frac{<-1,-17,11>}{\sqrt{1^2+17^2+11^2}} \cdot 7 = < \frac{-7}{\sqrt{411}}, \frac{-119}{\sqrt{411}}, \frac{77}{\sqrt{411}} >$

$< \frac{-7}{\sqrt{411}}, \frac{-119}{\sqrt{411}}, \frac{77}{\sqrt{411}} >$

Ex: 4 Find the area of the parallelogram with vectors as adjacent sides $< 1, 3, 2 >$, $< 4, 5, 0 >$.

Take the cross product of the two vectors:

$\mathbf{i}(0-10)-\mathbf{j}(0-8)+\mathbf{k}(5-12)$
$-10\mathbf{i}+8\mathbf{j}-7\mathbf{k}$
To find the area, just find the magnitude of this vector: $\sqrt{10^2+8^2+7^2}$

$\sqrt{213}\approx 14.5945$

Ex: 5 Given the 3 vectors $X<5,-1,1>$, $Y<-2,3,4>$, and $Z<3,4,5>$ that make up the parallelepiped, find the volume. To find the volume of this parallelepiped, find the triple scalar product of the three vectors or basically the "determinant" of the vectors. The triple scalar product is the dot product of one vector and the cross product of the other two.

$$\begin{vmatrix} 5 & -1 & 1 \\ -2 & 3 & 4 \\ 3 & 4 & 5 \end{vmatrix}$$

This determinant is equal to:
$5(15-16)-(-1)(-10-12)+1(-8-9)$
$-5-22-17=-44$
Volume is positive so we take the absolute value. The reason why a negative number pops is that when the vectors are taken in different directions a negative area can show up.

44

Planes, Traces, and Lines

Ex: 1 Find the distance between plane $2x-4y+4z-6=0$ and the point $(0,3,6)$.
First we find the normal vector to this equation. The normal vector represents a perpendicular vector that we can use to find the closest distance. The normal vector is just the coefficients of the variables in the equation so it's:
$<2,-4,4>$. Now let's choose a line in the plane to be our point P. Plugging in $y=0, z=0$, we get the point $P(3,0,0)$. Therefore, the vector from this point to the point $(0,3,6)$ in component form is $<0-3,3-0,6-0>=<-3,3,6>$. Now the distance can be found by finding the dot product between these two vectors and dividing the magnitude of the normal vector.

$D=\frac{<2,-4,4>\cdot<-3,3,6>}{\sqrt{4+16+16}}$ By formula
$D=\frac{-6-12+24}{\sqrt{36}}$ Simplifying

$D=1$

Ex: 2 Find the angle between plane $x+2y-z+1=0$ and plane $x-y+3z+4=0$. The normal vectors for each of the equations can be found by just taking the coefficients of the equations in standard form:
$<1,2,-1>$ and $<1,-1,3>$.
Now we can find the angle between the two vectors by finding the dot product and dividing that by the magnitudes.
$\cos\theta=\frac{1-2-3}{\sqrt{1+4+1}\cdot\sqrt{1+1+9}}$
$\cos\theta=\frac{-4}{\sqrt{66}}$

$\theta\approx 60.5037915°$

Ex: 3 Find the xz trace of $(x-4)^2+(y-2)^2+(z+5)^2=6$ in standard form.
To find the xz trace, the y value must be 0. Therefore, we can just plug in $y=0$:
$(x-4)^2+(0-2)^2+(z+5)^2=6$
$x^2-4x+16+4+z^2+10z+25=6$ Expanding

$x^2-4x+z^2+10z+39=0$

Ex: 4 Find the parametric and symmetric equations for the line through the points $(4,-1,2)$ and $(1,1,5)$.
First let's find the direction vector by finding the vector with initial point $(4,-1,2)$ and terminal point $(1,1,5)$. This direction vector or the "slope" is $<-3,2,3>$. Plugging in the point $(4,-1,2)$ as the "starting" point, we get $x=4-3t$
$y=-1+2t$, $z=2+3t$. Solving for t for each, we get $t=\frac{x-4}{-3}=\frac{y+1}{2}=\frac{z-2}{3}$

Parametric: $x=4-3t$ $y=-1+2t$, $z=2+3t$
Symmetric: $\frac{x-4}{-3}=\frac{y+1}{2}=\frac{z-2}{3}$

Ex: 5 Find the equation of the sphere that has endpoints of a diameter at $(3,-2,2)$ and $(7,0,4)$. The midpoint of the diameter is the center. Therefore the center is at: $(\frac{3+7}{2},\frac{-2+0}{2},\frac{2+4}{2}) = (5,-1,3)$. By the distance formula, radius equals $\sqrt{(5-3)^2+(-1+2)^2+(3-2)^2} = \sqrt{6}$.

$$(x-5)^2+(y+1)^2+(z-3)^2 = 6$$

Ex: 6 Find the equation of the sphere with center $(4,-2,1)$ that is tangent to the plane $8x+4y-z=104$.

We need to find the radius of the sphere in order to find the equation. To do so, we need to find the point of tangency. We know the sphere is tangent to $8x+4y-z=104$, so the line that goes from radius to point of tangency must be perpendicular to this plane. Therefore, the slope vector of this line must be $<8,4,-1>$. Since, it goes through the center, we use these symmetric equations to represent this line: $\frac{x-4}{8} = \frac{y+2}{4} = \frac{z-1}{-1}$.

$\frac{x-4}{8} = \frac{y+2}{4}$ Taking the first two

$4(x-4) = 8(y+2)$ Cross multiplying

$y = \frac{1}{2}x - 4$ Finding y in terms of x

$\frac{x-4}{8} = \frac{z-1}{-1}$ Taking the first and last

$4 - x = 8z - 8$ Cross multiplying

$z = -\frac{1}{8}x + \frac{3}{2}$ Finding z in terms of x

Now we can use substitution into the equation of the plane in order to find the point of tangency.

$8x + 4(\frac{1}{2}x - 4) - (-\frac{1}{8}x + \frac{3}{2}) = 104$

$16x + 4x - 32 + \frac{1}{4}x - 3 = 208$ Multiplying by 2

$x = 12$ Solving for x

$y = \frac{1}{2}(12) - 4 = 2$ Solving for y

$z = -\frac{1}{8}(12) + \frac{3}{2} = 0$ Solving for z

Now let's find the distance from this point to the center to get the radius.

$r = \sqrt{(12-4)^2 + (-2-2)^2 + (1-0)^2}$

$r^2 = 64 + 16 + 1$

$r^2 = 81$

$$(x-4)^2+(y+2)^2+(z-1)^2 = 81$$

Ex: 7 Find the parametric and symmetric equations of the line that passes through the point $(1,2,-1)$ and is parallel to the line of intersection of the planes $2x+y-3z=3$ and $2x-5y+z=6$.

Remember that the line of intersection between two planes is parallel to the cross product of the normal vectors. (Think about how we know that.)

Crossing $<2,1,-3> \times <2,-5,1>$ we get:

$\mathbf{i}<1-15> - \mathbf{j}(2+6) + \mathbf{k}(-10-2)$

Simplifying, we get that the direction vector (since they are parallel) for our line is $<7,4,6>$. Therefore, the parametric equations can be found using $(1,2,-1)$. $x = 1+7t, y = 2+4t, z = -1+6t$. Solving for t gives us the symmetric equations.

Parametric: $x = 1+7t, y = 2+4t, z = -1+6t$
Symmetric: $\frac{x-1}{7} = \frac{y-2}{4} = \frac{z+1}{6}$

Ex: 8 Find the equation of the plane, in general form, that contains both the point $P(1,2,3)$ and the line $\frac{x-4}{2} = \frac{y+3}{-3} = \frac{z-1}{4}$.

Two points determine a line. Three points determine a plane. If we can find two points on our line, we'll have three points to find our plane. Let's first rewrite our line into parametric form.

$x = 2t+4, y = -3t-3, z = 4t+1$

If $t = 0: x = 4, y = -3, z = 1$ so we get $A(4,-3,1)$

If $t = 1: x = 6, y = -6, z = 5$ so we get $B(6,-6,5)$

Now, in order to find the equation of the plane we need to find the normal vector by taking the cross product of PA and PB.

$PA = <4-1,-3-2,1-3> = <3,-5,-2>$

$PB = <6-1,-6-2,5-3> = <5,-8,2>$

$PA \times PB = \mathbf{i}(-10-16) - \mathbf{j}(6+10) + \mathbf{k}(-24+25)$

$PA \times PB = -26\mathbf{i} - 16\mathbf{j} + \mathbf{k}$

Any vector with point P as initial point and (x,y,z) as terminal point could be represented by $<x-1,y-2,z-3>$. Since the cross product $(PA \times PB)$ gave us a normal (perpendicular) vector, the dot product of these two new vectors must be 0. We get the equation is:

$-26(x-1) - 16(y-2) + 1(z-3) = 0$

$-26x + 26 - 16y + 32 + z - 3 = 0$

$-26x - 16y + z + 55 = 0$

$$-26x - 16y + z + 55 = 0$$

Ex: 9 Find the equation of the plane that is tangent to $(x-5)^2+(y+7)^2+(z-6)^2=106$ and passes through the points $A(1,1,0)$ and $B(4,3,2)$.

Let the point of tangency be $P(a,b,c)$. The slope vector from the point of tangency to the center of the sphere would be $<5-a,-7-b,6-c>$. Another way to get this slope vector would be to find the cross product of the two vectors PA and PB. Remember the cross product gives us the vector that is normal to both PA and PB. Because the line that connects the point of tangency to the center of the sphere must be normal to the plane, this cross product will give us the same slope vector as $<5-a,-7-b,6-c>$.

$PA=<1-a,1-b,-c>, PB=<4-a,3-b,2-c>$ Definition of component form

$PA\times PB=\mathbf{i}(2-c-2b+bc+3c-bc)-\mathbf{j}(2-c-2a+ac+4c-ac)+\mathbf{k}(3-b-3a+ab-4+4b+a-ab)$

We get this by setting up a determinant and multiplying out the terms.

$PA\times PB=\text{i}(2+2c-2b)-\text{j}(2+3c-2a)+\text{k}(-1+3b-2a)$ Simplifying

Therefore, the normal vector of the plane would be $<2+2c-2b,-2-3c+2a,-1+3b-2a>$.

Now technically, the two vectors we have to represent our normal vectors could be scalar multiples of one another. However, if we go forward with this technicality, we would get a system of 3 by 3 quadratics. Therefore, let's assume $<2+2c-2b,-2-3c+2a,-1+3b-2a>$ equals $<5-a,-7-b,6-c>$.

$a-2b+2c=3$ Equating corresponding terms

$2a+b-3c=-5$ Equating corresponding terms

$-2a+3b+c=7$ Equating again

If we solve this system of 3 variables, we get $a=1, b=2, c=3$.

Our normal vector would be $<4,-9,3>$ by plugging in the a,b,c values.

$4(x-1)-9(y-2)+3(z-3)=0$ Definition of normal vector

$4x-9y+3z+5=0$ Simplifying

$4x-9y+3z+5=0$

Ex: 10 Find the equation of the lines that are tangent to $(x-1)^2+(y-2)^2+(z-1)^2=9$, pass through $(5,-2,-8)$ and are contained in the plane $-16x+12y-13z=0$.

Let the point of tangency to the sphere be (a,b,c). The slope vector from this point to the center would be $<a-1,b-2,c-1>$. The slope vector from this point to $(5,-2,-8)$ would be $<a-5,b+2,c+8>$. Remember that the tangent line is perpendicular to the line connecting the center to the point of tangency.

$<a-1,b-2,c-1>\cdot<a-5,b+2,c+8>=0$ Dot Product must equal to 0

$a^2-6a+b^2+c^2+7c=7$ Evaluating dot product

Because the point of tangency is on the sphere, $(a-1)^2+(b-2)^2+(c-1)^2=9$ as well.

$a^2-2a+b^2-4b+c^2-2c=3$ Simplifying

Now if you subtract the this from the first equation, we get:

$-4a+4b+9c=4$ Subtracting

Remember that this point must also be on the plane $-16x+12y-13z=0$.

$-16a+12b+13c=0$ Point contained in plane

By multiplying the first equation by 4 and eliminating, $b=\frac{16-49c}{4}$. By multiplying the first equation by 3 and eliminating, $a=3-10c$.

$(3-10c)^2-6(3-10c)+(\frac{16-49c}{4})^2+c^2+7c=7$. Substituting in a and b in terms of c.

$4017c^2-1456c=0$ Expanding and simplifying

$c(c-\frac{112}{309})=0$ Factoring

$c=0, \frac{112}{309}$ Solving for c

If $c=0, a=3, b=4$ Solving for a and b

If $c=\frac{112}{309}, a=\frac{-193}{309}, b=\frac{-136}{309}$ Solving for a and b

Now to find the equation of our line, we need to find the respective slope vectors.

$<5,-2,-8>-<3,4,0>=<2,-6,-8>$.

$<5,-2,-8>-<\frac{-193}{309},\frac{-136}{309},\frac{112}{309}>=<\frac{1738}{309},\frac{-482}{309},\frac{-2584}{309}>$.

By using our slope vectors and choosing the point of tagencies as a starting point, we get:

$\frac{x-3}{2}=\frac{y-4}{-6}=\frac{z}{-8}$ and $\frac{309x+193}{1738}=\frac{309x+136}{-482}=\frac{309z-112}{-2584}$

$\frac{x-3}{2}=\frac{y-4}{-6}=\frac{z}{-8}, \frac{309x+193}{1738}=\frac{309x+136}{-482}=\frac{309z-112}{-2584}$

Vectors and Planes Test 1

#1: (15 points) A ship sails 25 miles from the dock at a bearing of $N40^\circ W$. Then the ship begins sailing at a bearing of $S30^\circ E$. How many miles should the ship sail in this direction to be 25 miles away from the dock?

#2: (15 points) In the figure below, two ropes are supporting a load of 600 lbs. If angle 1 is 25° and angle 2 is 57°, what is the tension for each rope?

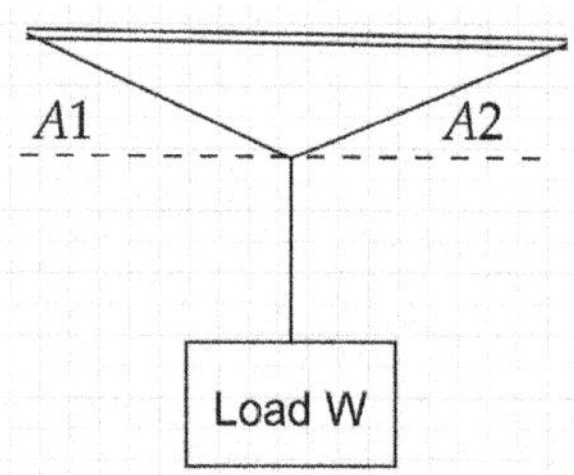

#3: (10 points) What is the closest distance from the point on the surface defined by $x^2 + 2x + y^2 + 6y + z^2 + 4z = 35$ to the plane $z = 20 - 2x - 3y$?

#4: (8 points) A toy wagon is pulled by exerting a force of 30 lbs on a handle that makes a 18° angle with the horizontal. Find the work done in pulling the wagon 55 feet.

#5: (8 points) Find the volume of the parallelepiped having adjacent sides $< 1,1,4 >$ $< 0,4,4 >$ and $< 4,0,4 >$.

#6: (10 points) Find the vector of length 9 that is orthogonal to the vectors -3**i**+4**j**-**k** and 3**i**-**j**.

#7: Given **u** $<-4,3,1>$ and **v** $<1,-1,5>$.

a) (3 points) Find the component form and magnitude of 3**u**-4**v**.

b) (3 points) Find the angle between vectors **u** and **v**.

c) (3 points) Find the projection of **u** onto **v**.

#8: (15 points) Find the equation that represents the set of all points that is equidistant from the plane $3x-4y=10$ and $(x-1)^2+(y+8)^2+z^2=4$.
<u>42</u>

#9: (10 points) Find the set of parametric equations for the line of intersection of $-2x+y-3z=0$ and $x-3y+2z=0$.

Vectors and Planes Test 2

#1: (15 points) A plane is traveling at an airspeed speed of 550 miles per hour with a bearing of $N35^{\circ}E$. A wind whose bearing is $S75^{\circ}E$ and speed is 45 miles per hour is blowing at the plane. What is the plane's true speed and bearing?

#2: (15 points) In the figure below, two ropes B and C are supporting a load of 400 lbs. Let angle 1 be 22° and angle 2 be 54°. What is the tension of the two ropes?

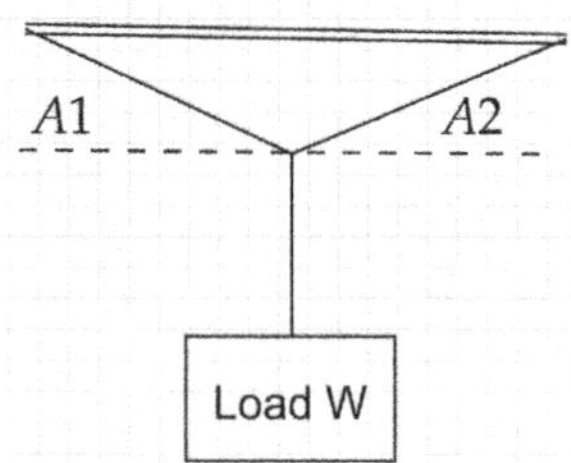

#3: (10 points) If the closest distance from the $(10,3,c)$ to $2x+4y-4z=c$ is 3, find all possible c.

#4: (8 points) A toy wagon is pulled by exerting a force of 40 lbs on a handle that makes a 20° angle with the horizontal. Find the work done in pulling the wagon 55 feet.

#5: (8 points) Find the volume of the parallelepiped having adjacent sides $<2,-2,3>$ $<0,2,2>$ and $<3,0,4>$.

#6: Given **u** $< -3,2,0 >$ and **v** $< 4,-2,6 >$.

a) (3 points) Find the component form and magnitude of 3**u**-4**v**.

b) (3 points) Find the angle between vectors **u** and **v**.

c) (3 points) Find the projection of **u** onto **v**.

#7: (10 points) Find the vector of length 7 that is orthogonal to the vectors -2**i**+7**j**-**k** and 2**i**-3**j**.

#8: (10 points) Find the coordinates of the foot of an altitude drawn from $(1,2,3)$ to the plane $5x - 3y + 2z = 2$. What is the length of this altitude?

#9: (15 points) Find the equation of the plane that contains the lines $\frac{x-4}{3} = \frac{y-1}{1} = \frac{z-6}{9}$, $\frac{x}{4} = \frac{y+1}{2} = \frac{z+2}{8}$, and $\frac{x}{1} = \frac{y+1}{1} = \frac{z+2}{-1}$.

Chapter 14 Introduction to Calculus

This chapter will go over the basic applications of the three core concepts of calculus: limits, derivatives, and integrals.

Limits and Continuity

Ex: 1 Use the graph of $f(x)$ to evaluate:

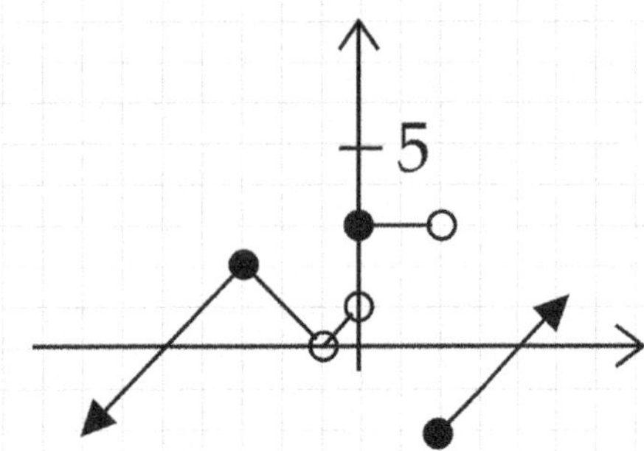

a) $\lim\limits_{x\to -1} f(x) - \lim\limits_{x\to 2^+} f(x) =$

We can use direct substitution. If we approach -1 from the either side, the graph approaches 0. So $\lim\limits_{x\to -1} f(x) = 0$. If we approach 2 from the right side only, we look at the line with slope 1. The graph approaches -2 so $\lim\limits_{x\to 2^+} =-2$.

$0-(-2)=2$

b) $\lim\limits_{x\to 0^-}[(x+1)^2 f(x)] =$

We can evaluate each factor of the limit separately and then multiply it together at the end.
$\lim\limits_{x\to 0^-}(x+1)^2 = 1^2 = 1$. We can directly substitute in 0 because $(x+1)^2$ is continuous at 0. Looking at the graph of $f(x)$, when we approach 0 from the left side, we get $f(x) = 1$. Multiplying them:

$1(1) = 1$

c) $\lim\limits_{x\to 2^-}[f(x) + \sqrt{2x}] =$

We can evaluate each part of the limit separately and then add them together. $\lim\limits_{x\to 2^+} f(x) = 3$ by analyzing the graph and $\lim\limits_{x\to 2^-}\sqrt{2x} = \sqrt{4} = 2$.

$3+2=5$

Ex: 2 Find the constants a and b such that the function is continuous.

$$f(x) = \begin{cases} ax^2 - bx & \text{if, } x < 2 \\ bx + 1 & \text{if, } -2 < x < 4 \\ a\sqrt{x-3} & \text{if, } x \le 4 \end{cases}$$

In order for the function to be continuous, the the limit from both sides at the "breaking points" ($x =-2$ and $x = 4$), must be the same.
$\lim\limits_{x\to -2^-} f(x) = \lim\limits_{x\to 2^+} f(x)$
We can use direct substitution because we know a parabola and linear equation are continuous.
$a(-2)^2 - b(-2) = b(-2) + 1$
$4a + 2b =-2b + 1$
$4a =-4b + 1$
Now for $x = 4$: $\lim\limits_{x\to 4^-} f(x) = \lim\limits_{x\to 4^+} f(x)$
$4b + 1 = a\sqrt{4-3}$
$4b + 1 = a$
Substitute in this a value into our first equation:
$4(4b+1) =-4b + 1$
$16b + 4 =-4b + 1$ Simplifying
$20b =-3$ Combining like terms
$b = \frac{-3}{20}$
Therefore, $a = 4(\frac{-3}{20}) + 1 = \frac{2}{5}$.

$a = \frac{2}{5}, b = \frac{-3}{20}$

Evaluating Limits

Ex: 1 Evaluate $\lim\limits_{x\to\frac{5\pi}{4}} \frac{\sec x - 2\sin x}{(\sin x - \cos x)^2}$

Checking $x = \frac{5\pi}{4}$, we see that the denominator becomes 0 so plugging it in does not work.
Let's expand the fraction to see what happens.

$\lim\limits_{x\to\frac{5\pi}{4}} \frac{\frac{1}{\cos x} - 2\sin x}{\sin^2 x - 2\sin x \cdot \cos x + \cos^2 x}$ Expanding/rewriting $\sec x$

$\lim\limits_{x\to\frac{5\pi}{4}} \frac{\frac{1}{\cos x} - 2\sin x}{1 - 2\sin x \cdot \cos x}$ Using pythagorean identity

$\lim\limits_{x\to\frac{5\pi}{4}} \frac{1 - 2\sin x \cdot \cos x}{\cos x(1 - 2\sin x \cdot \cos x)}$ Multiplying $\cos x$

$\lim\limits_{x\to\frac{5\pi}{4}} \frac{1}{\cos x}$ Cancelling out like terms

$\frac{1}{\cos(\frac{5\pi}{4})}$ Plugging it in

$-\sqrt{2}$

Note that we must keep the limit notation when we are simplifying our function. When we plug the x value in, that's when we stop.

Ex: 2 Evaluate $\lim_{x\to4}\frac{16x-x^3}{\sqrt{x}-2}$

Once again we can't plug in $x = 4$.

$\lim_{x\to4}\frac{x(4-x)(4+x)}{\sqrt{x}-2}$ Factoring the numerator

$\lim_{x\to4}\frac{x(4-x)(4+x)}{\sqrt{x}-2}\cdot\frac{\sqrt{x}+2}{\sqrt{x}+2}$ Multiplying the conjugate

$\lim_{x\to4}\frac{x(4-x)(4+x)(\sqrt{x}+2)}{x-4}$ Difference of squares

$\lim_{x\to4}x(-1)(4+x)(\sqrt{x}+2)$ Cancelling out factors

$4(-1)(8)(\sqrt{4}+2)$ Plugging $x = 4$

-128

Ex: 3 Evaluate $\lim_{x\to5}\frac{|25-x^2|}{x^2-6x+5}$

With an absolute value, we can't evaluate this limit typically. Instead, we must look at the right and left limits to see if they are the same. If we approach 5 from the left side, we know that $25-x^2$ will be positive.

$\lim_{x\to5^-}\frac{(5-x)(5+x)}{(x-5)(x-1)}$ Limit on the left side

$\lim_{x\to5^-}\frac{-(5+x)}{(x-1)}$ Cancel out factors

$\frac{-10}{4}=\frac{-5}{2}$ Plugging in $x = 5$

If we approach 5 from the right side, x will be a bit greater than 5 so $25-x^2$ will be negative.

$\lim_{x\to5^+}\frac{-(5-x)(5+x)}{(x-5)(x-1)}$ Limit on the left side

$\lim_{x\to5^+}\frac{(5+x)}{(x-1)}$ Cancel out factors

$\frac{10}{4}=\frac{5}{2}$ Plugging in $x = 5$

Since the limit is different from either side:

The limit does not exist

Ex: 4 Evaluate $\lim_{x\to27}\frac{\sqrt[3]{x}-3}{\sqrt{3x}-9}$

$\lim_{x\to27}\frac{\sqrt[3]{x}-3}{\sqrt{3x}-9}\cdot\frac{\sqrt{3x}+9}{\sqrt{3x}+9}$ Multiply the Conjugate

$\lim_{x\to27}\frac{(\sqrt[3]{x}-3)(\sqrt{3x}+9)}{3x-81}$ Multiply difference of squares

$\lim_{x\to27}\frac{(\sqrt[3]{x}-3)(\sqrt{3x}+9)}{3(x-27)}$ Factor

Notice that by difference of cubes we can factor $x-27=(\sqrt[3]{x})^3-3^3=(\sqrt[3]{x}-3)(\sqrt[3]{x^2}+3\sqrt[3]{x}+9)$

$\lim_{x\to27}\frac{(\sqrt[3]{x}-3)(\sqrt{3x}+9)}{3(\sqrt[3]{x}-3)(\sqrt[3]{x^2}+3\sqrt[3]{x}+9)}$ Factoring

$\lim_{x\to27}\frac{\sqrt{3x}+9}{3(\sqrt[3]{x^2}+3\sqrt[3]{x}+9)}$ Cancelling out common factor

$\frac{\sqrt{3(27)}+9}{3(\sqrt[3]{27^2}+3\sqrt[3]{27}+9)}$ Substituting $x = 27$

$\frac{18}{3(9+9+9)}$ Simplifying

$\frac{2}{9}$

Ex: 5 Evaluate $\lim_{x\to2}\frac{\sqrt{2x^2-x+1}-\sqrt{7}}{x^2-5x+6}$.

$\lim_{x\to2}\frac{\sqrt{2x^2-x+1}-\sqrt{7}}{x^2-5x+6}\cdot\frac{\sqrt{2x^2-x+1}+\sqrt{7}}{\sqrt{2x^2-x+1}+\sqrt{7}}$ Multiply Conjugate

$\lim_{x\to2}\frac{2x^2-x+1-7}{(x^2-5x+6)(\sqrt{2x^2-x+1}+\sqrt{7})}$ Difference of Squares

$\lim_{x\to2}\frac{(x-2)(2x+3)}{(x-2)(x-3)(\sqrt{2x^2-x+1}+\sqrt{7})}$ Factoring

$\lim_{x\to2}\frac{2x+3}{(x-3)(\sqrt{2x^2-x+1}+\sqrt{7})}$ Cancelling out common factor

$\frac{2(2)+3}{(2-3)(\sqrt{2(2^2)-2+1}+\sqrt{7})}$ Direct substitution

$\frac{7}{-2\sqrt{7}}$ Simplifying

$-\frac{\sqrt{7}}{2}$ Simplifying

$\frac{\sqrt{7}}{2}$

Ex: 7 Evaluate $\lim_{x\to2}\frac{2x^4-7x^3-2x^2+13x+6}{x^2-3x+2}$

$\lim_{x\to2}\frac{(x-2)(2x+1)(x-3)(x+1)}{(x-2)(x-1)}$ Factoring

$\lim_{x\to2}\frac{(2x+1)(x-3)(x+1)}{(x-1)}$ Cancelling out factors

$\frac{(4+1)(2-3)(2+1)}{2-1}$ Substituting in $x = 2$

-15

A strategy would to always factor out the term for which x is approaching. This is since the problem writer will probably make this a common factor.

Ex: 8 Find the value of k that will make the following limit exist. Then evaluate the limit:

$\lim_{x\to2}[\frac{2x+1}{x^2-3x+2}+\frac{k}{x^2+2x-8}]$

Let's first combine the fractions cause the limit does not exist for each individual fraction so we can't evaluate them separately.

$\lim_{x\to 2}[\frac{2x+1}{(x-2)(x-1)} + \frac{k}{(x+4)(x-2)}]$ Factoring

$\lim_{x\to 2}[\frac{(2x+1)(x+4)+k(x-1)}{(x-2)(x-1)(x+4)}]$ Common denominator

$\lim_{x\to 2}[\frac{2x^2+x(9+k)+(4-k)}{(x-2)(x-1)(x+4)}]$ Expanding

In order for the limit to exist, the $x-2$ factor must cancel out from the top and bottom. In order for the numerator to have this factor, plugging in $x=2$ must yield 0 by the factor theorem. Plugging this in, we get:

$2(2^2)+2(9+k)+4-k=0$. Solving, $k=-30$.

$\lim_{x\to 2}[\frac{2x^2-21x+34}{(x-2)(x-1)(x+4)}]$ Substituting $k=-30$

$\lim_{x\to 2}[\frac{2x-17}{(x+4)(x-1)}]$ Dividing Out Technique

$\frac{4-17}{6\cdot 1}$ Simplifying

$k=-30$ allows the limit to be $\frac{-13}{6}$

Limits at Infinity and Asymptotes

Ex: 1 Evaluate $\lim_{x\to -\infty}\frac{2-4x+3x^2}{2x^2+4x-9}$

$\lim_{x\to -\infty}\frac{2-4x+3x^2}{2x^2+4x-9}\cdot\frac{\frac{1}{x^2}}{\frac{1}{x^2}}$ Multiplying by $\frac{1}{x^2}$

$\lim_{x\to -\infty}\frac{\frac{2}{x^2}-\frac{4}{x}+3}{2+\frac{4}{x}-\frac{9}{x^2}}$ Simplifying

Remember that the $\lim_{x\to\pm\infty}\frac{n}{x^r}=0$. So only the 3 and 2 matter. From what we learned in the rational functions chapter, we know that this rational function has a horizontal asymptote at $y=\frac{3}{2}$ since the degree of the numerator and denominator is the same. So the limit is $\frac{3}{2}$.

$\frac{3}{2}$

Ex: 2 Evaluate $\lim_{x\to\infty}\frac{\sqrt{4x^2+3}}{4x-1}$

$\lim_{x\to\infty}\frac{\sqrt{4x^2+3}}{4x-1}\cdot\frac{\frac{1}{x}}{\frac{1}{x}}$ Factoring out x or $\sqrt{x^2}$

$\lim_{x\to\infty}\frac{\sqrt{4+\frac{3}{x^2}}}{4-\frac{1}{x}}$ Simplifying

$\lim_{x\to\infty}\frac{3}{x^2}$ and $\lim_{x\to\infty}\frac{-1}{x}$ approach 0 because as x gets larger and larger, the fraction gets smaller and smaller without bound. Therefore:

$\lim_{x\to\infty}\frac{\sqrt{4+\frac{3}{x^2}}}{4-\frac{1}{x}}=\frac{\sqrt{4}}{4}$

$\frac{1}{2}$

Ex: 3 Evaluate $\lim_{x\to -\infty}\frac{1+e^x}{3x-1}$

We must approach this problem intuitively. Looking at the numerator, as we approach negative infinity, $1+e^x$ will approach 1 because e^x becomes a smaller and smaller fraction as x increases and approaches 0. Looking at the denominator, as we approach negative infinity, $3x-1$ gets infinity smaller without bound. Therefore, this fraction will approach 0.

0

Ex: 4 Evaluate $\lim_{x\to -\infty}\sqrt{16x^2-x}+4x$

$\lim_{x\to -\infty}\sqrt{16x^2-x}+4x\cdot\frac{\sqrt{16x^2-x}-4x}{\sqrt{16x^2-x}-4x}$ Conjugate

We take the conjugate because we want to express things as ratios and "zero" parts out

$\lim_{x\to -\infty}\frac{16x^2-x-16x^2}{\sqrt{16x^2-x}-4x}$ Difference of Squares

$\lim_{x\to -\infty}\frac{-x}{\sqrt{16x^2-x}-4x}$ Simplifying

$\lim_{x\to -\infty}\frac{-x}{|x|(\sqrt{16-\frac{1}{x}})-4x}$ Factoring out x from bottom

Remember that $\sqrt{x^2}$ actually gets the absolute value of x, not the positive. Since in this case, x approaches negative infinity, $|x|=-x$.

$\lim_{x\to -\infty}\frac{-x}{-x(\sqrt{16-\frac{1}{x}})-4x}$

$\lim_{x\to -\infty}\frac{1}{\sqrt{16-\frac{1}{x}}+4}$ Cancel out common x factor

Remember that in the grand scheme of things, $\frac{-1}{x}$ does not matter because as x approaches negative infinity, these approach 0 anyways.

$\frac{1}{\sqrt{16}+4}=\frac{1}{8}$

Ex: 5 Evaluate $\lim_{x\to\infty}\frac{14n(n+1)(2n+1)}{6n^3}$

$\lim_{n\to\infty}\frac{7n(n+1)(2n+1)}{3n^3}$ Simplify

$\lim_{n\to\infty}\frac{14n^3+21n^2+7n}{3n^3}$ Expanding

$\lim_{n\to\infty} \frac{14+\frac{21}{n}+\frac{7}{n^2}}{3}$ Multiplying by $\frac{1}{n^3}$

$\frac{14}{3}$

Ex: 6 Evaluate $\lim_{x\to-\infty} \frac{(3x-7)^3(-x+2)^9}{(6x-5)^2(2x-1)^5}$

This is a mess to expand but for limits at infinity, we only care about the highest degrees.

$\lim_{x\to-\infty} \frac{(27x^3...)(-x^9...)}{(36x^2...)(32x^5...)}$ "Expanding"

$\lim_{x\to-\infty} \frac{-27x^{12}...}{1152x^7...}$ Simplifying

The limit does not exist since the degree of the top is more than the degree of the bottom. Now obviously the x^{12} grows at a faster rate than x^7. Even as the denominator is trying to make the $f(x)$ smaller, it won't do much at infinity. Since the degree of numerator is even, x^{12} goes toward positive infinity. However, with the negative sign, the numerator approaches negative infinity. For the denominator, it approaches negative infinity as well (odd degree) but at a much slower rate.

Limit does not exist, approaches ∞

Ex: 7 Find the horizontal asymptotes of $f(x) = 2\tan^{-1}(\frac{x+3e}{e^x-1})$.

To find the horizontal asymptotes, we need to find $\lim_{x\to\pm\infty} f(x)$. An important thing is that we can rewrite this limit expression into $2\tan^{-1}(\lim_{x\to\pm\infty} \frac{x+3e}{e^x-1})$ by the properties of composition of functions. As x approaches positive infinity, both $x+3e$ and e^x-1 approach positive infinity as well. However, e^x-1 increases at a much greater rate. Therefore, the denominator "trumps" the numerator and the fraction approaches 0 from the positive side. $2\tan^{-1}(0) = 0$ so there's a horizontal asymptote at $y=0$. As x approaches negative infinity, $x+3e$ approaches negative infinity. e^x will always be positive but because of negative exponents, it'll be a really small fraction, approaching 0. Subtracting 1, surely puts it on the negative side. If we divided a huge negative number, by a really small negative number, we'll end up approaching positive infinity. Based on inverse trig, we know that as the angle gets closer and closer to $\frac{\pi}{2}$, the tangent of that angle also approaches positive infinity. Therefore, our horizontal asymptote is at $2\cdot\frac{\pi}{2} = \pi$.

Horizontal Asymptotes: $y=0, y=\pi$

Finding Derivatives

Ex: 1 Find the derivative of $f(x) = \frac{1}{\sqrt{x-4}}$ and the line that is tangent to $f(x)$ at $(8, \frac{1}{2})$.

By definition, using the difference quotient gets us the derivative. $f'(x) = \lim_{h\to 0} \frac{f(x+h)-f(x)}{h}$.

$\frac{f(x+h)-f(x)}{h} = \frac{\frac{1}{\sqrt{x-4+h}}-\frac{1}{\sqrt{x-4}}}{h}$ Difference Quotient

$\frac{\sqrt{x-4}-\sqrt{x-4+h}}{h(\sqrt{x-4+h})(\sqrt{x-4})}$ Getting rid of complex fractions

$\frac{\sqrt{x-4}-\sqrt{x-4+h}}{h(\sqrt{x-4+h})(\sqrt{x-4})} \cdot \frac{\sqrt{x-4}+\sqrt{x-4+h}}{\sqrt{x-4}+\sqrt{x-4+h}}$ Conjugate

$\frac{x-4-x+4-h}{h(\sqrt{x-4+h})(\sqrt{x-4})(\sqrt{x-4}+\sqrt{x-4+h})}$ Difference of Squares

$\frac{-1}{(\sqrt{x-4+h})(\sqrt{x-4})(\sqrt{x-4}+\sqrt{x-4+h})}$ Factoring

$\lim_{h\to 0} \frac{-1}{(\sqrt{x-4+h})(\sqrt{x-4})(\sqrt{x-4}+\sqrt{x-4+h})}$ Finding the limit

$f'(x) = \frac{-1}{(x-4)(2\sqrt{x-4})}$ Substituting in 2

Now plug in $x=8$, to find that the slope at that point is $f'(8) = \frac{-1}{4(4)} = \frac{-1}{16}$. Using, point slope form the line is $y - \frac{1}{2} = \frac{-1}{16}(x-8)$

$y = -\frac{1}{16}x + 1$

Ex: 2 Find the derivative of $f(x) = x^3 - 5x^2 - 2$. Use that to find out at what ranges is $f(x)$ increasing.

$f'(x) = \lim_{h\to 0} \frac{(x+h)^3-5(x+h)^2-2-x^3+5x^2+2}{h}$ Definition

$\lim_{h\to 0} \frac{x^3+3x^2h+3xh^2+h^3-5x^2-10xh-5h^2-x^3+5x^2}{h}$ Expanding

$\lim_{h\to 0} \frac{3x^2h+3xh^2+h^3-10xh-5h^2}{h}$ Combining like terms

$\lim_{h\to 0} 3x^2 + 3xh + h^2 - 10x - 5h$ Simplifying

$f'(x) = 3x^2 - 10x$ Evaluating the limit

If $f(x)$ is increasing, the slope at the given point must be positive. Therefore, we are trying to solve the equation when the derivative is greater than 0: $3x^2 - 10x > 0$

$3x(x - \frac{10}{3}) > 0$

Plotting the critical points at 0 and $\frac{10}{3}$, we see that 1, a number between the critical points does not fulfill the inequality. Therefore, $x < 0, x > \frac{10}{3}$ are the ranges that would allow $f(x)$ to be increasing.

$x < 0, x > \frac{10}{3}$

Ex: 3 Using the power rule shortcut, find the derivative of $f(x) = 5x^4 - 3x^3 + 2x^2 - 7x + 9$.

By the power rule shortcut, we know if $f(x) = nx^a$, $f'(x) = anx^{a-1}$. Therefore:

$f'(x) = 4(5)x^{4-1} - 3(3)x^{3-1} + 2(2)x^{2-1} - 7(1)x^{1-1} + 0$

$f'(x) = 20x^3 - 9x^2 + 4x - 7$

Applications of Derivatives

Ex: 1 If $by - ax = b$ is tangent to $f(x) = 2x^2 - bx + a$ at a certain point and $3y - x = 13$ is the normal line at that same point, what is a and b?

$ax - by = 1$ can be rewritten as $y = \frac{a}{b}x + 1$.

$3y - x = 13$ can be rewritten as $y = \frac{1}{3}x + \frac{13}{3}$.

The tangent and normal line are perpendicular, so the slope of $y = \frac{a}{b}x + 1$ must be -3.

$\frac{a}{b} = -3$ Definition of Slope Intercept Form

$a = -3b$ Rearranging to solve for a

Now, if we want to find a and b, we need to find where the two lines intersect (point of tangency).

$\frac{a}{b}x + 1 = \frac{1}{3}x + \frac{13}{3}$ Point of Intersection

$-3x + 1 = \frac{1}{3}x + \frac{13}{3}$ Substituting $a = -3b$

$x = -1$ Solving for x

Using the powerful shortcut, we know $f'(x) = 4x - b$.

$f(-1) = 4(-1) - b = -3$ Slope of Tangent Line

$b = -1$ Solving for b

$a = -3(-1) = 3$ Solving for a

$a = 3, b = -1$

Ex: 2 An object's position on the x axis can be modelled by $s(t) = \frac{1}{3}t^3 - t^2 - 8t + 24$ for $t \geq 0$.

a) At what times is the object at rest?

The object is at rest when the velocity is 0. The equation of velocity is the derivative of $s(t)$.

$s'(t) = 3 \cdot \frac{1}{3}t^2 - 2t - 8$ by power rule

$s'(t) = t^2 - 2t - 8 = 0 = (t - 4)(t + 2)$

Solving this, we see that $t = 4, -2$.

The object is at rest when $t = 4$.

b) What is the total distance traveled by the object in the first 5 seconds?

Because the particle is at its turning point at $t = 4$, we must split the distance into two cases. At $t = 0$, $s(0) = 24$. At $t = 4$, $s(4) = -2\frac{2}{3}$. So the particle has moved a distance of $26\frac{2}{3}$. At $t = 5, s(5) = \frac{2}{3}$. So the distance traveled from $t = 4$ to $t = 5$ is $3\frac{1}{3}$.

30 Summing the distances together

c) At what velocities is the object traveling at when $s = 0$?

Solving $s(t) = 0$ by factor by grouping:

$s(t) = \frac{1}{3}t^2(t - 3) - 8(t - 3)$

$s(t) = (\frac{1}{3}t^2 - 8)(t - 3)$

Therefore, the ball is at the ground at $t = 3, 2\sqrt{6}$

Now, we just plug these values into our derivative equation. $v(3) = 3^2 - 2(3) - 8 = -5$.

$v(2\sqrt{6}) = 24 - 2(2\sqrt{6}) - 8 = 16 - 4\sqrt{6}$

$-5, 16 - 4\sqrt{6}$

d) At what time is the object's velocity at a minimum?

The equation of the velocity is $v(t) = t^2 - 2t - 8$. If rewrite this in vertex form we get:

$v(t) = t^2 - 2t + 1 - 9$

$v(t) = (t - 1)^2 - 9$. Therefore, the vertex is at $t = 1$

$t = 1$

e) At what time is the object's velocity constant (acceleration equals 0)?

To find the acceleration, find the derivative of the velocity function. $a(t) = v'(t) = 2t - 2$ by the power rule. Now we solve for when $a(t) = 0$. This is obvious by solving this linear equation that $t = 1$.

$t = 1$

When the object's acceleration is zero is equal to the minimum velocity. This is because when we graph the velocity function, the tangent line at the vertex (minimum) would be exactly horizontal.

Ex: 3 If a particle's position in space is modelled by the vector $< x(t), y(t) >$ where $x(t) = 2t^2 - 5t - 6$ and $y(t) = 2t^3 - 8t^2 + 10t - 3$, at what times is the particle moving right and down?
The particle is moving right when the rate of change for $x(t)$ is positive. It's moving down when the rate of change for $y(t)$ is negative.
$x'(t) = 4t - 5$ Using Power Rule Shortcut
$4t - 5 > 0$ Rate of Change is Positive
$t > \frac{5}{4}$ Solving for t
$y'(t) = 6t^2 - 16t + 10$ Using Power Rule Shortcut
$6t^2 - 16t + 10 < 0$ Rate of Change is Negative
$2(3t - 5)(t - 1) < 0$ Factoring
$t = \frac{5}{3}, 1$ Solving for Critical Values
Testing 0, a point less than 1, we see the inequality does not hold true. Therefore, times $1 < t < \frac{5}{3}$ allow for the function to be negative.

$\frac{5}{4} < t < \frac{5}{3}$ Intersection of Two Inequalities

Ex: 4 Find the local minimums and local maximums of $f(x) = x^3 + 4x^2 + 4x$.
Let's first find the derivative of $f(x)$.
$f'(x) = 3x^2 + 2(4x) + 4 = 3x^2 + 8x + 4$ by the power rule. Now if we find where the derivative equals 0, that's where the tangent line is horizontal aka a local maximum or minimum. Solving $f'(x) = 0$, we see that $0 = (3x + 2)(x + 2)$ so $x = \frac{-2}{3}$ and $x = -2$ are where we have a local maximum or minimum. Plugging this into our original function gets us the points $(-2, 0), (\frac{-2}{3}, -1.185)$. However, which is which? If we just plug in $x = 0$, a number just right of $\frac{-2}{3}$, we see that the slope is $f'(0) = 4$. Therefore, the graph decelerates, passes through $x = \frac{-2}{3}$, then quickly accelerates, gaining a greater slope. Therefore, $x = \frac{-2}{3}$ is a local minimum and $x = -2$ is the local maximum.

Local minimum: $(\frac{-2}{3}, -1.185)$ Local maximum: $(-2, 0)$

Ex: 5 Using the power rule shortcut on $f(x) = \sqrt{x}$, approximate the value of $\sqrt{3.9}$.
To utilize linear approximation, we want to find the tangent line through a point close to 3.9 (4). Using the tangent line and the function to evaluate for 3.9 would give us a close value.
Let's first find the derivative of $f(x) = \sqrt{x} = x^{1/2}$.
We use the power rule shortcut to get $f'(x) = \frac{1}{2}x^{-1/2} = \frac{1}{2\sqrt{x}.}$ Plugging in $x = 4$, we see that the slope will be $\frac{1}{4}$. Now we can find the equation of the line that goes through $(4, 2)$ and has slope $\frac{1}{4}$. Using point slope form, $y - 2 = \frac{1}{4}(x - 4)$ or $y = \frac{1}{4}x + 1$. Plugging in $x = 3.9$ into this tangent line, we get $\sqrt{3.9} \approx 1.975$

$\sqrt{3.9} \approx 1.975$

Ex: 6 A rectangle is inscribed within $\frac{x^2}{25} + \frac{y^2}{16} = 1$. What is the maximum area?

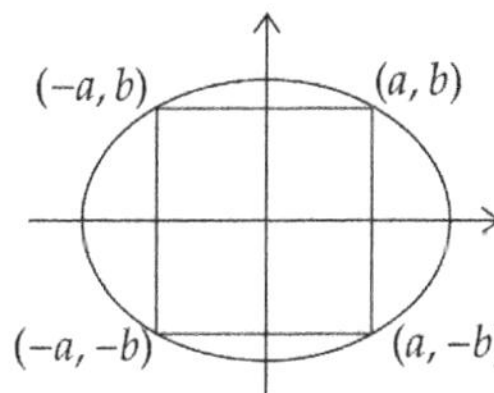

$\frac{x^2}{25} = 1 - \frac{y^2}{16}$ Manipulating ellipse's equation
$x^2 = \frac{25(16-y^2)}{16}$ Isolating x^2
$x = \frac{5\sqrt{16-y^2}}{4}$ Solving for x
The dimensions of rectangle are $2a$ by $2b$.
$A = 4ab$ Area of a rectangle definition
$A = 5b\sqrt{16 - b^2}$ Substituting in a in terms of b
Now we want to take the derivative in terms of b in order to optimize and find the maximum area.
$\lim_{h \to 0} \frac{5(b+h)\sqrt{16-(b+h)^2} - 5b\sqrt{16-b^2}}{h}$ Definition of derivative
$\lim_{h \to 0} \frac{5b\sqrt{16-(b+h)^2} - 5b\sqrt{16-b^2}}{h} + 5\sqrt{16 - (b + h)^2}$ Simplify

$\lim_{h \to 0} \frac{25b^2(16-(b+h)^2)-25b^2(16-b^2)}{h(5b\sqrt{16-(b+h)^2}+5b\sqrt{16-b^2})} + 5\sqrt{16-(b+h)^2}$

Multiplying conjugate.

$\lim_{h \to 0} \frac{-50b^3-25b^2h}{5b\sqrt{16-(b+h)^2}+5b\sqrt{16-b^2}} + 5\sqrt{16-(b+h)^2}$ Simplify

$A'(b) = \frac{-5b^2}{\sqrt{16-b^2}} + 5\sqrt{16-b^2}$ Plugging in $h = 0$

$\frac{-5b^2}{\sqrt{16-b^2}} + 5\sqrt{16-b^2} = 0$ Optimization

$-5b^2 + 5(16-b^2) = 0$ Multiplying $\sqrt{16-b^2}$

$10b^2 = 80$ Combining like terms

$b = 2\sqrt{2}$ Solving for b

$A = 5(2\sqrt{2})\sqrt{16-8}$ Plugging in $b = 2\sqrt{2}$ into area formula

$A = 40$ Simplifying

$A = 40$

Ex: 7 You form a cone by curling up a sector of angle 240° and attaching a circle at the bottom. What is the radius length of the sector that produces the maximum numerical difference when the volume is subtracted from the surface area? What is this difference?

Let the radius length of the sector be r. The arc length of the sector would be $\frac{240}{360} \cdot 2r\pi = \frac{4\pi r}{3}$. When we curl up the sector, this arc length forms the circumference of the base of the cone. If the circumference of the circular base is $\frac{4\pi r}{3}$, the radius of that base would be $\frac{2r}{3}$.

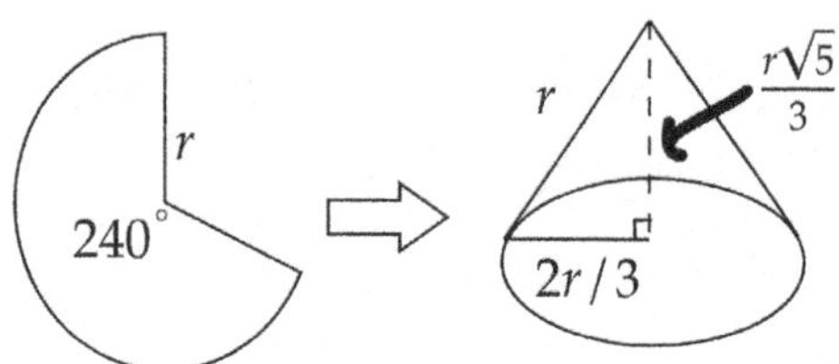

Using the pythagorean theorem, we find that the height of the cone is $\frac{r\sqrt{5}}{3}$. The volume of the cone would be $\frac{1}{3}\pi(\frac{2r}{3})^2(\frac{r\sqrt{5}}{3}) = \frac{4\sqrt{5}r^3\pi}{81}$. The surface area would be $\pi(\frac{2r}{3})(r) + \pi(\frac{2r}{3})^2 = \frac{10\pi r^2}{9}$. Remember that the lateral length would be r in the formula. The function for this difference would be

$f(r) = \frac{10\pi r^2}{9} - \frac{4\sqrt{5}r^3\pi}{81}$

$f'(r) = \frac{20\pi r}{9} - \frac{4\sqrt{5}r^2\pi}{27}$ Power Rule Shortcut

$f'(r) = 0 = \frac{20\pi r}{9} - \frac{4\sqrt{5}r^2\pi}{27}$ Process of Optimization

$0 = \frac{4\sqrt{5}\pi}{27}r(3\sqrt{5} - r)$ Factoring

$r = 3\sqrt{5}$ Solving for r, r must be positive

$f(3\sqrt{5}) = \frac{10\pi(45)}{9} - \frac{4\sqrt{5}(135\sqrt{5})\pi}{81} = \frac{50\pi}{3}$ r in $3\sqrt{5}$

$r = 3\sqrt{5}, \frac{50\pi}{3}$

Introduction to Integrals

Ex: 1 Approximate the area under the curve $f(x) = -x^2 + 4x + 2$ from $[0,4]$ with the four intervals $[0,1],[1,2],[2,3],[3,4]$.

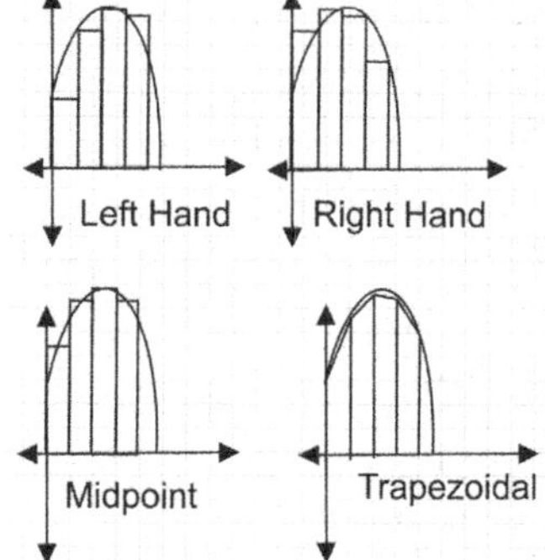

a) Using left-hand rule

The left-hand rule means that for each interval, the left-hand interval determines the height of the triangle. Therefore, the area would be approximated as $1(f(0)+f(1)+f(2)+f(3))$ since the width of each rectangle is 1. Evaluating we get:

$2+5+6+5 = 18$

b) Using right-hand rule

Now we use right endpoints to get height: $1(f(1)+f(2)+f(3)+f(4))$. Evaluating we get:

$5+6+5+2 = 18.$

c) Using midpoint rule

Now, instead of using the left or right, we use the midpoint of each interval to find the height of the rectangle. Therefore, the area would be: $1(f(0.5)+f(1.5)+f(2.5)+f(3.5))$

$3.75 + 5.75 + 5.75 + 3.75 = 19$

d) Using trapezoidal rule

Now instead of rectangles, we create trapezoids whose height is constant at the width (1), while the base lengths are determined by the left and right endpoints on the curve. The area would be $\frac{f(0)+f(1)}{2} + \frac{f(1)+f(2)}{2} + \frac{f(2)+f(3)}{2} + \frac{f(3)+f(4)}{2}$ $\frac{2+5}{2} + \frac{5+6}{2} + \frac{6+5}{2} + \frac{5+2}{2}$.

18

e) Limit as $n \to \infty$ (definite integral)

Now we find the area, if the number of rectangles we use approaches infinity.

Now our width of each rectangle would be $\frac{4}{n}$. This is cause the total interval is 4, so we divide by the number of intervals to get the width of each rectangle. The height of each rectangle is given by $f(0 + \frac{4i}{n})$. This is since we start at $x = 0$ and with each interval x increases by $\frac{4}{n}$. We evaluate that for $f(x)$ to get the height.

$A = \lim_{x\to\infty} \sum_{i=1}^{n} f(\frac{4i}{n})(\frac{4}{n})$

$A = \lim_{x\to\infty} \sum_{i=1}^{n} (\frac{-16i^2}{n^2} + \frac{16i}{n} + 2)(\frac{4}{n})$ Evaluating $f(x)$

$A = \lim_{x\to\infty} \sum_{i=1}^{n} (\frac{-64i^2}{n^3} + \frac{64i}{n^2} + \frac{8}{n})$ Multiplying

$A = \lim_{x\to\infty} (\sum_{i=1}^{n} \frac{-64i^2}{n^3} + \sum_{i=1}^{n} \frac{64i}{n^2} + \sum_{i=1}^{n} \frac{8}{n})$ Splitting apart

$A = \lim_{x\to\infty} (\frac{-64n(n+1)(2n+1)}{6n^3} + \frac{64n(n+1)}{2n^2} + \frac{8n}{n}$ Summations

$A = \frac{-128}{6} + \frac{64}{2} + 8$ Evaluating the limits separately and considering the leading coefficients

$A = \frac{56}{3}$

Ex: 2 Using the fundamental theorem of calculus, find the area under $f(x) = x^3 - 2x^2 - 8x$ from [-2,0]. Remember that the fundamental theorem of calculus states that the area under $f(x)$ in the interval from $[a, b]$ is $\int_a^b f(x)dx = F(b) - F(a)$. So if we find the antiderivative of $f(x)$ and evaluate -2 and 0, we're done. We can use the power rule shortcut to find the antiderivative that states for $f(x) = ax^n$, the antiderivative is $F(x) = \frac{a}{n+1}x^{n+1}$.

Therefore, $F(x) = \frac{1}{4}x^4 - \frac{2}{3}x^3 - \frac{8}{2}x^2$.

$F(-2) = \frac{16}{4} - \frac{2(-8)}{3} - 4(4) = 4 + \frac{16}{3} - 16 = \frac{-20}{3}$

$F(0) = 0$ obviously.

$0 - (-\frac{20}{3}) = \frac{20}{3}$

Ex: 3 Using the fundamental theorem of calculus, find the area between $f(x) = x^2 - 4x + 5$ and $g(x) = x + 1$.

We have to first find their points of intersections to see the interval we must calculate the area for.

$x^2 - 4x + 5 = x + 1$

$x^2 - 5x + 4 = 0$

$(x - 4)(x - 1) = 0$

Therefore, we want to find the area from $[1, 4]$. We can find the area under the curve of each. Then find the difference to find the area between the curves. For $f(x)$ we can find the integral with:

$\int_1^4 (x^2 - 4x + 5)dx$

Finding the antiderivative of $x^2 - 4x + 5$, we get $F(x) = \frac{1}{3}x^3 - 2x^2 + 5x$ using the power rule.

$\int_1^4 (x^2 - 4x + 5)dx = F(4) - F(1)$

$F(1) = \frac{1}{3}(1^3) - 2(1^2) + 5(1) = \frac{10}{3}$

$F(4) = \frac{1}{3}(4^3) - 2(4^2) + 5(4) = \frac{28}{3}$

Therefore, $\int_1^4 (x^2 - 4x + 5)dx = 6$

For $g(x)$ we can find the integral with:

$\int_1^4 (x + 1)dx$ Finding the antiderivative of $x + 1$ using the power rule shortcut, we get $G(x) = \frac{1}{2}x^2 + x$.

$\int_1^4 (x + 1)dx = G(4) - G(1)$

$\int_1^4 (x + 1)dx = 12 - \frac{3}{2} = \frac{21}{2}$. Now that we have gotten the two areas under the curve, we subtract the area under $f(x)$ from $g(x)$.

$\frac{21}{2} - 6 = \frac{9}{2}$

Limits Test 1

#1: (10 pts each) Find the limit.

a) $\lim_{x \to 4} \frac{4-x}{\sqrt{13-x}-3}$

b) $\lim_{x \to 3} \frac{x^3+2x^2-9x-18}{x^3-4x^2+x+6}$

c) $\lim_{x \to \pi/6} \frac{4\cos^3 x+\sin 2x-4\cos x}{2\cos 2x-1}$

d) $\lim_{x \to +\infty} [\frac{x}{2x+1} + \frac{2x^2}{(x+2)^2}]$

e) $\lim_{x \to \infty} \frac{\sin(2x)}{x}$

#2: (2 pts each) Use the graph $f(x)$ to evaluate:

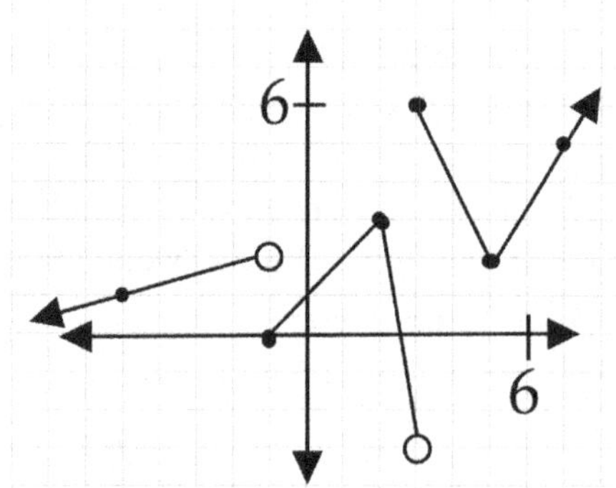

a) $\lim_{x \to -1^-} f(x)$

b) $\lim_{x \to -1^+} f(x)$

c) $\lim_{x \to -5} f(x)$

d) $\lim_{x \to 3^+} f(x)$

e) $\lim_{x \to 3^-} f(x)$

f) $f(-1) + f(3)$

#3: (12 pts) Given positive c such that $\lim_{x \to c} \frac{\sqrt{x^2+5}}{3x^2} = \frac{1}{4}$. Find $\lim_{x \to 4} \frac{\sqrt{8-x}-c}{\sqrt{3x+2c}-4}$. **30**

#4: (12 pts) Given continuous function $f(x)$.

$f(x) = cx^2 + (c+1)x,\ x < 3$

$f(x) = cx + x^2\sqrt{c^2+1},\ x \geq 3$

a) What is the value of c?

b) What is the limit as x approaches 3 for $f(x)$?

#5: (14 points) Find the coordinates of the hole for the function $f(x) = \frac{\sqrt[3]{27-2x}-3}{16-4\sqrt[4]{256+4x}}$.

Limits Test 2

#1: (10 points) Evaluate the limits.

a) $\lim\limits_{x\to 3} \frac{2x^3-3x^2-8x-3}{x^2+x-12} =$

b) $\lim\limits_{x\to 4} \frac{2x^3-128}{\sqrt{x}-2} =$

c) $\lim\limits_{x\to -4} [\frac{\sqrt{x^2+9}-5}{x+4} + \frac{x^2+4x}{x^2+3x-4}] =$

d) $\lim\limits_{x\to -\infty} \frac{\sqrt{16x^8-x}}{x^4+3} =$

e) $\lim\limits_{x\to \infty} e^{x-x^2} =$

#2: (12 points) Find the horizontal asymptotes of $f(x) = \frac{1-e^{-x}}{2+3e^{x}}$

#3: (12 points) Find a and b such that $\lim\limits_{x\to 0} \frac{\sqrt{ax+4}-b}{(a-b)x} = \frac{3}{4}$ **32**

#4: (12 points) If $\lim_{x \to a} \frac{x^3-a^3}{x^2-a^2} = a^2 - 10$, what are the possible values of a? **35**

#5: (14 points) Let $f(x) = \frac{ax+1}{x^2+b}$ and $g(x) = \frac{bx+2}{x^2+a}$.
Find the value of a and b if
$\lim_{x \to 0} \frac{f(x)-g(x)}{x} = f(2)$

Limits Test 3

#1: (10 points each) Evaluate the limit.

a) $\lim_{x\to 4} \frac{x^{3/2}-8}{x+2x^{1/2}-8}$

b) $\lim_{x\to 0} \frac{\sin(3x)}{\sin(2x)}$

c) $\lim_{x\to 1} \arccos(\frac{\sqrt{x}-1}{x-1})$

d) $\lim_{x\to 3} \frac{x^3+2x^2-9x-18}{x^3-4x^2+x+6}$

e) $\lim_{x\to\infty} \ln(\frac{11+8x}{x^3+6x})$

#2: (12 points) Find $\lim_{x\to a} \frac{\sqrt[3]{x}-\sqrt[3]{a}}{\sqrt{x}-\sqrt{a}}$ in terms of a.

#3: (12 points) Find a and b such that
$\lim_{x\to 2} \frac{b-\sqrt{a-x}}{\sqrt{18-x}-4} = \frac{-4}{3}$.

#4: (12 points) Let $f(x) = \frac{ax^3+bx^2+10x-20}{x^2-4}$. If $\lim_{x\to\infty} f(x) = 10$, find $\lim_{x\to -2} f(x)$.

#5: (14 points) If $f(x) = \lim_{n\to x} \frac{n^3-n^2-14n+24}{n-x}$, find the maximum and minimum values of $f(x)$ and its corresponding x values.

Derivatives and Integrals Test 1

#1: (15 points) Use the definition of derivatives to find the derivative of $f(x) = 2x^2 - 3x + 4$. Then find the equation of the tangent line at $x = 2$.

#2: (15 points) Using the definition of a definite integral, determine the approximate area under the curve for $f(x) = x^3 - 2x$ from $[-1,0]$.

#3: A particle's position is modelled by $s(t) = t^3 + \frac{5}{2}t^2 + 2t - 1$

a) (6 points) Find the formula for the instantaneous rate of change of the particle.

b) (6 points) What is the instantaneous rate of change at 2 seconds.

c) (6 points) Find the formula for the acceleration of the particle

d) (6 points) At what times is the particle at rest?

#4: Let the position (height) of a ball tossed in the air be modeled by $s(t) =- 16(t-2)^2 + 24$

a) (3 points) Find the position when the ball is released.

b) (8 points) Find the initial velocity of the object.

c) (6 points) Find the maximum height the object will reach.

d) (3 points) Find the time the ball takes to reach the ground.

e) (4 points) Find the velocity when the ball hits the ground.

f) (6 points) Find the acceleration when the ball hits the ground.

5: (4 points each) Given the graph of $f'(x)$.

a) Over which interval(s) is $f(x)$ increasing?

b) Over which interval(s) is $f(x)$ decreasing?

c) For what value(s) of x does $f(x)$ have a local maximum?

d) For what value(s) of x does $f(x)$ have a local minimum?

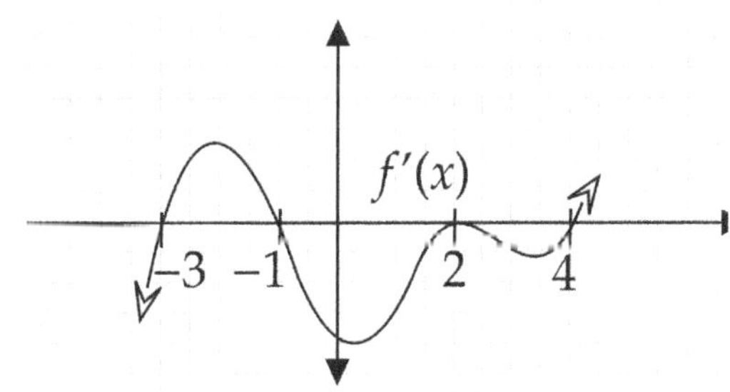

Derivatives and Integrals Test 2

#1: (20 points) Using the definition of a derivative, find the equation of the line tangent to $f(x) = 2\sqrt{x} + x$ at $x = 9$. Then use linear approximation to approximate $\sqrt{9.2}$.

#2: (20 points) Using the definition of a definite integral, determine the area formed by the intersection of $f(x) = 2x + 3$ and $g(x) = x^2 + 2x + 2$.

#3: (15 points) Alice is trying to construct a box whose has dimensions $x, x+5, 3-x$. What should the dimensions of the box approximately be to maximize the volume of the box?

#4: (15 points) Use the limit of summation as $n \to \infty$ to determine the area under the curve of $f(x) = 2x^3 + 6x^2 - 3$ from $[-2, -1]$.

#5: A particular flying fish's position relative to the surface of the ocean in feet can be modelled by $s(t) = -2t^4 + 15t^3 - 34t^2 + 24t$ where t is in seconds. The fish leaps out from the ocean two times, the first time at $t = 0$.

a) (5 points) At what times is the fish breaking the surface of the ocean?

b) (5 points) Find the equation $v(t)$ that represents the fish's velocity at a given time.

c) (5 points) At what velocity is the fish traveling when it plunges back into the ocean the first time? Second time?

d) (5 points) Find the equation $a(t)$ that represents the fish's acceleration at a given time.

e) (5 points) At what times is the fish's velocity constant?

f) (5 points) At what time is the fish's acceleration the highest? What is the fish's velocity at that time?

Derivatives and Integrals Test 3

#1: (15 points) Find the derivative of $f(x) = \sqrt{2x^2 + 7} + x$. Then find the equation of the tangent line to $f(x)$ at $x = 3$.

#2: (15 points) Find the area of under the curve bounded by $f(x) = x^2 + 1$ and $g(x) = 3x^2 - 5x - 2$.

#3: (15 points) If r_1, r_2, r_3 are the not necessarily real roots of $f(x) = ax^3 - (a-1)x^2 + (a+1)x + d$. Find the minimum value of $r_1^2 + r_2^2 + r_3^2$.

#4: (15 points) If the area bounded by $f(x) = x^2 + kx + 2$ and $g(x) = x + 2$ is $\frac{9}{2}$, find the possible value(s) of k.

#5: (20 points) A slice of cake is in a shape of a 3D circular sector with radius r cm, central angle of $\frac{\pi}{3}$ radians, and height h cm. The volume of the slice of cake is $\frac{8}{3}\pi^2$ cm cubed. What should r be so that the surface area (including the bottom) is minimized?

#6: (10 points each) A particle's position on the x axis can be modelled by $s(t) = \frac{1}{3}t^3 - 3t^2 + 8t$ for t $[0, 5]$.

a) How much has the particle traveled in the time interval?

b) At what time intervals is the particle moving away from the origin?

Chapter 15 Hints

1 This one is hard. Plug in the two y values and use the discriminant twice to get two equations. Eliminate the hk term and you'll get $(h-3)^2 = (k-2)^2$.

2 By Vieta's formulas, remember that the sum of roots is a. Product of roots is -12 and paired sum is -4. Try to combine the fractions into one.

3 Remember that a matrix multiplied by its inverse is the identity matrix. Find the inverses of the matrices that are being multiplied to X.

4 Remember $\sin x = \cos(x - 90^\circ)$ and use $\sin 2x = 2\sin x \cos x$.

5 Remember by Vieta's Formulas $r_1 + r_2 = 4\sin(\theta + \frac{\pi}{4}), r_1 r_2 = 2\cos(4\theta)$. Do some squaring and manipulation!

6 Find angle EDC first. Use that to set up an equation to solve for AE.

7 What happens if you split it into two cases: $-2 < x < 2$ and $x < -2, x > 2$?

8 $\sqrt[3]{3} = 3^{1/3}, \sqrt[3]{\sqrt[3]{9}} = 3^{2/9}, \sqrt[3]{\sqrt[3]{\sqrt[3]{27}}} = 3^{3/27}$... Notice a pattern here?

9 Let $AP = a, AQ = b$. $\frac{1}{2}ab\sin 60^\circ = \frac{169\sqrt{3}}{48}$. Then use the Law of Cosines on the same triangle.

10 Remember that the average of the 1st and 3rd term is equal to the 2nd term. Use that to set up 2 equations.

11 Hmm. What is the relationship between $4, 6, 9$? Is there a pattern here?

12 $A = (a, 4a^2 + 2a - 3), B = (b, 4b^2 + 2b - 3)$ Now set up two equations to represent the midpoint.

13 Sorry about this one. Using the infinite sum formula, set up a system of two equations. Use elimination to cancel out the part involving S_a.

14 I apologize in advance. Let $F_1B = y$ Then, $x^2 + y^2 = 4c^2$ by the pythagorean theorem. Use the properties of foci to get that $x + y = 2a$. Remember that $a^2 = b^2 + c^2$ in an ellipse. In this case, $b = \sqrt{6}$ from the minor axis length.

15 The parameters of our domain represent the zeroes of $-x^2 + ax + b$.

16 For domain, remember $bx^2 - 2x + a \geq 0$. Also try expressing this in vertex form.

17 Find the arclength AB to find the radius AO_2. Use you the sector area formula $\frac{1}{2}r^2\theta$ to find the area of $CABD$.

18 Let the first radical be in the form $x + y\sqrt{2}$. Let the second radical in the form $a + b\sqrt{2}$. Then solve for x, y, a, b. Think about why we can do this?

19 After simplifying, multiply both sides by the inverse of X. Remember that $X^{-1}(X)$ equals the identity matrix.

20 Don't isolate the radical just yet. Cube both sides and simplify!

21 Use Law of Cosines on triangle ABE and triangle BEC because you know they share a common angle. Use the Angle Bisector Theorem to find the length of ED.

22 If the circle is the smallest possible, the tangency points will be at the hyperbola's vertices. Find the coordinates of the vertices by first finding it in $x'y'$ form.

23 Let $S = \sum_{n}^{\infty} \frac{n(n+1)}{3^n}$. What happens when you subtract $\frac{1}{3}S$ from S? List out some terms!

24 Rewrite the expression as $\frac{(\sin 12^\circ + \sin 48^\circ) + (\sin 42^\circ + \sin 78^\circ)}{\sin 27^\circ + \sin 63^\circ}$

25 $1 = \log_b b$. Try completing the square.

26 Extend lines BC and AD to form an equilateral triangle.

27 Remember that the maximum or minimum of a function occurs at the "vertex". The vertex is also always halfway between two points that have the same y coordinate due to symmetry.

28 Divide out the $1 - \cos 2x$. Express each factor as a square and then take the square root.

29 Simplify $\frac{1-\cos 2x}{\cot x}$ first.

30 Solve for c through direct substitution. Then solve the limit using the rationalization two times.

31 Let the terms of matrix X be a, b, c, d. Use that is to set up a system of equations. Don't multiply out inverses!

32 Multiply by the conjugate first. Remember that the x factor must cancel from the top and bottom.

33 Solve $3x^2 + x = 2$ and $2x^3 + 3x^2 - 2x - 1 = 2$.

34 Remember that $h(h^{-1}(x)) = x$. What happens when you trying plugging in $h^{-1}(x)$ into the function?

35 Factor the difference of cubes and squares. Simplify and then use direct substitution.

36 Simplify $\frac{1-\cot x}{1+\cot x}$ by multiplying $\sin^2 x(1 - \cot x)$ on the top and bottom.

37 Express $\tan(\frac{a+b}{2})$ as $\frac{\sin(\frac{a+b}{2})}{\cos(\frac{a+b}{2})}$. Multiply the top and bottom by $\cos(\frac{a+b}{2})$ then use double angle formulas to simplify.

38 Find the coordinates of X and Y. Then use the distance formula with pythagorean theorem to set up equations. Remember $9 = b^2 + c^2$ in this case.

39 Sorry, this is really geo heavy. Just construct 30-60-90 triangles and use change of base

40 Remember $\log_a b = \frac{1}{\log_b a}$. Try squaring now?

41 What is the relationship between $4x - 1, 4 - x$, and $3x + 3$?

42 The distance from a point to a circle is basically the distance to the center minus the length of the radius.

43 What this problems really is asking is $\lim_{x \to 0} f(x)$. First, use the difference of cubes to "rationalize" the numerator. Then change the difference in quartics to the difference of squares to "rationalize" denominator. The x factors will cancel out.

44 The polar graph listed is a circle with radius 2. The distance (x, y) to the pole is $\sqrt{x^2 + y^2}$. The distance to the circle is the distance to center minus the radius length.

45 The length of the lactus rectum is $\frac{2b^2}{a}$. Then use properties of $30 - 60 - 90$ triangle. Try to express things in terms of c and a. Finally, you'll have to use the quadratic formula at the end after a bunch of simplifying.

46 Let b be the common difference for b_n. Rewrite b_4 as $b_3 + b, b_6$ as $b_5 + b$, etc.

47 The area of the curved part would be the arc length of the sector times the height. Use the formulas you know to sum up the surface areas for the two cases. You'll get a nonlinear system of equations.

48 Let $g(x) = ax + b$. Think about why we know $g(x)$ is a linear function?

49 Try simplifying $\tan(\tan^{-1}0.5 + \tan^{-1}\frac{1}{3})$.

50 First use the discriminant to find r. If the circle intersects the hyperbola at two points of the same y coordinate, think about what this means about the hyperbola's center in relation to the circle's center.

Chapter 16 Answer Keys

Chapter 1 Diagnostic Test

#1a) $32x^2(x-2)(x^2+2x+4)$

b) $(16x-1)(3x+5)$

c) $(x-y)(x^2+xy+y^2)(x+y)(x^2-xy+y^2)$

d) $(x+1)(2x+3)(x+2)$

#2a) $x=3, y=-1, z=0$

b) $x=3,-1,2,\frac{-1}{2}$

c) $\sqrt{6}-1 \le x \le 3$

#3 Axis of Symmetry: $x=-6$
Vertex: $(-6,-33)$
y-intercept: $(0,3)$
x-intercept: $(-6 \pm \sqrt{33},0)$
Additional Points: $(1,16)(2,31)$
Transformation: Horizontal Translation 6 units left, Vertical Translation 33 units down

#4 $k=2 \pm 2\sqrt{2}$

#5 18 upcharges, \$19220

#6 $a=-3$

If you weren't able to complete all the questions in this test, I would recommend reviewing these Algebra 1 and 2 concepts before beginning. Quadratics and polynomials in "disguise" pop up a lot in Pre-calculus problems and finding the "maximum" of functions is frequent as well. Note that I didn't really include any geometry problems. However, you should have a basic knowledge of geometry figures for this book.

Chapter 2 Radical Functions

Test 1:

#1a) $9+3\sqrt{7}$

b) $\frac{8-2\sqrt[3]{3}}{61}$

c) $\frac{1}{256}$

d) $\frac{27+3\sqrt{3}+9\sqrt[4]{3}+\sqrt[4]{27}}{78}$

#2 $g^{-1}(x)=\frac{1+\sqrt{12x+25}}{6}$

#3 Domain: $x \le -4, x \ge \frac{3-\sqrt{65}}{2}$ Range: $y \ge 2$

#4 $a=3, b=-1$

#5a) $-3 \le x \le \frac{1-3\sqrt{5}}{2}$, $x \ge \frac{1+3\sqrt{5}}{2}$

b) $x=1$

c) $x=0,4,-4$

d) $x=\frac{1}{4},4$

Test 2:

#1a) $3-\sqrt{7}$

b) $\frac{32+\sqrt[3]{9}}{61}$

c) 2

#2 $f(2)=\frac{-11}{27}, 2\ f^{-1}(2)=\frac{-1\pm\sqrt{13}}{6}$

#3 1

#4 7

#5a) $-\sqrt{5} \le x \le -1, 2 \le x \le \sqrt{5}$

b) $x=13$

c) $x=-1/3,-1/2$

d) $x=8$

#6a) $g(x)=x^2-x-3$

b) $b=4$

Test 3:

#1a) $3-2\sqrt{7}$

b) $-\frac{3\sqrt[3]{9}+14\sqrt[3]{3}+40}{61}$

c) 4

#2a) 1

b) 1

c) 16

#3 $$f(x)=\begin{cases}\sqrt{x^2+3x-4} & \text{if, } x \ge 2\\ \sqrt{-x^2+3x+4} & \text{if, } -1 \le x < 2\\ \text{Undefined} & \text{if, } -4 < x \le -1\\ \sqrt{x^2+3x-4} & \text{if, } x \le -4\end{cases}$$

#4 $g(x)=\frac{2}{3}x^2-7x+16$

#5 $f^{-1}(x)=-\frac{1}{9}x^2-2$ Range: $y \ge 0$, Domain: $x \ge 0$

#6a) $x=5$

b) $x=3, \frac{25}{8}$

c) $-3 \le x \le \frac{5-\sqrt{117}}{2}, x \ge \frac{5+\sqrt{117}}{2}$

#7 3

#8 Domain: $x \le -2, x \ge 3/2$ Range: $y \ge 4$

Chapter 3 Exponential/Logarithmic Functions

Test 1:

#1a) $\frac{-5}{6}$

b) $\frac{1}{(3-2x)^2}$

c) $\log(\frac{a^3c}{b^6\sqrt{243}})$

d) $\frac{12x+1}{3}$

#2 Domain: $-1 \le x \le 7/4$ Range: $4 \le y \le 2^{11/2}+3$

#3 18

#4 $g(x) = f^{-1}(2x^2 - x - 1)$ Domain: $x < -\frac{1}{2}, x > 1$

#5a) $x = \frac{1}{5}$

b) $x = 0, \frac{1}{2}$

c) $x = 3^{3/4}, x = 9$

d) $\frac{-26}{7} < x < \frac{-3-\sqrt{13}}{2}$ $x > \frac{-3+\sqrt{13}}{2}$

#6 $\frac{5}{2}$

#7 $\log_{1.01} 1.25$

Test 2:

#1a) $\ln(\frac{128x^3}{(x^2-2)^9})$

b) $(1+6x)^{-6\sqrt{5}}$

c) $\log \frac{1}{16(a+3b)}$

d) $\frac{16x+23}{6}$

#2 Domain: $-2-\sqrt{15} \le x \le -2+\sqrt{15}$

Range: $0 \le y \le 2$

#3 $a = 8, b = 16; a = 16, b = 8; a = \frac{1}{8}, b = \frac{1}{16}$

$a = \frac{1}{16}, b = \frac{1}{8}$

#4a) $x = \log_{3/2}(\frac{1+\sqrt{5}}{2})$

b) $x = \log_2 3$, $x = -1$

c) $x = 3, \log_3 54$

d) $10^{\pm\sqrt{3}}$

#5a) $3\log_{0.83} 0.2$

b) $(0.83)^{5/3}$

#6 $b = 6$

Test 3:

#1a) 24

b) 6

c) $(x^2+1)^6$

d) $8x+1$

#2 $\log_{0.82} 0.5$

#3 Range: $-1 \le y \le 4$ $(a = 2, b = 3)$

#4a) $x = 11$

b) $x = 2, 1, 0$

c) $\frac{3}{2} < x < 2$

d) $x = \frac{1}{16}, 16, 1$

#5 $\frac{4}{3}$ $(x = 4, a = 16^{2/3})$

#6 $C + \frac{5}{4}A - B + \frac{1}{2}$

Chapter 4 Rational Functions

Test 1:

#1a) $\frac{1}{x}$

b) $\frac{2x(2x^2+2x+1)}{(x+1)(x-1)}$

c) $\frac{2b^2(2a-3b)}{a-b}$

#2 Hole: $(-6, 20/7)$, VA: $x = -3, 1$, HA: $y = 1$, SA: None, x-intercept: $(6,0)$, $(-1,0)$ y-intercept: $(0,2)$ Intersection: $(-3/7, 1)$

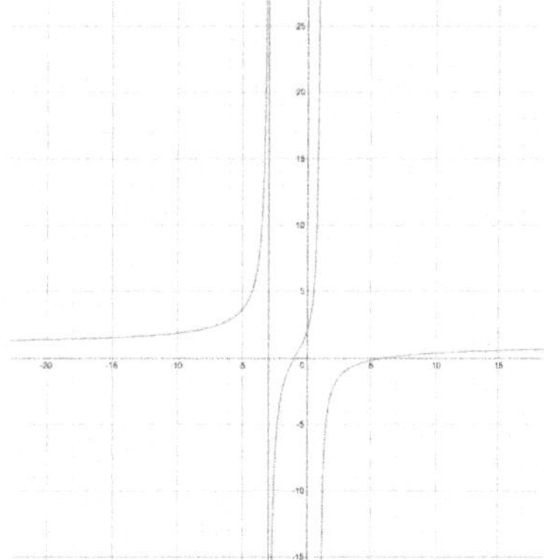

#3a) $x + 5 + \frac{234/7}{x-6} - \frac{3/7}{x+1}$

b) $\frac{5}{x} - \frac{4}{x+1} - \frac{9}{(x+1)^2}$

#4a) Matthew: 7.2 hours Ryan: 9 hours

b) 4.95 hours

#5a) $F = \frac{kwv}{r^2}$ (Varies)

b) 22.5

c) 2700 Newtons

#6 $(-\infty, 2) \cup [7, +\infty)$

Test 2:

#1a) $\frac{(m+2)(m+3)}{(m-2)(m+1)}$

b) $\frac{(3y-2)(y-2)}{2(y-1)^2}$

c) $\frac{3x^2-3x-14}{(2x-1)(3x-7)(x+1)}$

#2 Hole: $(-2, -7/3)$, VA: $x = -1, 1$, HA: $y = 0$, SA: None, x-intercept: $(3/2, 0)$, y-intercept: $(0,3)$ Intersection: $(3/2, 0)$

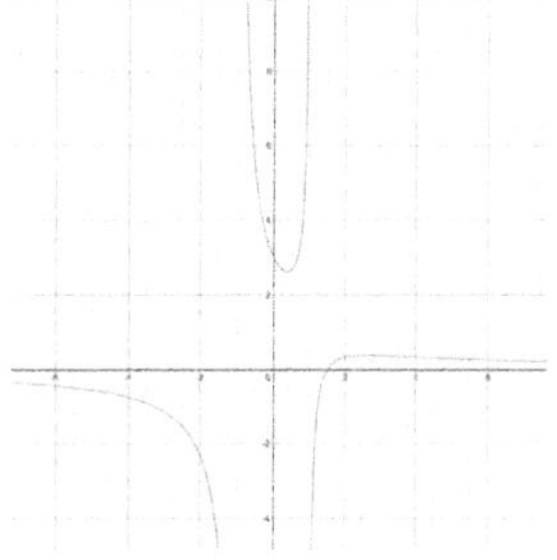

#3a) $\frac{1/2}{x} + \frac{1/2}{x-6} - \frac{1}{x+1}$

b) $\frac{-4}{x+1} - \frac{2}{x^2+3} - \frac{2}{(x^2+3)^2}$

#4a) $\frac{120}{19}$ hours

b) $\frac{84}{9}$ hours

#5a) $I = \frac{kG^3SE^2}{A}$ (Varies)

b) 1/30

c) 11520

#6 $(-\infty,-3/2) \cup [-8/7,+\infty)$

Test 3:

#1a) $\frac{(m-3)(m-4)}{m+1}$

b) $\frac{-(a+b)^2}{a-b}$

c) $\frac{7x^2+12x+9}{(3x+5)(x-1)(x+1)}$

#2 Hole: $(-1,-6)$, VA: $x=-3$, HA: None, SA: $y = 2x - 13$, x-intercept: $(3,0),(\frac{1}{2},0)$, y-intercept: $(0,1)$, Intersection: None

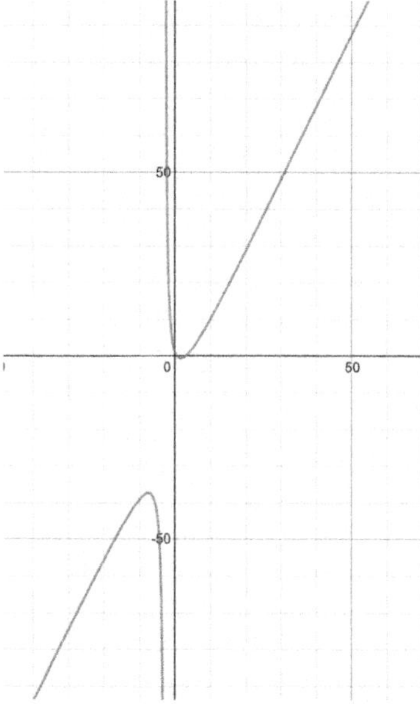

#3a) $\frac{-1/3x+5/3}{x^2+2} + \frac{1/3}{x-1}$

b) $\frac{2}{x} + \frac{2}{x^2+1} + \frac{1}{x^2-5}$

#4a) 40

b) 48 miles per hour

#5a) $G = \frac{k \cdot S \cdot E^2 \cdot A^3}{O \cdot R^2}$ (Varies)

b) 2/3

c) 75

#6 $(-\infty,1) \cup [2,3]$

Test 4:

#1a) 5

b) $\frac{(m+4)(2m+1)(n-5)}{2n}$

c) $\frac{5x-2}{4x^2-2x+1}$

#2 Hole: $(2,\frac{28}{9})$, VA: $x=-1, x=\frac{1}{2}$, HA: $y=\frac{3}{2}$, SA: None, x-intercept: $(-2,0),(-\frac{1}{3},0)$, y-intercept: $(0,-2)$, Intersection: $(-\frac{7}{11},\frac{3}{2})$

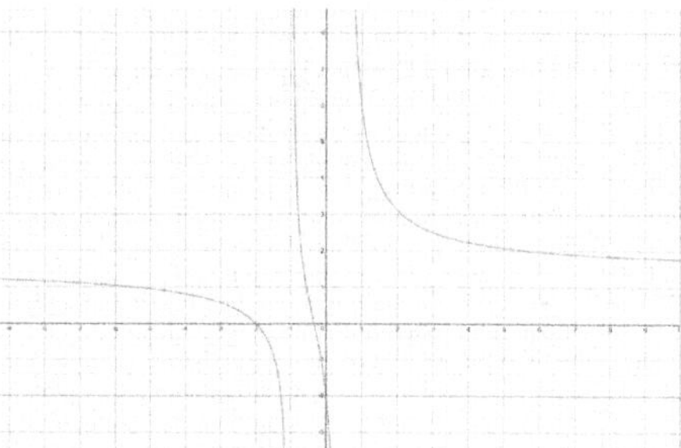

#3a) $\frac{3}{x} + \frac{2}{x+1} - \frac{1}{2x-1}$

b) $\frac{2}{x+2} - \frac{2x+3}{x^2+1} + \frac{1}{x-2}$

#4 1040 seconds

#5a) $W = \frac{C}{kh}$ (Answers Vary)

b) 40 coders

#6 $(-\infty,-3] \cup,(-2,1]$

Chapter 5 Sequences and Series

Test 1:

#1a) $a_n = \frac{(-1)^n(\frac{1}{2}n^2-\frac{1}{2}n+2)}{n \cdot n!}$

b) $a_n = n^3 \cdot (\frac{1}{2}n^2 + \frac{1}{2}n + ((-1)^n \cdot 2n!)$

c) $a_n = (-1)^{n-1} \cdot \sqrt[n]{n^2 \cdot 3n!}$

#2 $\frac{13}{4}$

#3 $a_n = 2n+5, b_n = 3n-1$

#4 16

#5a) $n = 2 : 5^2 + 9 < 6^2$

$34 < 36$ So it is true for $n = 2$.

$n = k$: Assume it is true for $n = k+1$ for $k \geq 2$

Now we want to prove it's true for $n = k+1$:

$5^k + 9 < 6^k$ From assumption

$6(5^k + 9) < 6^{k+1}$ Multiplying 6 on both sides

$(5+1)(5^k + 9) < 6^{k+1}$ Rewriting the 6

$5^{k+1} + 9 + (5^k + 45) < 6^{k+1}$ Expanding

Since $k \geq 2, 5^k + 45$ is obviously greater than 0.

Thus $5^{k+1} + 9 < 6^{k+1}$ is true, finishing the proof.

b) $n = 1 : 17(1^3) + 103(1) = 120 = 6(2)$

So it is true for $n = 1$.

$n = k$: Assume $17k^3 + 103k = 6a$ for integer a

Now we want to prove it's true for $n = k+1$:

$17(k+1)^3 + 103k$

$17k^3 + 51k^2 + 51k + 17 + 103k + 103$ Expanding

$17k^3 + 103k + 51k^2 + 51k + 120$ Simplifying

$6a + 51k(k+1) + 6(20)$ Factoring

$6a + 6(8)k(k+1) + 3k(k+1) + 6(20)$ Rewriting

We can prove this part by induction if we wanted, but we know that the product of any two consecutive numbers has to be even, so:

$6a + 6(8)k(k+1) + 3(2b) + 6(20)$ for integer b

$6(a + 8k(k+1) + b + 20)$ Factoring

Since a, k, b are all integers, the proof is finished.

c) $n = 1 : 1^2 = \frac{4(1)-1}{3}$ so it's true for $n = 1$.

$n = k$: Assume $1^2 + 3^2 + 5^2 + \ldots + (2k-1)^2 = \frac{4k^3-k}{3}$

Now we want to prove it's true for $n = k+1$: If we add $2(k+1) - 1$ to both sides of our assumption, our right side becomes:

$\frac{4k^3-k}{3} + (2(k+1)-1)^2$

$\frac{4k^2-k}{3} + 4k^2 + 4k + 1$ Simplifying

$\frac{4k^3-k+12k^2+12k+3}{3}$ Combining Fraction

$\frac{4k^3+12k^2+12k+4-k-1}{3}$ Rewriting

$\frac{4(k+1)^3-(k+1)}{3}$ Factoring

This shows how the equation holds true for $n = k+1$ and our proof is finished.

#6 $4, 6, 9$ or $9, 6, 4$

#7a) 2450

b) $\frac{88}{7}$

Test 2:

#1a) $a_n = (n^2 - 2n + 8)(\sqrt[n+1]{2n!})$

b) $a_n = \frac{|3-n|}{\frac{1}{2}n^2 - \frac{1}{2}n + 3}$

c) $a_n = \frac{(-1)^n \cdot n^3}{(n-1)!}$

#2 $x = 11$

#3 $x = 60$

#4 820

#5a) $n = 1 : 9 = 1(2(1)+7)$ so it's true for $n = 1$.

$n = k$: Assume $9 + 13 + 17 \ldots + (4k+5) = k(2k+7)$

Now we want to prove it's true for $n = k+1$: If we add $4(k+1)+5$ to both sides of our assumption, our right side becomes:

$2k^2 + 7k + 4k + 4 + 5$ Simplifying

$2k^2 + 11k + 9$ Combining like terms

$(k+1)(2k+9)$ Factoring

$(k+1)(2(k+1)+7)$ Rewriting, finishing proof

b) $n = 1 : 5^1 - 3^1 = 2(1)$

So it is true for $n = 1$.

$n = k$: Assume $5^k - 3^k = 2a$ for integer a

Now we want to prove it's true for $n = k+1$:

$5^{k+1} - 3^{k+1}$ What we must prove true

$5(5^k) - 3(3^k)$ Exponent rules

$2(5^k) + 3(5^k) - 3(3^k)$ Rewriting $5(5^k)$

$2(5^k) + 3(5^k - 3^k)$ Factoring

$2(5^k) + 3(2a)$ From assumption

$2(5^k + 3a)$ Factoring

Since k and a are integers, this proves it holds true for $k+1$ and finishes up our proof.

c) $n = 1 : 8^1 \geq 4(1)$ so it's true for $n = 1$.

$n = k$: Assume $8^k \geq 4k$ for integer $k \geq 1$

Now we want to prove it's true for $n = k+1$: From assumption: $8^k \geq 4k$.

$8(8^k) \geq 32k$ Multiplying 8 on both sides

$8^{k+1} \geq 4k + 28k$ Splitting $32k$

Since $k \geq 1$, $28k \geq 28 \geq 4$, therefore, $8^{k+1} \geq 4k+4$.

$8^{k+1} \geq 4(k+1)$. This is what we wanted to prove so this proof is finished.

#6 $\frac{3}{4}$

#7 $\frac{-117}{40}$

Chapter 6 Counting and Probability

Test 1:

#1 10264320

#2 0.4419

#3 72

#4 0.4905

#5 0.2950

#6 1/3

#7 0.1608

#8 0.4720

#9 231600

#10 16

#11 17280

#12 0.0768

#13 0.3177

#14 343980

#15 5/11

#16 0.1678

#17 840

#18 1/10

#19 5/12

Test 2:

#1 3602776320

#2 5/11

#3 17/200

#4 $\frac{3}{10}$

#5 0.1406

#6 3069
#7 5/9
#8 0.8809
#9 0.3297
#10 0.4370
#11 960
#12 7/18
#13 5160
#14 5/12
#15 1/6
#16 0.2513
#17 264
#18 180180
#19 19399380

Test 3:
#1 $253440x^7$
#2 0.2966
#3 0.0541
#4 1/8
#5 30
#6 0.6625
#7 100%
#8 400
#9 46200
#10 2/3
#11 0.0016248
#12 0.4355
#13 28800
#14 0.4286
#15 120
#16 0.01727
#17 19/56
#18 8
#19 $1.599 \cdot 10^{10}$

Chapter 7 Trigonometric Functions

Test 1:
#1a) $\frac{\sqrt{2}}{2}$
b) $\frac{-2\sqrt{3}}{3}$
c) -1
d) $\frac{-\sqrt{3}}{2}$
e) $\sqrt{2}$
f) $\sqrt{3}$
g) $\frac{1}{2}$
h) 2
i) Undefined
#2 Period: 1 Mideline: 1 Phase Shift: $\frac{-1}{2}$
Asymptotes at $x = \frac{\pm k}{2}$ where k is odd.

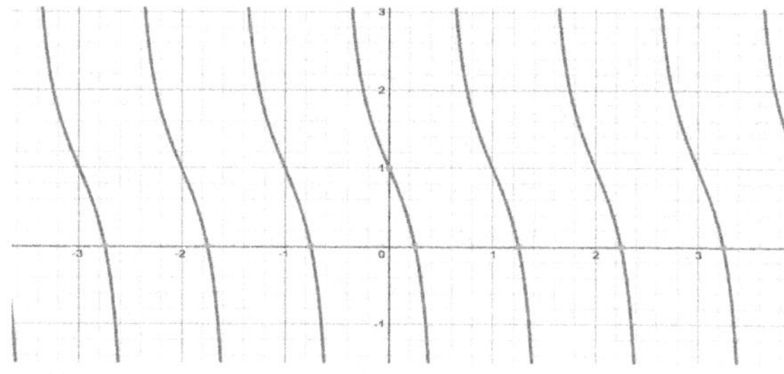

#3a) $4000\pi\frac{rad}{min}$
b) $\frac{20}{9}yd/sec$
c) $y =- \cos(\frac{20\pi}{3}t) + 1, y =- \sin(\frac{\pi}{2} - \frac{20\pi t}{3}) + 1$
#4a) $60\,ft$
b) $60 + 60\sqrt{3}ft$
c) $60 - 2\sqrt{3}ft$
#5 $\theta = 1, h = 2$
#6a) $\frac{4\,rad}{sec}$
b) $\frac{2}{\pi}rev/sec$
c) $y =- 12\sin(\frac{\pi}{2} - 4t) + 12 =- 12\cos(4t) + 12$
#7a) $4 + 4\sqrt{3}km$
b) $8 + 8\sqrt{3}km^2$

Test 2:
#1a) $\frac{-\sqrt{2}}{2}$
b) -2
c) -1
d) $\frac{1}{2}$
e) $-\sqrt{2}$
f) $\frac{\sqrt{3}}{3}$
g) Undefined
h) 2
i) 0
#2 Period: 1 Phase Shift: $x =- \frac{1}{4}$ Midline: -1
Asymptotes: $x = \frac{\pm k}{4}$ where k is odd, Amplitude: 1

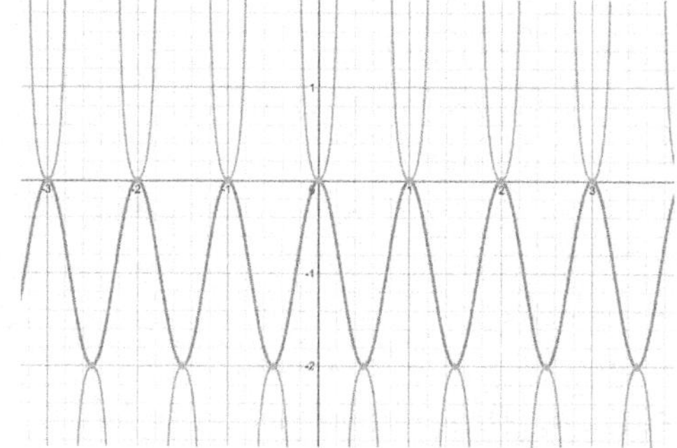

#3 El Toro: $100\sqrt{3}$ ft, Kingda Ka: $100\sqrt{3} + 300$ ft

#4a) $\frac{21\pi}{4}$

b) $\frac{15\pi}{8}$

c) $\frac{6615\pi}{4} in^2$

#5a) $\frac{360\pi\ rad}{min}$

b) $4 yd/sec$

c) $y = -cos(6\pi t) + 2$

d) $y = -sin(6\pi t - \pi) + 2$

#6a) $3\ rad/sec$

b) $\frac{3}{2\pi} rev/sec$

c) $y = -11\sin(\frac{\pi}{2} - 3t) + 11 = -11\cos(3t) + 11$

#7 $AO_1 = 3, AC = 2$

Test 3:

#1a) $-\sqrt{2}$

b) $-\frac{1}{2}$

c) 1

d) $\frac{-2\sqrt{3}}{3}$

e) $\frac{\sqrt{2}}{2}$

f) $-\sqrt{3}$

g) 0

h) $\frac{-\sqrt{3}}{2}$

i) Undefined

#2 Period: 4 Amplitude: 2 Phase Shift: $x = 3$

Asymptotes: $x = 2k$ where k is an integer

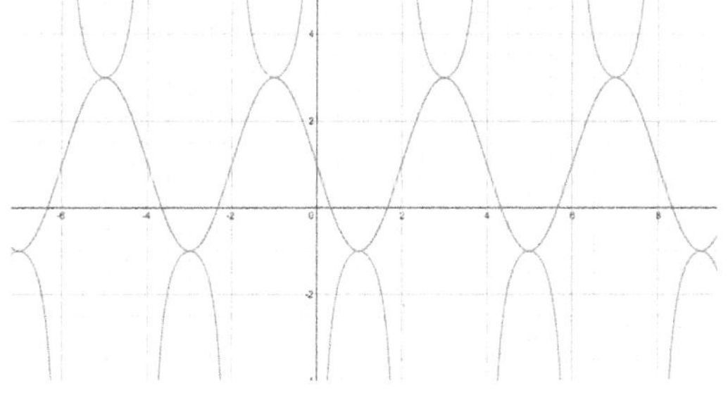

#3a) $1584\ yd/min$

b) $\frac{594\ rad}{35\ min}$

c) $\frac{7128^\circ}{\pi}$

d) $\frac{1400\pi}{9}$

#4 $\frac{6\pi}{\pi+9} \approx 1.55247$

#5a) $\frac{\pi/360}{minute}$

b) $\frac{\pi\ ft}{hour}$

c) $h = -6\sin(\frac{\pi}{30}t - \frac{1}{2}) + 107 = 6\cos(\frac{\pi}{30}t) + 107$

#6a) $y = -70\cos(\frac{1}{5}x) + 80 = -70\sin(\frac{\pi}{2} - \frac{1}{5}x) + 80$

b) $115\ feet$

#7a)

$\sqrt{(120\sin 20^\circ + 80\sin 40^\circ)^2 + (120\sin 70^\circ - 80\sin 50^\circ)^2}$

b) $N\tan^{-1}(\frac{120\sin 20^\circ + 80\sin 40^\circ}{120\sin 70^\circ - 80\sin 50^\circ})W$

Chapter 8 Trig Equations/Identities

Test 1:

#1a) $\frac{5}{6}$

b) $\frac{-\sqrt{29}}{5}$

c) $\frac{5}{\sqrt{26}}$

#2 $\sqrt{2+\sqrt{3}}$

#3 $\frac{\sqrt{3}+3\sqrt{2}-3}{3-\sqrt{6}+\sqrt{3}}$

#4a) $x = \frac{\pi}{6}, \frac{2\pi}{3}, \frac{\pi}{12}, \frac{7\pi}{12}$

b) $x = \frac{\pi}{3}$

c) $x = \frac{\pi}{2}$

d) $x = \frac{\pi}{18}, \frac{\pi}{6}, \frac{7\pi}{6}, \frac{7\pi}{18}, \frac{\pi}{2}, \frac{11\pi}{18}, \frac{13\pi}{18}, \frac{5\pi}{6}, \frac{17\pi}{18}, \frac{\pi}{12}$

$\frac{\pi}{4}, \frac{5\pi}{12}, \frac{7\pi}{12}, \frac{3\pi}{4}, \frac{11\pi}{12}$

#5 $\frac{28}{3}$

#6a) LHS: $(1 + 2\sin x \cdot \cos x)(1 + 2\sin x \cdot \cos x)$

$(1 + \sin(2x))(1 - \sin(2x))$

$1 - \sin^2(2x)$

$\cos^2(2x)$

$(2\cos^2 x - 1)^2$

b) LHS: $2\tan x(1 - \sin^2 x)$

$2\tan x \cdot \cos^2 x$

$\frac{2\sin x}{\cos x} \cdot \cos^2 x$

$2\sin x \cdot \cos x$

$\sin(2x)$

$\frac{\sin(2x)}{\cos(2x)} \cdot \cos(2x)$

$\tan(2x) \cdot \cos(2x)$

Test 2:

#1a) $\sqrt{-x^2 - 4x - 3}$

b) $\frac{\sqrt{-x^2+4x}}{x-2}$

c) $\frac{-3}{5}$

#2 $\cos^2(2x)$

#3 $\frac{-\sqrt{6+3\sqrt{2}}+\sqrt{2-\sqrt{2}}}{4}$

#4a) $V = \sin(\frac{\theta}{2})\cos(\frac{\theta}{2})$

Max at $\theta = 90^\circ$ Max Volume: $\frac{1}{2}m^3$

b) $V = \frac{1}{2}\sin\theta$

#5a) $x = \frac{\pi}{4}, \frac{7\pi}{4}$

b) $x = \frac{\pi}{4}, \frac{5\pi}{4}, \frac{\pi}{3}, \frac{2\pi}{3}, \frac{4\pi}{3}, \frac{5\pi}{3}$

#6a) LHS: $\frac{1-\cot x}{(1+\cot x)(1-\cot x+\cot^2 x)}$

$\frac{1-\cot x}{1+\cot x} \cdot \frac{1}{\csc^2 x - \cot x}$

$\frac{(1-\cot x)(1-\cot x)}{(1+\cot x)(1-\cot x)} \cdot \frac{\sin^2 x}{1-\sin x\cos x}$

$\frac{1-\frac{2\cos x}{\sin x}+\frac{\cos^2 x}{\sin^2 x}}{1-\frac{\cos^2 x}{\sin^2 x}} \cdot \frac{2\sin^2 x}{2-\sin 2x}$

$\frac{\sin^2 x-2\sin x\cos x+\cos^2 x}{\sin^2 x-\cos^2 x} \cdot \frac{2\sin^2 x}{2-\sin 2x}$

$\frac{1-\sin 2x}{-\cos 2x} \cdot \frac{2\sin^2 x}{2-\sin 2x}$

$\frac{2\sin^2 x(\sin 2x-1)}{2\cos 2x-\sin 2x\cos 2x}$

$\frac{4\sin^2 x(\sin 2x-1)}{4\cos 2x-\sin 4x}$

b) LHS: $(-2\sin(3x)\sin(-x))^2+(2\sin(3x)\cos(x))^2$

$4\sin^2(3x)\sin^2 x+4\sin^2(3x)\cos^2 x$

$4\sin^2(3x)(\sin^2 x+\cos^2 x)$

$4\sin^2(3x)$

#7 $\frac{29\sqrt{46}}{142}$

Test 3:

#1a) $\frac{\sqrt{-x^2-2x}}{\sqrt{-x^2-2x+1}}$

b) $\frac{2\sqrt{-x^2+4x}}{-x^2+4x}$

c) 0.6

#2 $2-2\cos(4x)+\cos(2x)-\cos(6x)$

#3 $\sqrt{\frac{4+\sqrt{2}-\sqrt{6}}{8}}$ or $\frac{\sqrt{6+3\sqrt{2}}-\sqrt{2-\sqrt{2}}}{4}$

#4a) 60°

b) $\cos x=1-\frac{2}{M^2}$

#5 $x=0,\frac{\pi}{2},\frac{3\pi}{2},\frac{\pi}{4},\frac{3\pi}{4},\frac{5\pi}{4},\frac{7\pi}{4}$

#6 0.8

#7a) LHS: $[\sin(\theta+\frac{\pi}{4})]^2$

$[\sin\theta\cos\frac{\pi}{4}+\sin\frac{\pi}{4}\cos\theta]^2$

$[\frac{\sqrt{2}}{2}(\cos\theta+\sin\theta)]^2$

$\frac{1}{2}(\cos^2\theta+2\sin\theta\cos\theta+\sin^2\theta)$

$\frac{1}{2}(1+\sin 2\theta)$

b) LHS: $\frac{\cos(2x)\cos x-\sin(2x)\sin x}{\cos x}$

$\cos(2x)-\sin(2x)\cdot\frac{\sin x}{\cos x}$

$1-2\sin^2 x-2\sin x\cdot\cos x\cdot\frac{\sin x}{\cos x}$

$1-2\sin^2 x-2\sin^2 x$

$1-4\sin^2 x$

#8 90°

Test 4:

#1a) $\frac{1}{\sqrt{-x^2-2x}}$

b) $\frac{\sqrt{x^2-2x+5}}{x-1}$

c) $\frac{44}{125}$

#2 $A=3, B=\frac{\pi}{4}$

#3 $\frac{-6}{7}$

#4 $\frac{-\sqrt{6+3\sqrt{2}}-\sqrt{2-\sqrt{2}}}{4}$

#5 $\pm\frac{\sqrt{39}}{8}$

#6 $x=30^\circ,150^\circ,210^\circ,330^\circ$

#7 $\theta=\frac{\pi}{12}$

#8a) LHS: $\frac{1}{\tan(2x+x)}$

$\frac{1-\tan(2x)\tan x}{\tan(2x)+\tan x}$

$\frac{1-\frac{2\tan x}{1-\tan^2 x}\cdot\tan x}{\frac{2\tan x}{1-\tan^2 x}+\tan x}$

$\frac{1-\tan^2 x-2\tan^2 x}{2\tan x+\tan x-\tan^3 x}$

$\frac{1-3\tan^2 x}{3\tan x-\tan^3 x}$

b) LHS: $2(\sin(4x)+\sin(2x))(\sin(4x)-\sin(2x))$

$2(2\sin(3x)\cos x)(2\cos(3x)\sin x)$

$2(2\sin(3x)\cos(3x))(2\sin x\cdot\cos x)$

$2\cdot\sin(6x)\cdot\sin(2x)$

$2\cdot\frac{1}{2}(\cos(4x)-\cos(8x))$

$\cos(4x)-\cos(8x)$

Test 5:

#1a) $\frac{\sqrt{6}-\sqrt{2}}{4}$

b) $\frac{24}{7}$

#2a) LHS: $\frac{(\sec x+\tan x+1)}{(\sec x+\tan x-1)}\cdot\frac{\cos x}{\cos x}$

$\frac{1+\sin x+\cos x}{1+\sin x-\cos x}\cdot\frac{1+\sin x+\cos x}{1+\sin x+\cos x}$

$\frac{2+2\sin x\cos x+2\sin x+2\cos x}{(1+\sin x)^2-\cos^2 x}$

$\frac{2+2\sin x\cos x+2\sin x+2\cos x}{\sin^2 x+2\sin x+1-\cos^2 x}$

$\frac{2(\sin x+1)(\cos x+1)}{\sin^2 x+2\sin x+\sin^2 x+\cos^2 x-\cos^2 x}$

$\frac{2(\sin x+1)(\cos x+1)}{2\sin x(\sin x+1)}$

$\frac{\cos x+1}{\sin x}$

$\csc x+\cot x$

b) 7

#3 $\frac{21}{121+10\sqrt{142}}$

#4 $\frac{\sqrt{2+\sqrt{2}}+\sqrt{6-3\sqrt{2}}}{4}$

#5 $\frac{2\pi}{3}$

#6 $x=7.5^\circ,37.5^\circ,90^\circ,97.5^\circ,127.5^\circ$

#7a) LHS: $\cos(2\theta+\theta)$

$\cos 2\theta\cos\theta-\sin 2\theta\sin\theta$

$(2\cos^2\theta-1)\cos\theta-2\sin^2\theta\cos\theta$

$2\cos^3\theta-\cos\theta-2\cdot\frac{1-\cos 2\theta}{2}\cdot\cos\theta$

$2\cos^3\theta-\cos\theta-\cos\theta+\cos\theta\cos 2\theta$

$2\cos^3\theta-\cos\theta-\cos\theta+\cos\theta(2\cos^2\theta-1)$

$2\cos^3\theta-2\cos\theta+2\cos^3\theta-\cos\theta$

$4\cos^3\theta - 3\cos\theta$

b) $\cos 54^\circ = 4\cos^3 18^\circ - 3\cos 18^\circ$

c) $\sin 36^\circ = 2\sin 18^\circ \cos 18^\circ$

d) $4\sin^2 18^\circ + 2\sin 18^\circ - 1 = 0$

$\sin 18^\circ = \frac{-1+\sqrt{5}}{4}$

e) $\cos 36^\circ = \frac{1+\sqrt{5}}{4}$ $\cos 72^\circ = \frac{-1+\sqrt{5}}{2}$

f) $\frac{1}{2}$

Test 6:

#1a) $\sqrt{x^2+2x+2}$

b) $\frac{\sqrt{x^2+4x+5}}{x+2}$

c) $\frac{56}{65}$

#2 $k = 89$

#3 $\frac{\sqrt{6+3\sqrt{2}}+\sqrt{2-\sqrt{2}}}{4}$

#4 $\frac{11}{24}$

#5 $x = 0^\circ, 30^\circ, 60^\circ, 90^\circ, 120^\circ, 150^\circ, 180^\circ, 210^\circ$
$240^\circ, 270^\circ, 300^\circ, 330^\circ$

#6a) LHS: $2\sin(2x)\cos(2x)$

$2 \cdot 2\sin x \cdot \cos x \cdot \cos(2x)$

$4\sin x \cdot \cos x(1 - 2\sin^2 x)$

b) LHS: $\frac{\sin(\frac{a+b}{2})(2\sin(\frac{a+b}{2}))-1}{\cos(\frac{a+b}{2})2\sin(\frac{a+b}{2})\cos(\frac{a-b}{2})\sin(\frac{a-b}{2})}$

$\frac{\sin(\frac{a+b}{2})(2\sin(\frac{a+b}{2}))-1}{\sin(a+b)(\frac{1}{2})\sin(a-b)}$

$\frac{2\sin^2(\frac{a+b}{2})-1}{\sin(a+b)(\frac{1}{2})\sin(a-b)}$

$\frac{-2\cos(a+b)}{\sin(a+b)\sin(a-b)}$

$\frac{-2\cot(a+b)}{\sin(a-b)}$

#7 $x = 1$

#8 $\frac{7}{4}$

Chapter 9 Geometry Trig/Complex Numbers

Note: I approximated values to the best of my ability but some answers may have slight rounding errors.

Test 1:

#1a) 210.0170722 miles

#2 $-13122 - 13122\sqrt{3}i$

#3 $z = 2cis\frac{\pi}{4}, 2cis\frac{11\pi}{12}, 2cis\frac{19\pi}{12}$

#4a) $B = 38.78^\circ$ $C = 107.22^\circ$ $c = 42.70$
$B' = 141.22^\circ$ $C' = 4.78^\circ$ $c' = 3.73$

b) $a = 11.51, b = 17.30, c = 17.19$

#5a) $AB = \sqrt{19}$

b) 10.680980

#6a) 6.855023 ft

b) $\theta \approx 25.41922359^\circ$

#7 1230.181 miles squared

#8a) 105.83 feet

b) $N60.89339^\circ W$

Test 2:

#1 212.1039281 miles

#2 $8192 + 8192\sqrt{3}i$

#3 $z = 2cis\frac{3\pi}{16}, 2cis\frac{11\pi}{16}, 2cis\frac{19\pi}{16}, 2cis\frac{27\pi}{16}$

#4a) $B = 59.75^\circ C = 77.25^\circ c = 21.45$
$B' = 120.25^\circ C' = 16.75^\circ c' = 6.34$

#5 $2\sqrt{7}$

#6 $AB \approx 9.14285, BE \approx 6.8571$

#7a) 342.53 feet

b) Original Route

c) 5832.132 feet squared

Test 3:

#1 7.12282934

#2 $32.768i$

#3 $z = \sqrt[3]{6\sqrt{6}cis\frac{2\pi}{9}}, \sqrt[3]{6\sqrt{6}cis\frac{8\pi}{9}}, \sqrt[3]{6\sqrt{6}cis\frac{14\pi}{9}}$

#4a) $B = 52.36^\circ C = 90.64^\circ c = 31.57$
$B' = 127.64^\circ C' = 15.36^\circ c' = 8.36$

b) $b = 30.00$ $c = 13.35$ $a = 24.65$

#5 858 miles

#6 $\frac{84}{17}$

#7 $5\sqrt{3}$

#8 90.39789°

Test 4:

#1 2.900 hours

#2 $209952 + 209952\sqrt{3}i$

#3 $\sqrt[6]{8}cis\frac{\pi}{36}$ $\sqrt[6]{8}cis\frac{13\pi}{36}$ $\sqrt[6]{8}cis\frac{25\pi}{36}$ $\sqrt[6]{8}cis\frac{37\pi}{36}$
$\sqrt[6]{8}cis\frac{49\pi}{36}$ $\sqrt[6]{8}cis\frac{61\pi}{36}$

#4a) $B = 54.897, C = 86.103, c = 15.853$
$B' = 125.103,\ C' = 15.897,\ c' = 4.352$

b) $b = 7.8817, a = 14.063, c = 14.992$

#5a) $D = 79.233, A = 122.452, B = 103.315$

b) 46.988

#6 $BA' = 2, A'C = 5$

#7a) 0.765 mi b) 1.872 mi c) $N16.996^\circ W$

Test 5:

#1 $AC = 314.563$ miles $N83.432E^\circ$

#2 $-524288 + 524288\sqrt{3}i$

#3 $z = 2cis\frac{\pi}{24}, 2cis\frac{9\pi}{24}, 2cis\frac{17\pi}{24}$

$2cis\frac{25\pi}{24}, 2cis\frac{33\pi}{24}, 2cis\frac{41\pi}{24}$
#4a) $B = 76.761^\circ, C = 51.239^\circ, c = 16.8220$
$B' = 103.239^\circ, C' = 24.761^\circ, c' = 9.036$
b) $b = 87.022, a = 49.413, c = 63.564$
#5 35.2475°
#6 143.5941235
#7a) 0.8221676 miles
b) 0.781479 miles
c) 0.660438 miles, $S12.7032352^\circ W$

Chapter 10 Matrices

Test 1:
#1 $x = -1$
#2

$$\begin{bmatrix} 2/5 & -5 \\ -2/5 & 12 \end{bmatrix}$$

#3a) $(4, 3, -1)$
b) $(-2, 1, -1)$
c) $(3, 2, 0)$
#4 $\frac{9}{2}$
#5 $a = 2, b = -1, c = 1, d = -4$

Test 2:
#1 -97
#2

$$\begin{bmatrix} 1 & 3 \\ -2 & 4 \end{bmatrix}$$

#3a) $(2, 1, 5)$
b) $(-1, 2, 3)$
c) $(1, 2, -3)$
#4 $x = 3$
#5 Jessie: 48 marbles, Tenny: 116 marbles, Jonathan: 52 marbles, Jerry: 144 marbles

Test 3:
#1 -105
#2

$$\begin{bmatrix} 0 & -1 \\ 2 & 3 \end{bmatrix}$$

#3a) $(5, 1, -1)$
b) $(1, 2, -3)$
c) $(2, -1, 1)$
#4 12
#5 Classics: 360 pages, Comics: 540 pages, Fantasy: 240 pages, Science Fiction: 360 pages

Chapter 11 Conics

Test 1:
#1 Center: $(1, -3)$ Vertices: $(1, -3 \pm \sqrt{2})$ Foci: $(1, -3 \pm 2\sqrt{5})$ Co-vertices: $(1 \pm \sqrt{2}, -3)$
Asymptotes: $y = -3 \pm \frac{1}{3}(x-1)$ Eccentricity: $\frac{\sqrt{10}}{2}$
#2 $y = \frac{-1}{3}x + \frac{7}{3}$
#3 $(\frac{4}{3}, 4)$
#4 $\frac{399\pi}{4}$
#5 $\frac{(x')^2}{4} + \frac{(y')^2}{1} = 1$
Vertices: $(\frac{4}{\sqrt{5}}, \frac{2}{\sqrt{5}})(-\frac{4}{\sqrt{5}}, -\frac{2}{\sqrt{5}})$
Covertices: $(-\frac{1}{\sqrt{5}}, \frac{2}{\sqrt{5}})(\frac{1}{\sqrt{5}}, -\frac{2}{\sqrt{5}})$
Foci: $(\frac{2\sqrt{15}}{5}, \frac{\sqrt{15}}{5})(-\frac{2\sqrt{15}}{5}, -\frac{\sqrt{15}}{5})$

Test 2:
#1 Center $(3, -1)$ Vertices: $(8, -1), (-2, -1)$
Co-vertices: $(3, -1 \pm \sqrt{7})$ Eccentricity: $\frac{3\sqrt{2}}{5}$ Foci: $(3 \pm 3\sqrt{2}, -1)$
#2a) 14.4286 inches b) 89.7949
#3 $\frac{x^2}{49/4} + \frac{y^2}{6} = 1$
#4 $(x+6)^2 + (y-11)^2 = 25$ $(x+13)^2 + (y-4)^2 = 25$
#5 $\frac{(x')^2}{4} - \frac{(y')^2}{16} = 1$

Test 3:
#1 Center: $(-\frac{2}{3}, 2)$ Vertices: $(-\frac{2}{3}, 1)$ $(-\frac{2}{3}, 3)$
Covertices: $(-\frac{7}{6}, 2)$ $(-\frac{1}{6}, 2)$ Foci: $(-\frac{2}{3}, 2 \pm \frac{\sqrt{3}}{2})$
Eccentricity: $\frac{\sqrt{3}}{2}$
#2 $y = -x$
#3 $(x - 2 + 2\sqrt{5})^2 + (y - 8 - \sqrt{5})^2 = 25$
$(x - 2 - 2\sqrt{5})^2 + (y - 8 + \sqrt{5})^2 = 25$
#4 $\frac{(x+4)^2}{100} + \frac{(y-3)^2}{36} = 1$
#5 $\frac{(x')^2}{2} - \frac{(y')^2}{10} = 1, x^2 + y^2 = 2$

Test 4:
#1 Center: $(-4, 4)$ Vertices: $(-\frac{5}{2}, 4)$ $(-\frac{11}{2}, 4)$
Covertices: $(-4, 3)$ $(-4, 5)$ Foci: $(-4 \pm \frac{\sqrt{10}}{2}, 4)$
Eccentricity: $\frac{\sqrt{10}}{3}$ Asymptotes: $y - 4 = \pm \frac{1}{3}(x+4)$
#2 $0 = x^2 + y^2 - 2xy - 22x - 26y + 121$
#3 $(\pm\sqrt{\frac{3}{2}}, \pm\sqrt{\frac{5}{2}})$

#4 $\sqrt{34}$

#5 $\frac{(x')^2}{20/7} + \frac{(y')^2}{10} = 1$

Test 5:

#1 Center: $(3,-3)$ Foci: $(3 \pm \sqrt{19},-3)$ Vertices: $(3 \pm \sqrt{17},-3)$ Covertices: $(3,-3 \pm \sqrt{2})$

Asymptotes: $y + 3 = \pm \frac{\sqrt{34}}{17}(x-3)$

Eccentricity: $\sqrt{\frac{19}{17}}$

#2 $\frac{(x-10^2}{114} + \frac{y^2}{2} = 1$

#3 $(\frac{34}{3}, \frac{661}{36})$

#4 $(x+2)^2 + (y+3)^2 = 5,\ (x-8)^2 + (y-7)^2 = 5$

$(x - \frac{14}{3})^2 + (y - \frac{1}{3})^2 = 5, (x - \frac{4}{3})^2 + (y - \frac{11}{3})^2 = 5$

#5 $\frac{(x')^2}{24/35} - \frac{(y')^2}{5/8} = 1$

Test 6:

#1 Center: $(5,-7)$ Vertices: $(8,-7)(2,-7)$

Covertices: $(5,-12)(5,-2)$ Foci: $(5 \pm \sqrt{34},-7)$

Asymptotes: $y + 7 = \pm \frac{5}{3}(x-5)$ Eccentricity: $\frac{\sqrt{34}}{3}$

#2 $(-6, 15)$

#3 $(\frac{3}{2}, 9)\ (\frac{5}{2}, 27)$

#4 $\frac{256}{5}$

#5 $\frac{(x')^2}{24/11} + \frac{(y')^2}{24} = 1$

Test 7:

#1 Center: $(5,-3)$ Vertices: $(11,-3)\ (-1,-3)$

Covertices: $(5,-3 \pm \sqrt{6})$ Foci: $(5 \pm \sqrt{30},-3)$

Eccentricity: $\frac{\sqrt{30}}{6}$

#2 $x^2 + 2xy + 32x + y^2 = 0$

#3 $\frac{x^2}{2} - \frac{(y+4)^2}{6} = 1$

#4 $\frac{3-\sqrt{3}}{3}$

#5 $\frac{(x')^2}{5} + \frac{(y')^2}{45} = 1$

Chapter 12 Parametric/Polar Equations

Test 1:

#1 $y = 2x^2 + 2$ Domain: $-1 \le x \le 1$.

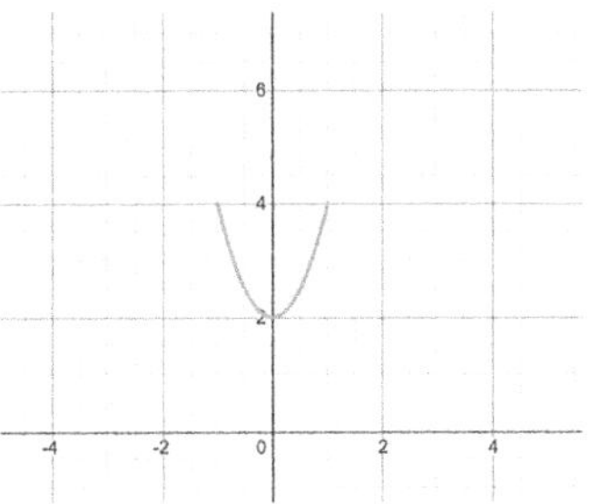

#2 $7, r = \frac{45}{24 \sin \theta + 2\sqrt{3} \cos \theta}$

#3 $t = 3, D = 2\sqrt{2}$

#4 $(x^2 + y^2)^5 = 9y^2(x^2 + y^2)^2 - 24y^4(x^2 + y^2) + 16y^6$

#5a) Pole: Symmetric pole, $\theta = \frac{\pi}{2}$: Inconclusive

b) Maximum: $(2, \frac{\pi}{4})(2, \frac{5\pi}{4})$ Zeros: $(0,0)(0,\pi)(0,\frac{\pi}{2})(0,\frac{3\pi}{2})$

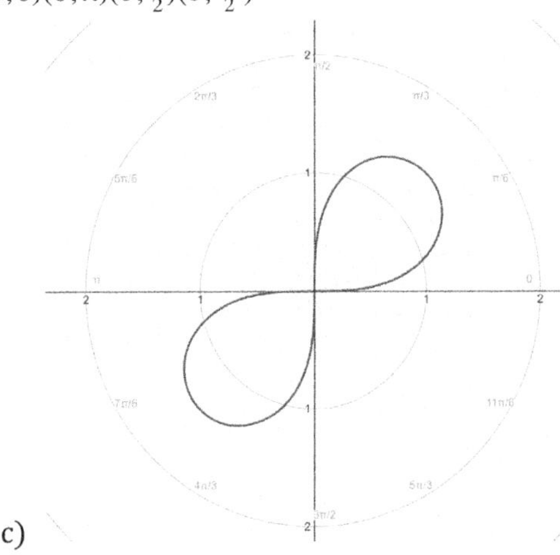

c)

#6a) $r = \frac{6}{4+\sqrt{2} \cos \theta + \sqrt{2} \sin \theta}$

b) Center: $(1, \frac{5\pi}{2})$ Covertices: $(2, \frac{11\pi}{12})(2, \frac{19\pi}{12})$ Foci: $(2, \frac{5\pi}{4})$ Directrix: $r = \frac{6}{\sqrt{2} \cos \theta + \sqrt{2} \sin \theta}$

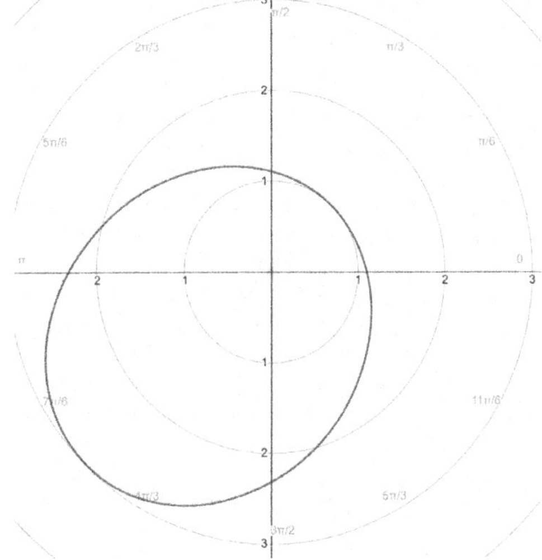

Test 2:

#1 $x^2 - 2xy + y^2 - 3x - 6y = 0$

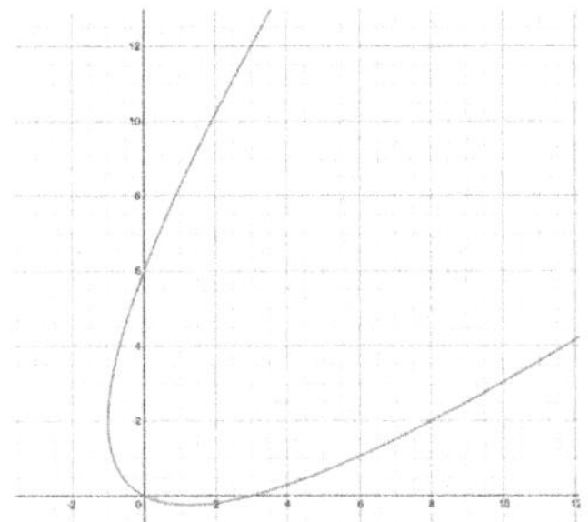

#2 $t = -3, D = \sqrt{5}$
#3 $K = 308$
#4 $r = \frac{1}{2\cos\theta + 2\sin\theta - \sin 2\theta}$ for $x < 1$
#5a) $\theta = \frac{\pi}{2}$: Symmetric, Pole: Inconclusive
b) Max: $(3, \frac{\pi}{2})$, Zeroes: $(0, \frac{7\pi}{6})(0, \frac{11\pi}{6})$
c)

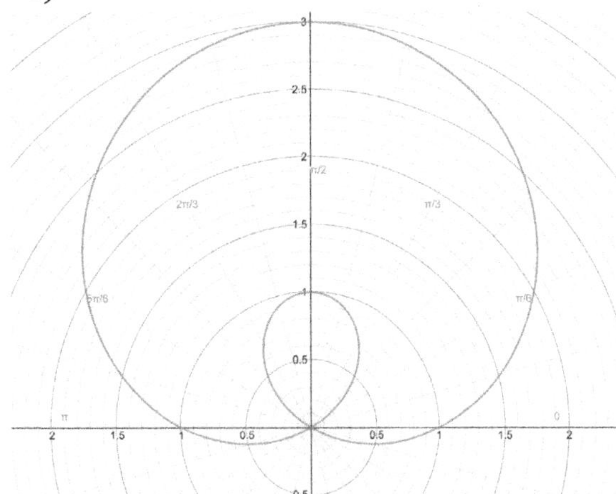

#6a) $r = \frac{3}{1-2\sin\theta}$
b) Center: $(2, \frac{3\pi}{2})$ Foci: $(4, \frac{3\pi}{2})$ Directrix: $r = \frac{-3}{2\sin\theta}$,
Covertices: $(\sqrt{7}, -0.85707)$ $(\sqrt{7}, 3.99866)$
Vertices: $(1, \frac{3\pi}{2}), (3, \frac{3\pi}{2})$
c)

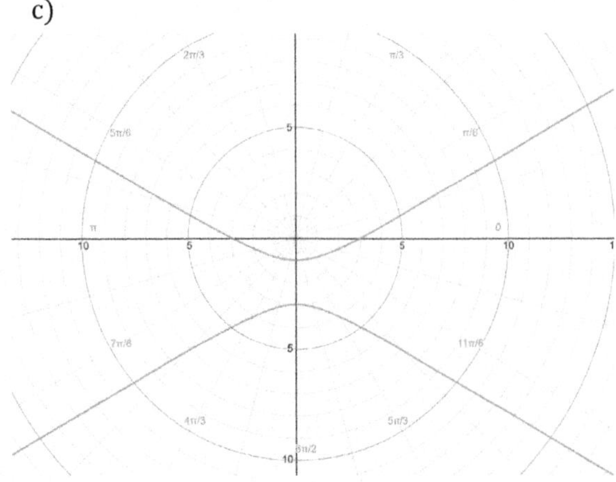

Chapter 13 Vectors and Planes

Test 1:

#1 49.24036 miles
#2 330,549.136 lbs
#3 1.8196
#4 1569.24325 ft-pounds
#5 32
#6 $0.9435\mathbf{i} + 2.83037\mathbf{j} + 8.491104\mathbf{k}$
#7a) $<-16, 13, -17>$, Magnitude: 26.72077
b) $\theta = 94.32909^{\circ}$
c) $< \frac{-2}{27}, \frac{2}{27}, \frac{-10}{27} >$
#8 $0 = 16x^2 + 24xy - 50x + 9y^2 + 400y + 25z^2 + 1625$
#9 $x = -7t, y = t, z = 5t$

Test 2:
#1 Speed: 566.9700 mph, Bearing: $N39.2772^{\circ}E$
#2 242.392, 382.354 lbs
#3 $c = -\frac{6}{5}, 6$
#4 2067.33238 ft-pounds
#5 14
#6a) $<-25, 14, -24>$ Magnitude: 37.37646
b) $\theta = 126.3701^{\circ}$
c) $<-\frac{8}{7}, \frac{4}{7}, -\frac{12}{7}>$
#7 $-2.3932\mathbf{i} - 1.59545\mathbf{j} - 6.38179\mathbf{k}$
#8 $(\frac{23}{38}, \frac{85}{38}, \frac{54}{19}), \frac{3}{\sqrt{38}}$
#9 $5x - 6y - z - 8 = 0$

Chapter 14 Introduction to Calculus

Limits Test 1
#1a) 6
b) $\frac{15}{2}$
c) $\frac{\sqrt{3}}{4}$
d) $\frac{5}{2}$
e) 0
#2a) 2
b) 0
c) 1
d) 6
e) -3
f) 6
#3 $-\frac{2}{3}$
#4a) $c = \frac{4}{3}$
b) 19
#5 $(0, \frac{32}{27})$

Limits Test 2
#1a) 4
b) 384

c) 0
d) 4
e) 0
#2 $y = 0$
#3 $a = 3, b = 2$
#4 $a = 4, -5/2$
#5 $a = 4, b = 2$

Limits Test 3
#1a) 2
b) $\frac{3}{2}$
c) $\frac{\pi}{3}$
d) $\frac{15}{2}$
e)Does not exist, $-\infty$
#2 $\frac{2\sqrt{a}}{3\sqrt[3]{a^2}}$
#3 $a = 11, b = 3$
#4 $\frac{15}{2}$
#5 Min: $(2, -6)$ Max: $(-4, 42)$

Derivatives and Integrals Test 1:
#1 $f'(x) = 4x - 3, y = 5x - 4$
#2 $\frac{3}{4}$
#3a) $v(t) = 3t^2 + 5t + 2$
b) 24
c) $a(t) = 6t + 5$
d) $t = \frac{-2}{3}, -1$
#4a) -40
b) 64 ft/s
c) 24 feet
d) $\frac{4 \pm \sqrt{6}}{2}$
e) $-32\sqrt{6}$ ft/s
f) -32 ft per second squared
#5a) $[-3, -1], [4, \infty]$
b) $[-1, 2], [2, 4]$
c) $x = -1$
d) $x = -3, 4$

Derivatives and Integrals Test 2:
#1 $y = \frac{4}{3}x + 3,\ 3.0333$
#2 $\frac{4}{3}$
#3 $\frac{5}{3}, \frac{20}{3}, \frac{4}{3}$
#4 3.5
#5a) $t = 0, 4, \frac{3}{2}, 2$
b) $v(t) = s'(t) = -8t^3 + 45t^2 - 68t + 24$
c) $\frac{-15}{4}$ ft/s and -40 ft/s
d) $a(t) = v'(t) = -24t^2 + 90t - 68$
e) $t = 1.04899, 2.701$ sec
f) $t = 1.875$ sec $v(1.875) = 1.96875$ ft/s

Derivatives and Integrals Test 3:
#1 $f'(x) = \frac{2x}{\sqrt{2x^2+7}} + 1, y = \frac{11}{5}x + \frac{7}{5}$
#2 $14\frac{7}{24}$
#3 $-\frac{33}{4}$
#4 $k = 4, k = -2$
#5 $2\sqrt[3]{6 + \pi}$
#6a) $\frac{28}{3}$
b) $0 < t < 2, t > 4$

About the Author:
Jonathan Cheng is a high school student who is passionate about learning and teaching math. In his free time, he also loves to read, write, and watch TV shows. When quarantine is over, you can find him at a local amusement park, riding his favorite roller coasters. He is currently working on another project that he hopes to have published by December 2020.

Made in the USA
Las Vegas, NV
21 December 2021